A Mom's Guide to Home Organization

Simple Solutions to Control Clutter, Schedules and Stress

A Mom's Guide to Home Organization

Simple Solutions to Control Clutter, Schedules and Stress

DEBBIE LILLARD

BETTERWAY HOME

CINCINNATI, OHIO
WWW.BETTERWAYBOOKS.COM

PART V: NO MORE SCATEGORIES

Introduction

In my experience as a professional organizer, I've noticed two things about the moms I've worked with: first, they need organizing help not because they are lazy, but because they are busy, and second, they are usually very hard on themselves. Let's face it, the job of a mother is multi-faceted. Maybe you're not the most organized mom on the block, but you may be the best cook, or the most fun to be with, or the one who gets involved in your child's school. Recognize your strengths along with your weaknesses. If you need help organizing, you've come to the right place.

Do you feel stressed out at home, can't find anything, are always rushing and being late, and have numerous unfinished projects in your house? If you feel like a mess, then congratulations! You've taken the first step toward improving your situation. The next step is to find your motivation. This is what will keep you going in the middle of a big project. Do you want to simplify your life so you can relax more? Do you want to arrange your home so you're not embarrassed to have guests over? Do you want to get rid of the excess in your life so others can benefit? Write down your motivation and look at it every day.

This book will help you organize your daily routines, your belonging (along with your children's belongings) and every room in your home. Make it a game and have fun. Be realistic with what you can save and toss. Above all, realize that organizing is like dieting. You can't do it fast and furious for two weeks and think you are done. You have to incorporate organizing into your daily life if you really want to change the way you are living.

Part I: Organize Your Time

PLAN YOUR WORK AND WORK YOUR PLAN. Mary Kay Ash, founder of one of the world's largest cosmetic companies, taught her directors to "plan their work and work their plan." I learned this as an Independent Beauty Consultant, one of the many part-time jobs I had as a young mom. All you need to accomplish something is to plan the work. The work might be decorating a house, packing for vacation, or starting your own business. Once you have a solid plan—a list of what needs to be done—you must work that plan. In other words, just do it—and don't second-guess yourself. Many times I venture into a project and start doing things not in my plan. Then I get distracted and everything takes longer than anticipated. At some point I make myself refocus and go back to my list. If I stick to the plan, I usually accomplish my goal.

"He who every morning plans the transaction of the day and follows out that plan, carries a thread that will guide him through the maze of the most busy life. But where no plan is laid, where the disposal of time is surrendered merely to the chance of incidence, chaos will soon reign."

—VICTOR HUGO

1. The Housework Never Ends!

THE PROBLEM

Maybe you were an organized woman B.C. (Before Children). Many of us were. When you only have yourself to care for, things are pretty simple. Even if you weren't the most organized person, all you needed to get back on track was a Saturday morning cleaning frenzy. Now that you're a mom, your time is not your own. You are at the mercy of your children's schedules and their basic needs. Each day you must consider the household responsibilities, the family social schedule, the medical needs of the children and often your own work obligations. Get back on track? That could take months! It often seems impossible to handle. Does this sound like you?

You find yourself forgetting appointments

You're always running late

You run around but never feel like you accomplish anything

You can't find time to talk to or see your best friends

You have no time for yourself

You dream about things you'd like to do but never get around to doing them

The first thing you need to work on is your time management.

Time management boils down to two things: planning and finding balance.

THE STORY

I have worked with several mothers who do not work and do not have young children at home. So when I hear that their excuse for being unorganized is "I just don't have the time," I have to hold back my scream. They're last-minute shoppers for gifts and food for dinner, and they just can't get to their paperwork piles. They have projects that they have been meaning to get to but just can't. They are not lazy people. They are constantly moving and doing, but they never seem to accomplish an end result. The problem is that they don't have a schedule or a plan to achieve goals.

THE SOLUTION

I believe time management boils down to two things: planning and finding balance. A mom who plans her time carefully can achieve balance between:

- household chores and mothering
- being a mom and being a wife
- family time and personal time

This balance brings happiness and contentment to your life. Sounds ideal, I know, but it is possible. Think about when you feel your worst as a mom. Does it happen when you've only been doing one thing? If all you do is household chores, do you feel like a maid? If you work outside the home too much, do you feel like your mothering is lacking? And if you are always with your husband and children, do you feel like you've lost the individual woman you once were? If you are never alone with your husband do you lose the romantic feeling you had when you were dating or first married? Balance is the key and if you want it to happen, you have to plan it! Most things don't happen by accident.

Start the Day Off Right

The most important time management skill involves how you start your day. Think about what you need to do or would like to do each morning to get yourself off to a good start. It might be exercise, showering, walking or having a cup of tea or coffee, or it might be simply to sit in quiet to read or pray. Answer this question for yourself: "What do I wish I could do every morning before the rest of the family is up?" Then get up at least thirty minutes before your earliest riser and do it. Take care of yourself before you have to take care of everyone else for the day. Too many moms wake up, roll out of bed and start right in on taking care of the children, making breakfast and packing lunches. Before they know it, they have to drive someone to school and they haven't even brushed their teeth yet! It's worth getting up a little earlier to start each day on your own terms.

Another morning ritual is to make sure the bedrooms are tidy before you go downstairs for breakfast. This includes: making the bed, putting clothes away and picking up any stray items that need to go downstairs. As the children get older they can help with their own rooms.

Absolute of Organizing: Daily routines are a must.

Work When You Are at Your Best

When establishing your new organizing habits, consider your own energy levels and your schedule. Are you a night owl or an early bird? If you need to be out of the house early in the morning, it makes sense to accomplish as much as possible in the evening. You can tidy up, set the coffee maker, make the children's lunches and plan your next day after the children go to bed. Then you can relax and not worry about tomorrow. One mom I know has a great tip for making lunches ahead of time: When she buys lunch meat, she immediately divides it into sandwich-size portions and freezes them in little sandwich bags. Each night, she takes one portion out and puts it in the refrigerator. By morning it is thawed and ready to make a quick sandwich. This also saves money because it keeps the meat fresh and you never have to throw out slimy meat at the end of the week!

If you work in the evening, or simply have more energy in the morning, then kick up your feet at night and follow my suggestion of rising before the children. People sometimes ask me, "What should I do first in the morning to be organized?" I tell them there is no right or wrong way to organize your time. There is only what works and what doesn't. Everyone's family is on a different schedule with work, school and little ones' sleep habits. Determine your best energy time and plan your day around it.

Use a Daily Planner

Another important step in organizing your time is choosing a daily planner in a size that works well for you. It could be an electronic organizer or a paper one. I use a Franklin Planner that has a month-at-a-glance, daily pages with plenty of room for my list of things to do and a clean page for notes. I started using

Daily planners are a great way to keep track of your appointments, tasks and errands.

a planner like this when I was working at a large company. When I decided to be a stay-at-home mom, I thought I would never need that level of detail again since my days would be spent in domestic bliss. Taking my child to the park and making wonderful dinners for my family would be my focus. I could watch TV and play blocks

I think about how to group tasks together to be more efficient.

at the same time. Who needed a list of things to do for that? It didn't take me long to realize how wrong I was. A few years and a few kids later, I was making doctor's appointments right and left, signing up for kiddy activities, starting my own business, undertaking home decorating projects and doing all the usual household chores. How could I fit it all in? I quickly ordered the refills for my planner and began to write it all down. I also formed the habit of taking a few minutes every morning to make a list of things to do in my planner. Now it's as habitual as my morning coffee. I think about how to group tasks together to be more efficient. I usually do my errands in the morning and plan which store to go to first if there is more than one. My toddler naps in the afternoon, so that is when I can do important things at home such as computer work or phone calls.

Absolute of Organizing: Group like things (or tasks) together.

To kick off this habit, limit your list to the five most important things you must do each day. A longer list may be too overwhelming to achieve. This will also help you focus on priorities. The daily planning process takes about ten minutes. You can do it either first thing in the morning or right before you go to bed, whenever you can think clearly. If your list is longer than five items, I suggest using the FranklinCovey method of prioritization:

Items marked A = must get done today

Items marked B = should get done today

Items marked C = would be nice to get done today

Then number the tasks with 1-2-3, etc., within each category in the order they should be completed. Check your progress around lunch time and re-prioritize if necessary. At the end of the day, if something is not done, move it to tomorrow's list or to the next logical day that it could be done. If all five things get done before the end of the day, you can add some less important items to the list, or take the rest of the day off to do some fun things.

If you decide to use an electronic planner, the method is the same. Use the "calendar" to plug in appointments or places you have to be. Then use the "tasks" list to put in the things you have to do each day.

You can also create other lists in your planner such as "Books to read," or "Places to go when friends come to town"—any lists you can imagine that will help you remember things. Many people create lists, but if these lists are on little pieces of paper throughout the house, they get lost and there's no continuity from day to day.

With a planner you can refer back to what you did yesterday or last month. Many times I've used my planner as a reference guide. If I can't remember if I called someone or sent a thank you note, I check back in my planner to see if I did. If a bill comes in with a late fee, I check to see when I mailed it. All these things are recorded in my planner along with other vital information. This level of detail may not work for you right now. Remember there is no "right" or "wrong" way to organize. Start simply and decide how you can make a planner work for you.

Keep a Notebook Handy

If you write lists and reminders to yourself all over the house and can never seem to find the right one on the right day, try this trick. Put a notebook and pen wherever you do your best thinking. For some it's in the car, or in the bathroom, or in bed at night. Have a note pad handy so you can write down the little tidbits that pop into your head. Then transcribe them into your daily planner or electronic organizer. Once it's written down, you don't need to think about it anymore, and once it's in your planner, you know that it will get done.

Tracking Expenses With Your Planner

HAVE YOU EVER started the week with $100 and by Friday you're down to $5? Where did the money go? Cash has a way of slipping through our hands, doesn't it? My husband, who is an accountant, taught me a simple trick when we were first married. Write it down in your daily planner! For instance, today I started with $20 in my wallet. I spent $5 on food and $7 on greeting cards. I should have $8 left at the end of the day. Once you have captured this information for a year, you can use it along with your checkbook ledger and credit card statements to create a family budget. But even if you don't strictly budget, you will have a sense from day to day where your money is spent. If you are ever questioned by your spouse—where did that $100 go?—you'll have an exact answer. This is a step that takes minutes to do each day and will give you vital information in the long run.

Absolute of Organizing: Start with a good list.

A daily planner is your best planning tool to use at the beginning and end of every day. You will feel accomplished as you check things off your list. You may even find that by planning things out, you have more free time than before. In other words, you'll be looking for things to do! That's when you can balance your time with things you like to do or want to do.

OCTOBER

SUN	MON	TUES	WED	THURS	FRI	SAT
	1 mom works 6-8	2 dance 5	3 mom works 10-2	4 ortho 4	5 soccer 6	6 soccer 12
7	8 **kids off** COLUMBUS DAY	9 dance 5	10	11 mother's club 10-2	12 soccer 6	13 soccer 2
14 church picnic 12-3	15 mom works 9-11	16 dance 5	17 mom works 10-2 PTA 7	18	19 mom works 9-1 soccer 6	20 soccer 9 smith's 8
21	22 mom works 9-4	23 dance 5	24	25 mom works 9-4	26 soccer 6	27 soccer 10
28	29	30 dance 5	31 HALLOWEEN			

A family calendar can cut down on paper piles by storing important information from incoming mail.

Family Calendar

Another tool that will help you on a day-by-day basis is the family calendar. I don't know how any mom can live without one. Choose an attractive calendar to hang in a prominent place in your home where everyone can see it or add to it. The kitchen is the most likely location for most families. You don't have to have a huge block for each day, just an average size will do for writing where you have to be. Abbreviate as much as possible, especially for things that occur several times a month. If you really want to be detailed, you can use different colored pens for each member of the family.

The family calendar is also where you can transfer information from incoming mail such as invitations or flyers about special events. There's no need to save an invite from a child's party once you have RSVP'd and you have the address or party location registered in your daily planner. Simply write on the family calendar "Ryan's B-day 3-5" and throw out the invitation. This will save you piles of paper in the long run!

SCHEDULE THE WEEKLY CHORES

As moms, we know there are things that have to be done on a weekly basis for the family to function. Yes, I'm talking about those household chores like cleaning, food shopping, doing the laundry and taking out the trash. For these tasks, I take my example from days gone by.

I had already decided to limit my big chores to one per day when my way of thinking was confirmed by a tour guide at a colonial plantation near my house. I was on a class trip with my daughter and we were learning about how they lived in colonial times. "You moms today are crazy," the tour guide said. "You'll wash and clean every day and run to the market several times a week. Back in colonial times, they would do one chore per day and on Sunday they would rest." Ahhh, simpler times! I would like to rest on Sunday, wouldn't you? So here's what I do to simplify my weekly chores:

Cleaning thoroughly each week may seem like a lot to do, but I look at it this way: I clean for my family, I straighten up for company.

Cleaning

I clean the whole house on Mondays. Weekends are usually a messy time in my house so it's better to clean after the hubby and kids have gone back to work and school. It's also a great way to start off the week. If you have small children at home, I suggest cleaning while they watch a video or take naps. Toddlers have a way of slowing you down with their "help." Now that my youngest child is in preschool a few mornings a week, I clean while he's gone so I can spend time with him when he's home.

By cleaning I mean scrubbing bathrooms and floors, dusting, and vacuuming. When not interrupted, I can clean the whole house in two hours. That includes four bathrooms, four bedrooms, a living room, dining room, kitchen and family room. Cleaning thoroughly each week may seem like a lot to do, but I see it as part of my overall job of keeping my family healthy. I look at it this way: I *clean* for my family, I *straighten up* for company. Cleaning every week has several other benefits:

- it forces you to keep clutter to a minimum
- you can see what needs to be repaired throughout the house
- you can find misplaced items as you clean
- if you miss a week for an emergency, it's okay.

Laundry

I wash all our clothes on Friday. Everyone has clean clothes for the weekend, when we dress up more than during the week. We usually have about six loads, so it's an all-day project, but it doesn't stop me from doing something fun with the kids that day. I sort the dirty laundry in my bedroom first thing in the morning. Then I put a load in before breakfast and continue to "swap the wash" between washer and dryer in between other things I do that day. I choose not to fold as I go but move the clean laundry bins to the family room. Then at the end of the day, or during the baby's nap time, I sit and fold as I watch TV. It's actually very relaxing. If you're someone who has a lot of ironing to do each week, you could fold as you go and iron in the evening. Or do the wash one day and the ironing the next. Friday night, my husband and I deliver each child's basket to his or her room and all but the three-year-old put their clothes away. If everyone in your family has at least seven pairs of underwear and socks, you can do this too! One bit of advice is to have a laundry bin in each person's room. One bin per household fills up very quickly! And if your family likes to deposit dirty laundry in the laundry room all week, then have separate bins set up for whites, dark colors and light colors.

Food Shopping

I usually shop for food after church on Sundays. Yes, I know I'm supposed to be resting but I like to have fresh food to start out the week. My husband is home then, so I can go by myself, which is a lot faster and less costly. I use a list that remains on our refrigerator at all times. I call it the perpetual food list. Anyone who finishes something or who has a request can write it on the list. I also think about what meals I will make for the week and check my recipes for ingredients we might not have. If planning meals is difficult for you, try to make a list of fourteen meals that your family will eat. If you can't think of that many, try ten at least. Post this list in the kitchen or keep it with your coupon caddy so you can consult it before you go food shopping. Try to rotate between five to seven meals this week and five to seven different ones next week. That will prevent your family from getting bored with the same old meals. Before I go shopping, I pull out the coupons I will use. Then I stick to the list.

If planning meals is difficult for you, try to make a list of fourteen meals that your family will eat. Post this list in the kitchen or keep it with your coupon caddy so you can consult it before you go food shopping.

That leaves four days of the week free from big chores! Some people think this schedule is inflexible and regimented. I say it is quite the opposite. With the type of work I do, my schedule is always changing. Typically, I don't schedule clients for Monday or Friday, but if I must, I can do my cleaning or laundry on one of the other days. Recently, I spent an entire Monday with my son, going to doctors and getting a cast put on. And guess what? I easily skipped cleaning that week because I knew I could get it done the following week. I didn't have to worry about buying food for dinner that night or doing the laundry because it was already planned out for the week. I could focus on the situation at hand, which was taking care of my son.

LOOK AHEAD MONTH BY MONTH

Once you have your daily activities under control, you can start to plan farther out. This is where the month-at-glance part of your planner and the family calendar come in handy. My planner has a list of goals at the beginning of each month

> *Use a monthly goals list for bigger projects that haven't been scheduled yet or projects that require multiple steps. Use your "month-at-a-glance" to schedule these projects or goals and your daily pages to write down smaller tasks.*

that I find useful and easy to refer to. Ask yourself, "What do I want to accomplish this month?" Whether it's to get a haircut, paint a room, or plan a vacation, writing it down will help you remember and focus. Use the monthly goals list for bigger projects that haven't been scheduled yet or projects that require multiple steps. Use your "month-at-a-glance" to schedule these projects or goals and your daily pages to write down smaller tasks.

When you have household projects in mind, it's a good idea to plan them out by season. In the winter, you can work inside on painting and minor home improvements. In the spring, outdoor projects like planting, trimming hedges and fixing fences can get done before the summer vacation. Depending on where you live, early summer might be a good time for planting certain flowers or painting outside. The fall comes with its own chores, like putting away outdoor furniture and gathering leaves. Spread these seasonal projects across the "monthly goals" pages in your planner so you won't be overwhelmed when the time comes. You also can plan ahead for the cost of these projects. At the beginning of each month, write down exactly which day you are going to do these projects. I never like to talk about a project getting done "whenever we have time" because we all know when that is—never!

TIPS FOR WORKING MOMS

Moms working full time outside the home have a really tough job when it comes to organizing a family and house. If I were not at my house a good part of the day, things would suffer—I know that. Occasionally, moms who work full time outside the home will challenge my "daily routines" with questions like, "How can I dedicate a whole day to washing or cleaning when I'm at work?" The easy answer is this: hire someone to clean and give yourself a break! The more complex answer is to budget your time and delegate. Busy people may get more done, but everyone has a breaking point. You can't do it all. Let's look at the steps to getting the tasks of a working mom under control.

1. Make a list of daily, weekly and monthly chores/tasks.
2. Decide who does what. Involve your spouse and your children where possible, or look at what chores you can hire out.
3. Decide on what days the weekly and monthly chores will take place.

HOW OFTEN	CHORE	WHO?
Daily	Kitchen clean-up	All
	Make kids' lunches	Mom
	Cook dinner	Dad
	Go through mail	Mom and Dad
	Do homework with kids	Mom and Dad
	Pick up/straighten house	All
Weekly	Wash	All
	Food shop	Mom
	Clean	Dad
	Take out the trash	Mom and Dad
Monthly	Pay bills	Dad
	Miscellaneous shopping	Dad

Note: You may not be able to do all the wash in one night, but try to limit it to two nights. Some working moms also make cooking dinner a weekly event by putting together meals on Sunday and freezing them for the week.

BRAINSTORM ANNUAL VACATION PLANS

A great way to make sure you have a vacation plan is to start off the year with one. Our family typically does this the week between Christmas and New Year's. Decide how much money and time you can budget for vacations and then brainstorm with the whole family how you would like to spend it. Give the children parameters such as places within driving distance or one day trips. Get out a white board or a big piece of paper and write down everyone's ideas. Even if you can't do all the trips this year, you can save the ideas and re-evaluate them next year. Save the list in your planner of course!

CREATE ONE-ON-ONE TIME WITH YOUR CHILDREN

If you have more than one child, you know that one-on-one time doesn't always happen. From time to time, it's a good idea to plan "dates" with your children. Just a couple hours together doing something that they enjoy is all it takes. You could take your daughter ice skating, or your son to a make-your-own-pottery place. Or your husband could take one of them to a workshop at a home improvement store. In the hectic pace of life these days, this may sound ideal, but the special dates you have will be wonderful. The trick is to remember to keep making time for these activities. Many couples who have a son and a daughter tend to let Dad take the son and Mom take the daughter, but mixing it up can also be fun and beneficial for everyone in the family.

Absolute of Organizing: If you don't plan it, it won't happen!

SQUEEZE IN SOME TIME FOR YOU

Many moms I know complain that they never get time to themselves away from their children. It might seem selfish at first, but let's face it, we all need a break sometimes to be better mothers. Time away from your children will truly help you appreciate them and lower your stress level. It's just another means to balancing your life. First, ask yourself what you enjoy doing. Then think about how you can incorporate that activity into your life now. Maybe you could join a group that shares your talent, or take a class. Or plan a weekend doing what you enjoy. Time away from your children can be time spent with your husband or your girlfriends. I love going to the theater, so a few years ago, I bought subscription tickets to a local theater and rounded up a few girlfriends to go with me. It's not a lot of time or money but it is something we all enjoy. All it took was an idea, a few phone calls and some forward planning.

2. We're at the Baby's Beck and Call

THE PROBLEM

You have a new addition to your family, and now you are not getting a full night's sleep. You can't get anything done without the baby interrupting, and you have no time for yourself. Even your most basic needs take a back seat. Does this sound like your life? Take heart. It will get better. If you are a first time mom, know that millions of others have gone before you in this endeavor and survived. Everyone has a different approach to mothering, and you'll hear lots of advice. I will share with you my family's approach to the early years of having children and hope that you can adopt the main concept of my "schedule" and incorporate it into your life.

THE STORY

My mother raised six children and the only pediatrician I can remember seeing was also my mom's pediatrician when she was a child. When Mom found something that worked, she stuck with it. Her pediatrician had a plan for every baby. It included when to feed them, how much, when to put them to sleep and for how long. Some call it rigid, I call it genius.

THE SOLUTION

When my older sister and I started having our own children, my mother taught us to do the only thing she knew—follow the doctor's schedule. Since then, my sister and I typed it up, added editorial advice, and gave copies to hundreds of friends and cousins. I have friends who run into my mom at church and talk about how their baby is up all night, eating all the time, etc. She whips out a copy of the doctor's schedule and if they follow it, lives are transformed. I met another mother through my local mom's club who was raised by the same schedule. Also a patient of this doctor in Philadelphia, she hands out copies of the doctor's schedule to her friends and cousins and they all swear by it. Because I am not an expert on nutrition, I will not include the "what to feed them" portion of the plan beyond the first few months. Discuss your child's diet with your pediatrician. As an organizational expert, I feel this schedule can bring some sanity to a new mother's life, so I will focus on the baby time management.

SET THE SCHEDULE

When a baby is newborn, he basically needs to eat and sleep. You can use this plan whether you breast feed or give your baby formula. I went with breast feeding every four hours pretty early on with my children but most women feel comfortable with every three hours for the first two months. Then you can stretch it to every four hours as the baby gets older.

My mother used to say the goal is to have your baby up for two hours and then down for two. If you're feeding him or her every three hours, it's up for 1 ½ and down for 1 ½ hours. Try to follow this routine every day, remembering it takes three weeks to form a habit. Some days may be completely out of whack because of your life or the baby's mood. But having a routine that you can get back to is what gives a new mom sanity. If your baby wakes up at a time other than 6 AM, just start with that time and do the "up for two/down for two" routine. Sometimes you may need to wake your baby for a feeding to keep them on schedule the rest of the day. Some say this is crazy but it does pay off in the long run. The baby will take better naps and have more hearty feedings with this routine.

Manage the Baby's Routine

6 AM   *Baby wakes up.* Feed her for 10 minutes on each breast or 4-5 ounces of formula. Keep her up for about 1 ½ to 2 hours.

> *Note:* Keeping the baby awake at this point means having him or her around you, noise, and lights, in the baby carrier or swing, basically receiving some stimulation even though his or her eyes may be closed.

8 AM   *Put baby back to sleep* in the crib, darken the room.

> *Note:* This change in the environment to quiet and dark signals to the baby that it's time to sleep.

10 AM   *Feeding time.* Wake baby about 30 minutes before if she is still sleeping. Feed baby as mentioned above and keep awake again for 1 ½ to 2 hours.

12 PM   *Put baby back to sleep* in the crib and darken the room.

2 PM   *Feeding Time.* Wake baby about 30 minutes before feeding time if she is still sleeping. Feed as mentioned above and keep awake again for 1 ½ to 2 hours. This is a great time (2–4 PM) to get fresh air in the nicer weather.

4 PM   *Put baby back to sleep* in the crib; darken room.

6 PM   *Feeding time.* Wake baby about 30 minutes before if she is still sleeping. Feed for 20 minutes or 4-5 ounces and keep baby awake until 8 PM.

8 PM   *Put baby to bed* in the crib after a bath.

10 PM   *Feeding time.* Wake baby for feeding and put back to bed immediately.

2 AM   *Baby should wake up* in the middle of the night around 2 or 3 AM. Do not wake her: let her wake you for this one! And then put her right back to sleep after burping. Also, try to feed her in a quiet, darker environment at this feeding.

CREATE A ROUTINE FOR YOURSELF

As you can see there are three naps during the day for the baby. These times are strategic for you to take care of yourself and get things done. For example:

8–10 PM   *Eat breakfast*, shower and do something around the house.

12–2 PM   *Eat lunch*, make phone calls, pay bills, etc.

4–6 PM   *Prepare dinner* and rest!

The flip side of that is the time you have when the baby is awake. Then you can do things outside of the house with him or her:

10–12 PM   *Run errands*, visit with friends, go for a walk.

2–4 PM   *Play outside*, shop, pick up other kids from school.

I always felt the night time had some normalcy to it when the baby went to bed at 8 PM. Even though the baby would get up again around 10 or 11 PM, I felt like the day was winding down at this point, and my husband and I actually looked forward to that one-on-one time with the baby. If your husband is willing, I suggest letting him do the 10 PM feeding so you can get some rest. You can take the 2-3 AM shift.

My children were so accustomed to this schedule that at a summer party at a friend's house, my two-year-old son lay on a hammock and began sucking his thumb despite the people around and blaring music. I looked at my friend and said, "It must be 8 o'clock." I was exactly right.

Change as They Grow

Be sure to adapt the schedule to include notable benchmarks as your baby begins to grow. Not all babies follow this pattern but mothers who have followed this sleeping and feeding schedule agree that their babies begin to sleep through the night at about six to eight weeks. Be sure to adhere to your pediatrician's advice and follow common sense.

AGE	NOTABLE BENCHMARKS
6-8 Weeks	Baby should sleep through the night from 11 PM to 6 AM. No more 3 AM feedings!
5 Months	Baby should sleep through the night from 8 PM to 6 AM as long as she is getting enough to eat during the day (cereal, vegetables, fruit, etc.). You no longer should wake him or her for the 10 PM feeding. Generally speaking, once your doctor says to give the baby solid foods, the 6 AM feeding is just formula (or breast milk), 10 AM is breakfast, 2 PM is a big lunch, and 6 PM is formula, cereal and fruit.
9 Months	Baby becomes what I call a regular member of the family. In other words, she eats three meals a day at normal times and takes two naps a day for about 2 hours at a time. I used the 9-11 AM morning nap and 3-5 PM afternoon nap until my children were about 15 months old. Then I went to one afternoon nap a day until they absolutely wouldn't take it anymore, which was about four years old.

3. When Will They Learn...?

THE PROBLEM

All parents intend to teach their children well, but when it comes to time management and organizing, many of us fail the course. In an effort to give our kids a happy childhood, moms often end up doing too much for them and consequently turn them into non-functioning adults. The idea is to let go of certain things little by little, allowing the child to make some choices and take on some responsibilities. Sometimes the child will let you know when he or she wants to make decisions and sometimes you will have to let the child know.

THE STORY

Mom A has three children who are very independent. At age three each made it very clear that they would pick out their own clothes each day. So instead of arguing over what they would wear, Mom A decided to give the children parameters like: today is a pants and long-sleeved shirt day. The child could decide which pants and which shirt to wear. In this example, the clothing is appropriate for the weather and the child has the independence and decision-making power he or she desires.

The more your children can do for themselves, the less you have to do for them! It's a win-win situation—you free up your time, and you teach the children to take care of themselves.

In contrast, Mom B laid out her children's clothing each night so they only had to get dressed in the morning. This lasted until the children were about ten years old. One day the mother thought, "Why am I still picking out their clothing?" The answer is that she never passed on that responsibility, and the children never asked for it.

THE SOLUTION

Here are some guidelines about different responsibilities you can give to your children at various ages. Getting back to the idea of "time management," the more your children can do for themselves, the less you have to do for them! It's a win-win situation—you free up your time, and you teach the children to take care of themselves and eventually to help you around the house. Children who grow up like this are more independent and often develop better decision-making skills along the way. If you never had to clean your own room, make your own meal, earn your own money or plan how you would get your chores done, what kind of an adult would you be? Of course every child is different, so adapt these guides to suit your child's natural characteristics and abilities.

INCREASE CHILDREN'S RESPONSIBILITIES

The following chart offers a guideline of responsibilities you can give to children at different ages. Try some of these and test their limits. The key is to accept that at first (and maybe forever) they are not going to do it as well as you would. It's all part of letting go. Perfectionism will get you nowhere as a mom. And if you insist upon being perfect, you will end up with all the work back on your shoulders. Let them try, and teach them how to do it "as well as you." Then let them settle into their own ways of doing things. It's amazing how even the little ones will develop their own sense of style and personality.

Make Clean-up a Game

Here's a game you can play with your children: Right Room, Right Area, Right Container. This can be done in the morning for the bedroom area and at night for the downstairs or main areas of the house. It represents the three basic levels of organizing. I call it a "game" but the rules are very loose. Even a two-year-old can help clean up and get things to the right room. For instance, ask them to take all their toys to the toy room. That's the "right room." As the children get older they

AT AGE	TEACH THEM TO...
3-4	• Clear plates after meals. • Get dressed by themselves. • Match up socks when you're folding wash. • Put their toys away with a simple instruction such as "Put all the blocks in the red bin."
5-6	• Join in a family chore like picking up leaves or straightening up the house. • Follow a morning routine to get ready for school. (Write it down in on an index card and place it where the child can see it.) • Set the table. • Put their clean laundry away. • Straighten their rooms.
7-10	• Clean their own rooms. • Help serve meals. • Bathe or shower by themselves. • Decide which activities and sports they will join.

continued on next page

AT AGE	TEACH THEM TO...
11-13	• Take on certain weekly chores like taking out the trash, doing the dishes, folding the wash, mowing the lawn, etc. • Plan out how they will complete long term projects for school by setting interim deadlines on a calendar.
14–18	• Baby-sit younger siblings. • Make a meal for the family. • Have a part-time job and budget their money. • Make important decisions about college and their future.
18 & up	• Be an independent adult—at this point the "child" should be treated like a roommate with regard to sharing the household workload and contributing to the household budget.

can determine where the "right area" would be, such as getting the toys into the toy box or on a shelf. The next level of detail is to have all the pieces of a particular toy or game in the right container. If your children aren't old enough, then "right container" is your responsibility. At least you had help on the first two steps! Use this game as a quick way to tidy up before company comes over, and as an everyday task to keep things in order. If you are so exhausted at the end of a day that you can't imagine putting one more thing away, try to push yourself to at least get things to the right room. It will make things better in the morning. Also you can reverse the game as the children get older: Mom gets the items to the right room and the children put the items in the right area and container.

Use a Stair Basket to Save You Steps. As part of your game of getting things to the right room, I highly recommend a stair basket if you have stairs in your house. A stair basket is simply a temporary place to store items that are on the wrong floor and a vehicle for making your cleanup easier. The caution here is that many people fill the basket and forget about it for days. Then the basket becomes merely another junk drawer. Develop the habit of emptying it each night when you go upstairs and each morning when you come down, and make sure the children help you put the items away.

LIMIT ACTIVITIES

Another valuable time-management lesson we can teach our children is to limit their activities. In today's society children are extremely overbooked. It is a rare neighborhood where you can find children playing outside after school. Most are running here and there for sports, lessons, etc. Some have to cram in homework before they go

A stair basket will save you time and effort when tidying up. Just remember to empty the basket every day.

to their activities in the evening. Hence the popularity of the scheduled "play date." We have to plan our children's play time around their busy schedules.

Activities are great. They expand our children's minds, exercise their bodies, and teach them teamwork. However, doing too many activities can cause stress, leave little time for homework, and take away their freedom to use their imagination to figure out how to play on their own.

I recommend limiting activities to one sport per season and maybe one other organized activity like scouting, music lessons or community service. There's no magic number but you should consider the time commitment involved in each activity.

When children are young (ages four to six) is the time to experiment with different activities. They will probably want to try everything their friends are doing at that stage. As they get a little older (ages seven to eleven) they will discover what they are good at and what they enjoy. You can ask their opinion about what sports they like to play, what instrument they would like to play and what groups they would like to be a part of. As your children move from middle school to high school (ages twelve to eighteen) their options will change about sports and activities. You can help them make decisions by narrowing their choices and asking them to choose. You can also help by showing them on paper what their schedule will look like with all the extra-curricular activities plugged in. Children know what they want *now*; they aren't accustomed to thinking in long term. Sometimes you have to think for them and involve them in the decision. Limiting activities for your children also will have benefits for the whole family, such as:

1. You won't have to drive them somewhere every night of the week.
2. They will have ample time after school to do homework.
3. They will have free time to use their imagination and just play!
4. It will save you money.
5. They may remember this lesson as adults and not become stressed out and over-committed.

FINISH ONE THING BEFORE YOU START THE NEXT

In the age of Attention Deficit Disorder, finishing one thing before you start the next is so important that it's one of my Absolutes of Organizing. As parents we can be a good example and a teacher on this matter. I have developed the habit of saying, "I will be there as soon as I finish what I'm doing" whenever the kids yell "Mom!" from the other room or ask me to do something when I'm in the middle of something else. I let them know that I've heard them but I also indicate that what I'm doing is important.

I believe this gives the children a good example of limiting distractions, and it teaches patience. Also, if I'm playing with the children and they go on to

Work From Left to Right

ANOTHER TIP THAT CAN HELP you with anything from putting on make-up to making a recipe is to work from left to right whenever possible. Spread out your ingredients on your left, and as you use an item, move it to your right. When your left side is empty, you're done. This is a simple routine with big impact. Think about how many times you are interrupted by your children throughout the day. Have you ever stopped in the middle of a recipe, left the room to take care of a child then returned and thought, "Did I put the sugar in?" If it's on your left, the answer is no. Likewise, have you ever been in the middle of your beauty routine and thought, "Now, did I put on my deodorant yet?" Moving from left to right helps us stay on track when our lives are full of distraction.

something else, I ask, "Are you finished with this?" If the answer is yes, I suggest they put the toys or game away before we go on to something else.

This rule also applies to items that you are using like ketchup, toothpaste or a bottle of bubbles. How many times have you looked in the bathroom cabinet and seen three tubes of toothpaste all half full? What happened? Did you start a new one because the flavor was better? Or did the old one dry up? Whatever the case, finish the old one or throw it out before opening a new one. This prevents clutter and waste.

Absolute of Organizing: Finish one thing before you start another.

4. Are We Having Fun Yet?

THE PROBLEM

Certain times of the year are supposed to be joyous and magical for your family, like Christmas and vacations. But for us moms, the planning and wrapping and packing for these events can be so time-consuming and stressful that when the special day arrives, we just want to curl up in a ball and sleep!

THE STORY

Here's a tale of two Christmases. A mother of six frantically runs to the store at 5 PM on Christmas Eve. Her teenage children are baking cookies and trimming the tree. Frozen pizza is the meal for that night. As the children are dreaming of the wonderful toys that will appear tomorrow morning, Mom and Dad are up until 2 AM wrapping presents and putting toys together. The children awake at 6:30 AM ready to see what Santa has left. Mom and Dad beg them to stay in bed one more hour.

Another Christmas, Mom has done all her shopping online by December 6. The house and tree were decorated by December 17, when they had a little cocktail party for couples in the neighborhood. On Christmas Eve, the family has a nice lasagna dinner and they go to church at 7 PM for the candlelight service. After the children are in bed, Mom and Dad place the presents around the tree, put one toy together and have a glass of wine. They go to bed at 11 PM and awake at 6:30 AM with the children.

THE SOLUTION

My solution is to plan ahead, be efficient with preparation time, and keep it simple. Then you can enjoy yourself when that magical day arrives.

TAKE THE "BAH-HUMBUG" OUT OF YOUR CHRISTMAS SEASON

Our society makes such a big deal about the Christmas season that red and green decorations appear in stores before all the Halloween candy has been eaten. I've told myself many times that I'm not going to think or worry about Christmas until after Thanksgiving. But if you go shopping, you can't avoid it. So think about the holiday in a "planning ahead" way as opposed to a "buying frenzy" way. In planning any big event, you should start with a good list and a budget.

Create Christmas card labels. Right now, you probably have a good idea of who you like to send Christmas cards. If you are working from a handwritten address book that is wearing out, it's time to join the age of technology and put your Christmas card list on the computer. Find a way to create a sheet of mailing labels. If you don't have the skills to create one yourself, have a friend or one of your children create one for you. Name the file "Christmas Cards" or "Addresses" or something simple, and update it throughout the year. I usually print out this file on regular paper in late November. My husband and I look it over to see who we want to add or subtract, or if there are any addresses we need to get. I mark the changes on paper, key them into the file, and print out the labels. I use a decorative type font and clear mailing labels that can be purchased at any office supply store. When it comes time to send Christmas cards, we have an assembly line where I sign the card, someone stuffs the envelope and someone else puts the mailing label and stamp on. This can be done in one evening early in December.

Make two gift lists. An essential list for Christmas is the list of people you want to buy gifts for. This list should include family members, teachers or neighborhood helpers (like the baby-sitter or the bus driver), office Pollyannas, and charity donations. Put the list in your daily planner so you can add to it as you go about your normal day.

Remember, the more you buy, the more you have to organize.

The second gift list I keep in my planner all year long is a list of gift ideas for my family members and close friends. Sometimes I see a book or a clever toy and think, "My nephews would like this." If I don't write it down, I'm at a loss for what to get them when it comes time to shop. Like the perpetual food list, it's a perpetual gift list which can be used for Christmas and birthday ideas.

Set a budget. Remember, the more you buy, the more you have to organize! So look at your list and set a reasonable limit for your family. Write down the budgeted amount next to each name, and when you buy the present, record the actual price. Keep in mind that younger children do not know the prices of things. If you're trying to keep it even among the children in your family, look at the number of presents instead of the cost. It's normal to spend more on the older children and less on the little ones. Don't feel bad, their time will come!

There are many sales around Christmas time, so if you buy a $25 sweater for $15 and your budget for that person was $25, don't feel like you have to spend $10 more. They are receiving a $25 present. Keep the difference (you might need it for someone else's gift) and move on to the other people on your list.

Once you decide your total budget, think about how you will pay for these items. Will you use one credit card for everything? Will you pay cash? Or will you do a combination of the two? Whatever the case, make a decision and stick to it. I also recommend saving all the Christmas receipts in one envelope in case someone needs to return something after the holidays.

Shop efficiently. In this age of technology you really can make your shopping easy if you want to. First, decide what type of shopper you are: do you like to take

One way to shop efficiently is to buy the same type of present for several people.

your time and be inspired as you browse, or do you know exactly what you want for each person and it's a matter of getting it? If you enjoy going out to the stores, start looking at the newspapers in November and keep ads from stores that you want to go to. Map out which stores are close together. If you want to spread out the shopping, plan to go to one or two stores each day. That way you won't feel rushed. Some people like to pick up Christmas gifts all year long, but if you do this you have to have a hiding place where you can store them and not forget about them!

If you are someone who doesn't buy until you know exactly what you want, I suggest shopping online whenever possible. You can shop at several stores in one hour if you do it that way! Another way to shop efficiently is to buy the same type of present for several people. For example, if you are buying gifts for four teachers, give them all the same thing.

Try to finish your shopping a few days before Christmas. It will give you time to wrap presents, prepare the holiday meal and enjoy the beauty of the season.

Decorations. One of the first things I do to get ready for Christmas is to pull out the decorations around the first weekend in December. I love to put the electric candles and wreaths in the windows so our house is decorated from the outside. Then I have the kids help me spread our inside decorations through-out the house. The last decorating we do is the Christmas tree, which usually happens one week before Christmas. We typically take it down one week after New Year's Day.

When packing away the decorations, I keep them separated by where they will go. All the little ornaments are carefully wrapped in smaller boxes inside a big plastic storage container. The outside wreaths, candles and extension cords are put into plastic garbage bags. The inside decorations fit into two other plastic storage bins. By separating them this way, I can take out one box at a time to do the decorating and leave the tree ornaments where they are until the tree is up in its stand. We decorate in stages, setting aside one day for each. Use your month-at-a-glance calendar to schedule these activities at the beginning of the month.

Decide where and when the festivities will take place. For many families, a source of the stress is where to go for the holiday meal. There are often two sides of the family to consider, and for some families, close friends or neighbors may want to celebrate with them. Decide where to go as early as possible. A standing tradition makes it much easier. When I was first married, my husband and I decided that we would alternate Thanksgiving, spending it with his family one year and mine the next. Christmas was more important to us, so we decided to spend Christmas Eve with his family and Christmas Day with mine. It's not always at the same place or the same time of day, but everyone in our family knows what to expect. This is especially important if you come from a family where guilt comes into play. First and foremost, you should consider how your immediate family wants to spend the holidays and how your children will feel about traveling on Christmas Day. Do what makes you happy and not necessarily what you think you "should" do.

Keep the meals simple. Where there are families and holidays, there is eating! A traditional Christmas meal of turkey or ham with all the trimmings looks wonderful in the magazines, but is it realistic? And if you have two or more get-togethers over the holidays, can they all look picture perfect? Probably not. Sometimes it depends on what day of the week Christmas falls. If you are working until 4 or 5 PM on Christmas Eve, a big meal is not convenient. Have lasagna or pizza or sandwiches and save the big meal for Christmas Day. If you have a fancy Christmas Eve dinner,

If you are hosting the meal for a large group, there's nothing wrong with asking everyone to bring something.

serve cold cuts on Christmas Day. Like organizing, there's no right or wrong way to make the Christmas meal, there's only what works well for you. Keep this in mind before you set your expectations too high.

If you are hosting the meal for a large group, there's nothing wrong with asking everyone to bring something. You can take care of the main dish and other people can bring the wine, rolls, a vegetable dish and a couple desserts. If you're all going to Grandma's house, make sure you plan something for the children to do like a craft, a movie, or games. It will keep them from tearing apart Grandma's house and may give you some time to chat with the adults.

Follow these guidelines to plan ahead for your holiday season and your house will be decorated, presents will be wrapped, the meal will be easy to prepare and everyone will enjoy Christmas Day. Remember, it's the same time every year so there's no excuse for not being ready!

PACK UP YOUR FAMILY IN ONE WEEK

As a general rule, getting ready to go on vacation shouldn't take longer than the vacation itself. If you have implemented my tips for doing weekly household chores, you may have to switch things around a little the week before vacation. When you make your trip to the food store the week before vacation starts, include any special items that you will need to take with you. It's not an extra trip to the store, it's just a bigger order. When you wash clothes the week before vacation, pack everyone's clothes that night or the next day so they don't wear them before you leave.

A typical schedule the week before vacation may look like this:

Sunday – Check the weather for the place you are going so you can pack appropriate clothing. Cancel your newspaper and mail for the days you won't be home.

Monday – Clean the house. Print out your packing list.

Tuesday – Shop for sundries you will need.

Wednesday – Pack toys, books, music, etc.

Thursday – Wash and pack clothes.

Friday – Pack dry food. Drop off your pets if necessary.

Saturday – Pack cold food in cooler, and pack the car.

Be Adaptable to the Unexpected

I USUALLY PACK most of our food for the beach vacation we take every year. However, one year our refrigerator broke down and we had unexpected company the week before our vacation. Because it was such a stressful week, I cleared out the refrigerator into one cooler and packed whatever snacks we had in our cabinets. We ate dinner out the first night and I went food shopping the next morning when I was in a more relaxed state of mind. I don't usually like to go food shopping once my vacation has started, but in this case it was a necessity and it worked out just fine.

Make a packing list. Many families rent a house in the mountains or at the beach every year. If you take the same type of vacation every year, you can standardize your packing list so you don't have to start from scratch. Be general when you type up your list so you don't have to change it every year. For example, write "five shorts outfits, three pajamas" instead of "green shorts, tan T-shirt, blue pajamas, plaid boxers." I usually have my children, who are age six and older, pack their own clothes. I give them guidelines by telling them how many pajamas, short sets and bathing suits and let them decide which ones. I check the clothes before they go in the suitcase but they do most of the work. Then I give them each a bag to fill with toys, videos and books of their choosing. I give them the freedom to decide, but limit the space that all those items will take up.

For the food portion of the list, plan out dinners for the week and make sure you have some staples for lunch and breakfast. For the first night of vacation, it's convenient to pack something pre-made so you can just pop it in the oven. For the last night of vacation, don't plan a meal. Just eat the leftovers from the week so you don't have to bring them back home. Depending on where you are staying and how close you'll be to a supermarket, you'll want to decide ahead of time whether to pack all the food or go shopping once you get there.

If you are taking a plane trip instead of driving, the packing is easier. Airlines limit what you can bring on board and you won't have to pack food. As you're making your list for this type of trip, think about what the children will need for the traveling portion and what they will want once they are at your destination. Plane trips can take longer than expected, so it's a good idea to bring some surprise toys or crafts with you. For my children's first plane trip, a friend suggested I bring Crayola Color Wonder coloring books and paints. These are finger paints and magic markers that look clear but turn colors on the special paper. They don't make a mess. My children had a ball with them.

Once your packing list is printed out, take it with you on vacation. As you think of things you need, add to the list. As you find things you packed but didn't need or use, cross them off. You can even use this list to pack up when vacation is over so you don't forget any odds and ends. When you get home, update the list on your computer so you're ready for next year.

Weather. I once heard someone say, "There is no such thing as bad weather, only inappropriate clothing." How true this is! You don't have to let bad weather spoil your vacation. You just have to have a Plan B. Use the Internet to check the weather for wherever you are headed so you at least have an idea about the temperature and precipitation. Pack umbrellas and waterproof jackets for everyone in the family even if it's supposed to be dry. Also consider the weather at home for your return trip. Have you ever seen someone at the airport in shorts when there's a snowstorm outside? That person came from a tropical climate and didn't think through what the weather would be like when he or she landed! You don't have to pack a parka, but at least dress in layers.

Travel Information. The Internet is also a great place to start when planning your trip. Look up the city and surrounding areas for things to do, or go to a Web site for your hotel to see what amenities they have. You can also make reservations for special excursions or restaurants through some Web sites. Investigate your vacation spot, print out what you need and take it with you on the trip. When you get home you can trash it because it's all still there on your computer.

While you're there. Have you ever had a vacation that was so packed with activities that you needed another vacation when you came home? Think about that before you plan your next vacation. You want everyone to have fun, but you also want to build in some relaxation. In my experience, the children are usually worn out by midweek of the first week of vacation. Whether it's the experience of an amusement park, going to a beach or visiting friends out of town, the change in schedules affects the children, so plan on it. Take one day and don't do anything extra. Sleep late, go to bed early, lie around and watch movies or whatever suits your family. Take a "Sunday" in the middle of your vacation week and recharge everyone's energy.

When children are infants, I'm a stickler for regular eating and sleeping schedules, but as they get older, you can be more flexible. If a toddler still takes a nap at home, you'll want to keep that routine on vacation or you will have one cranky toddler. Sometimes it's nice for you and your husband or the other adults with you to rotate "nap duty." One adult stays at the house with the sleeping toddler or baby. If you have other children, the person with nap duty really has the easier job! You could also move the nap a little bit later in the day, like from 3-5 PM while you're preparing dinner. Or if you are out at a theme

Take a "Sunday" in the middle of your vacation week and recharge everyone's energy.

park, plan to head home during nap time so the child can sleep in the car. Be flexible, but plan some nap time for the little ones and the whole family will appreciate it.

If you're at your vacation destination and the weather is horrible, make the best of it. Remember, you're still on vacation and away from the daily grind and normal routines, so take advantage of it. Play games like charades or cards, or do skits or sing songs. Bundle up and take a walk in the rain or the snow if you must. The children will take their lead from Mom and Dad, so remember to stay relaxed and positive and don't complain.

My husband and I once had a crazy trip to Paris where everything went wrong on the first day. We started playing a game called "It could be worse, we could be..." and we took turns finishing that sentence with outlandish situations. In no time at all we were laughing hysterically. When you're packing for vacation, remember to bring along your sense of humor!

Make Your Time Work for You

Now you have the tools you need to make your time work for you. An organized schedule is the first step to an organized home, family and life.

REMEMBER

- Assign weekly chores such as cleaning, grocery shopping, and laundry to specific days of the week.
- Use a planner to plan your days, weeks and months.
- Delegate or outsource chores so you do not have to do it all.
- Keep infants on a regular sleeping and feeding schedule.
- Teach your children responsibility by giving them tasks and chores as they mature.
- Limit your children's extra activities.
- Simplify your holiday season by creating mailing labels for cards, a gift list, and a budget.
- Keep a packing list for family vacations on your computer and update it each year. Let the children help you pack before your vacation.
- Plan downtime in the middle of your vacation week.

After following these tips you will find you have more time in your schedule to spend with your children, your friends and your husband. If you still need to organize the stuff in your house, read on! We'll discuss how to handle what tends to accumulate over the years.

Part II: Organize Your Belongings

ADMINISTER C.P.R. There's a bumper sticker that reads, "The one who dies with the most stuff wins!" I disagree. The one with the most stuff probably doesn't even know what she has. She probably doesn't treasure it or use it. In some cases she can't even find what she really wants in all that clutter!

If you want to rid your home of clutter, you must pare down your belongings to the most essential items. I call my organizing method "C.P.R.", which stands for: Categorize, Purge and

Rearrange. You start by putting like things together (Categorize). Then you eliminate excess by trashing or donating whatever you don't use, need, or like (Purge). Then you put the items back in a logical place (Rearrange). Think of it as breathing new life into your possessions!

"Out of clutter, find simplicity; from discord, find harmony. In the middle of difficulty lies opportunity."

—ALBERT EINSTEIN

5. The Paper Pile Keeps Growing

THE PROBLEM

Your house is overrun by paper. It covers every available tabletop in every room and it keeps coming in. When you need to find something important, it takes an hour. Your method of straightening up the papers involves shoving everything into a plastic bag and tucking it away when you have guests. Sometimes you'll go back to these bags and pull out what you need. Sometimes these bags will be forgotten for years.

THE STORY

One of my clients has a lovely home complete with two home offices: one for herself and one for her husband. However, the dining room table, the kitchen table and the kitchen counters are always covered with papers. So for those of you who are thinking, "I just don't have enough room for all this paper," I say it's not always lack of space that is the problem. It's often the fact that papers are not being dealt with in a timely fashion. As Barbara Hemphill says in *Taming the Paper Tiger*, "Paper clutter is postponed decisions. Paper management is decision-making."

THE SOLUTION

First let's deal with the backlog of papers in your house. Let's make those decisions you've been postponing, and then I will give you some suggestions for maintaining a paperless, or a "less paper," environment going forward.

DIG OUT FROM YOUR BACKLOG OF PAPERS

Bring it all in. Bring all your papers to a location where you can go through them. If your designated office is messy right now, take the papers to the cleanest room of your house. It will help you to think clearly as you decide what to keep. Getting all of one category in one place gives me a feeling of control. I think, *Okay, this is all of it. Now I just have to deal with it.* Then I start my C.P.R. process (Categorize, Purge and Rearrange). For some people though, the thought of all that paper in one place is overwhelming. If you see it, you might need CPR! So, if you cannot physically manage all of your papers at once, clear one room at a time. If one room is still too much, sort one box at a time, but still take it to a clear room.

Categorize old paperwork. If your backlog of papers is older than a year, there are probably just a few categories to sort them into: tax files, memorabilia, and important documents. Get three cardboard boxes and label them with these categories.

Tax files should go back seven years if you want to be conservative. Most accountants will say you are safe from audit after three years.

Memorabilia is always a sketchy area but make sure when you save something it's not "just because." Ask yourself, *Am I saving this to put in a scrapbook? Do I get pleasure from looking at it? Will I look at it again?* If you answer no to all of these questions, throw it out and move on. Remember your goal is to rid your life of old papers and clutter!

Important documents would be birth certificates, a marriage license, papers regarding the purchase of your home or vehicle—any large purchase that you currently own.

Purge what you don't need. Anything that doesn't fall into one of these

> *Remember your goal is to rid your life of old papers and clutter!*

categories and cannot be filed in an existing file cabinet must be trash. Keep a shredder and trash bag handy to destroy any trash containing personal information. Shredding is a task you can delegate to another member of the family or you can do it yourself while you're watching TV.

Decide where old papers will be kept. Important papers can be kept in a safe deposit box or a fireproof safe that you will keep in your house. Decide with your spouse where it will be located and where the key will be kept.

Memorabilia papers can be kept in a scrapbook or a manila envelope inside a bigger "memory" box. If you've got years of these papers, you can separate by people or era.

Tax files can be stored in manila envelopes marked with the year. The last seven years of envelopes can be placed inside a plastic storage box. Decide where these will be stored. Possible options are the basement, the attic or a closet in your office. Most likely you will only need to access this box once a year when you put the new year in and take the oldest year out.

Memorabilia papers can be kept in a scrapbook or a manila envelope inside a bigger "memory" box (see chapter seven for ideas). If you've got years of these papers and don't know how to put them in any logical order for scrapbooking, you can separate by people or era. If you have several children and have clippings that pertain to each, make a pile for each child. Or if you have general papers that you want to keep, put them in order by the era of your life. Some might be from grade school and high school, others from college, and others from your early years of marriage. Only you know the best way to break it down, but don't get overwhelmed by the process. It doesn't have to be perfectly chronological to make an interesting and enjoyable scrapbook or memory box. Just remember to keep like things together.

Absolute of Organizing: Keep like things together.

GATHER AND PURGE MORE CURRENT PAPERS

Once again, gather all your current papers together. These might be the ones on the coffee table, the kitchen table, the mail table or the top of your desk. Most likely these will be from the last twelve months or so. Now get three boxes and label them: TO DO, TO READ, and TO FILE. Take each paper and decide whether you need to DO something with it, READ it, or FILE it. This is how you categorize in a big way. Any of the papers you come across that do not need to be read, worked with or filed must be trash. So, have a large trash bag and a shredder handy.

Once you have sorted every piece of paper in your house you will need to deal with one box at a time.

Absolute of Organizing: Organize from big to small.

A desk or work area is a good place to keep your TO DO file. Make sure this file has a permanent home.

CATEGORY	EXAMPLE
To read	• Newsletters • Magazines • Catalogs • Personal letters • School flyers
To do	• Bills to pay • Invitations to respond to • Address changes • Requests from school that require a response • Bank statements to be balanced • Projects that you are working on right now
To file	• Credit card statements (separated from bill stubs) • Bank statements that have been balanced • Catalogs that you like to keep on hand • Receipts for charitable contributions • Statements from financial investments • Statements from utility bills • School reference information

TO DO box

• Add these items to your TO DO list in your planner.

• Prioritize when to accomplish the tasks. Urgent items should go on the list for today or tomorrow; something you'd like to get done this month goes on your monthly goal list; a goal that is not time-sensitive belongs in your planner for a future month.

Organizing Your TO DO File

IF YOU ARE CREATING THIS TO DO FILE for the first time, it might seem overwhelming. You may want to divide it into sub-categories and tackle one at a time. However, once you make it a habit to address these things every day, the pile will dwindle quickly! At first it's a project, then it becomes a daily routine. A typical daily TO DO file might contain something like this: two phone calls, one invite to decide on, four bills, two school forms to fill out and one on-going project.

- Whenever possible, write down the pertinent information and discard the paper! If you must keep that paper, put it in the back pocket of your planner or in the file marked TO DO.

- Decide where your TO DO file will reside. Keep it in the same place every day. A logical place is on top of your desk or wherever you sit to make phone calls, pay the bills, etc.

- Create an action file for projects in progress, such as school functions, planning a party for your family, or investigating pre-schools. An action file is simply a file folder to hold all the relative papers that go along with that project. It can be left out on your desk or in your "in" bin because you are using it daily. Once the project is complete, however, weed out the unnecessary information and file away anything you will need for future reference. Then add that file to your file cabinet.

- When it comes to updating addresses and phone numbers, it is easiest to keep them in a computer file. Then you can easily update changes as you receive them. There are several types of electronic address books, or you can create a Word document set up for mailing labels. This makes sending holiday cards and invitations easy. If you have a traditional address/phone book, always write in pencil so it's easy to change.

- You might want to separate bills to pay out of your general TO DO box so they don't get forgotten. One suggestion is to put them in due-date order on top of your desk in a napkin holder or letter holder. If you don't have many paper bills, you could tuck them in your planner's back pocket.

TO READ box

- Simply put it in a place where you like to sit and read.
- If you want to force yourself to go through the box, put it on your bed!
- Carve out a little time each day to read. Even ten to fifteen minutes a day helps keep this pile down.
- Once you have read each piece, discard it or file it.
- Occasionally what you read may become a TO DO, in which case you should write it in your planner and toss the paper. Or put it in your planner pocket only if it has important information on it that can not be found elsewhere.
- If your TO READ pile gets too large or too outdated, it's time to let it go! Discard it and be assured there's more on the way.
- A great time to purge a large TO READ pile is while traveling by plane, train or riding in a car. Take a stack with you and vow not to bring it home!

TO FILE box

- This may be the largest pile, especially if you don't currently have a filing system.
- If you have current files, go through them first and purge what you don't need before you put any new papers in.

Be realistic. Only keep or create a file if you will refer back to it.

Start by sorting all papers into major categories such as:

- Financial
- Life Insurance
- Home
- Medical
- Educational
- Legal
- Car
- Charitable Contributions

As you sort, you may find certain categories are larger than others. If a file is too full, you might want to break it down into more specific sub-categories such as:

- bank accounts
- report cards
- kids' activities
- credit cards
- medical insurance
- contractors
- medical reports
- utility bills
- home owner's insurance
- investments
- home improvement receipts
- warranties and instructions
- car insurance
- school information
- car maintenance receipts

Decide where your files will be kept. If you have a desk with file drawers, use it for the most-used files. Reference files can be stored in a file cabinet that is either in your home office, a designated storage area, or in a closet. For school information that you will refer to throughout the year, have a folder for each child. Most importantly, be realistic. Only keep or create a file if you will refer back to it.

If you really want to be organized, put each major category of files in different colored hanging folders. Group like files together before you place them in your file cabinet.

MANAGE YOUR BUSINESS PAPERWORK

With so many network marketing companies and "home show" products, many moms run their own part-time business. If you are an independent consultant for a large company, the company may provide training about how to keep your books. Having done independent consulting myself, I will share some general guidelines for keeping this type of paperwork and bookkeeping under control.

Mileage Log: Keep a mileage log in your car for recording business miles. The log should include: date, starting mileage (from the odometer), ending mileage, total miles traveled and place or reason for the drive. At the end of the year, simply rip out these pages and total up the miles. Check with your accountant about the current mileage allowance you can claim on taxes.

Credit Card: Have a separate credit card for business expenses. Use it for things like office supplies, periodicals pertaining to your business, raw materials, and services such as Web site costs or cell phone charges. When the statement comes each month, file it in a "Business Expenses" file. Compile these at the end of the year for taxes.

Checking Account: Have a separate checking account for your business. Deposit your pay into this account and whenever possible write checks for your business expenses from this account. It will be easy to keep track of how much you are actually making at your part-time job! Again, your bank statements can get filed in "Business Expenses" so they can easily be compiled at the end of the year for taxes.

Contact Information: Contacts or leads can be kept in several different ways. The key is to consolidate names and contact information from business cards and little pieces of paper that you may accumulate. For many network-marketing businesses, following up is key. Possibilities for keeping your business contacts information include:

- A file box divided into categories like: new leads, call-backs, clients/customers
- An Excel spreadsheet
- A simple copybook

Cut Down on Junk Mail

ANOTHER WAY TO CUT DOWN ON YOUR PAPER FLOW is to remove your name from marketing lists. Each time you open a credit card or make a purchase via mail order or online, your name and address go on a marketing list. It's a good idea to contact the following agencies every five years to "clear the slate" and cut down on the sales offers you will receive by mail, phone or e-mail.

For credit card offers: Call 1-888-567-8688 to take your name off the credit information lists compiled by Equifax, TransUnion, Experian and Innovis.

For junk mail: Send a postcard with your name, address and the phrase "activate the preference service" to the following service: Mail Preference Service, Direct Marketing Association, P.O. Box 643, Carmel, NY 15012-0643. This will stop mail from all member organizations you have not specifically ordered products from in the last five years.

For general telemarketing calls: Call 1-888-382-1222 from all your phone lines or visit www.donotcall.gov online to be put on the National Do Not Call Registry set up by the Federal Trade Commission.

- Your e-mail program's address book
- A more sophisticated "contact" software program like ACT, GoldMine, Contact Manager Pro, Now Up-to-Date and FileMaker Pro, just to name a few
- Your "Contacts" list on your hand-held organizer

MAINTAIN YOUR PAPER SYSTEM EVERY DAY

Now that you have a place for all your papers, you need a plan to maintain your paper flow. Here are some daily habits to help keep the paper under control.

Mail: Deal with your mail every day. It requires making quick decisions but hopefully only a few each day. Sort into the same four categories mentioned before: TRASH, TO DO, TO READ, TO FILE. Take bills out of their envelopes, discard the excess paper, put the bill stub and return envelope in your TO DO or "bills to be paid" area, and the statement in your TO FILE area. Immediately trash junk mail, sales circulars that you're not interested in, and credit card offers—unless you are in the market for one of these products or services right now.

Children's Papers: Deal with your children's papers every day. Look at their schoolwork and ask them if they want to keep anything. If they do, each child should have a drawer in his or her desk or a box in his or her bedroom for schoolwork. Artwork can be displayed on the refrigerator, a bulletin board in the

Continued on page 70

A jute bin is an attractive way to store catalogs and newspapers.

How Long to Keep Statements

- *Utilities* – There's no need to keep these once the bill is paid, unless you want to compare year-to-year expenses. If so, two years is plenty.

- *Mortgage* – Save the last statement of the year if it has the "total interest paid" and "real estate taxes paid," which you may need for filing your taxes. Once it is paid off, keep the discharge statement as long as you own the property and six years after the sale.

- *Pay stubs* – Keep these for one year and check them against your W-2, then you may discard them and keep the W-2.

- *Car* – Save the sales contract and repair receipts for the life of the car.

- *Bank statements* – Keep for one year. Always balance your account on a monthly basis. If statements contain tax-deductible expenses, keep them with the tax information for that year.

- *Credit card statements* – If you use these for budgeting purposes, or if you will refer back to them, keep for one year. You may need to save the last statement of the year if you can claim the interest paid on your taxes.

- *Financial investments* – For tax purposes you will need to have proof of how much you paid for a stock and what you sold it for. Keep the purchase record as long as you own the stock and the sale record as backup information with your tax files for the year it was sold. If you have several dividends paid throughout a year, hold onto each until the investment company sends you an annual dividend statement. When in doubt, check with your accountant about what you need to keep.

- **Tax returns** – Keep a copy with all your backup information for seven years. Each year add one and discard the oldest one.

- **Medical bills** – Keep for the year if you itemize these on your tax return.

- **Medical reports/diagnosis** – Keep forever. As your children grow up and move out of the house, you can pass their medical file on to them.

- **Car/Health/Life/Homeowners insurance** – Keep current policies and claim information. In case of a claim against you, keep any previous homeowner and car insurance policies as long as the statute of limitations in your state.

- **Bill of purchase for property** – Keep for as long as you own the property.

- **Bill of sale for property** – Keep with tax information for the year in which it was sold.

Remember that most of these monthly and quarterly statements can now be electronically accessed. If you don't have a specific statement and you need it, you can usually contact that company to retrieve it.

playroom, or in a frame. The plastic box frames from art stores are great—they allow for easy updating. Throw out anything they don't want and you don't love. Read school flyers and treat them like any other mail. At the end of the school year, go through the box or drawer with your child. Anything you decide to keep will go into their memory box. Like your tax files, you can put papers in a manila envelope, and mark the grade or year.

Catalogs and Newspapers: Catalogs and newspapers tend to hang around the house for a while. I recommend having a specific, yet attractive place for each. Options include magazine racks, large baskets, leather carrying bins or some other decorative containers. Once the bin is full, however, it's time to weed out and recycle.

Sales Circulars: It's amazing how many of these we receive each week. I typically put these in the recycle bin immediately and here's why: They are designed to entice you to buy something you don't need! With my grocery list and other shopping lists that I keep in my planner, I know what I need to buy. Also, most grocery stores now have "clipless coupons." If you have a shopper's card for that store, you'll get the sale price anyway. However, with every rule there is an exception. If you are in the market for a gift or some clothing or household item and you want to find the best price for it, by all means look through the sales circulars, find the right store, cut out the coupon or ad that applies and place it in your TO DO file. You may even want to create a special envelope or folder to take with you when you are shopping.

When you return home from running errands, take five minutes to sort out your receipts from the day.

Receipts: While you're out running errands you will usually accumulate receipts. Take five minutes when you return home to sort them out. People often ask me, "How long do I need to keep certain receipts or bill statements?" Everyone's situation is different but I have some general guidelines that you can use:

- Receipts for cash expenses should be written down in your daily planner. Or if you keep your expenses on a computer system like Quicken, save the receipt in a small box or basket to record monthly.
- Credit card receipts should go in the file for that card and be stapled to the statement once it arrives.
- Check/debit card/ATM receipts should be entered into your check log each day. You can save the receipt in the back of your check log or in a file until the monthly statement arrives. Once you balance your account, you can shred those receipts.
- Receipts for gifts should either be kept with the gift or put in an envelope marked accordingly. Discard after you know it will not be returned.
- Receipts for major purchases should be kept stapled to the warranty or instruction book, in case of return.

6. So Many Photos—No Albums

THE PROBLEM

You have adorable, young children and you want to remember every precious moment of their lives—so now you are taking tons of pictures. But where do you put these photos? And when do you have time to organize them? Many of the mothers I speak with mention photographs as an area that they just cannot keep up with. If you are like them, maybe you are aiming for something too intricate and are ignoring simple solutions you can put in place right now to get your photos under control.

THE STORY

I once heard this tale at a Creative Memories scrapbooking demonstration: There was a family that cleaned out the parents' attic and fought over who would take the boxes of crumbled up and yellowed photos. No one wanted them!

Another family also cleaned out the parents' attic. This mother had meticulously put pictures in an album and wrote notes next to each one. This family also fought over who would take the old photo albums—they all wanted to take them!

THE SOLUTION

If you want to enjoy your photographs, you have to do something with them! Leaving them in their original envelopes is not an option. Every picture tells a story so make your story a beautiful one by putting pictures in a place where you and your family will enjoy them.

DECIDE HOW TO ORGANIZE

All organizing starts with a decision. In this case, decide how you want to keep your photos or how you like to look at them.

Slip-in photo albums. These albums are the easiest to maintain and therefore are a good starting point for people who have photos in big boxes or in the original drug store bag they came home in. These are simply photo albums with plastic sleeves that you slip your photos into. Many come in a binder format so it's easy to move pages around or add pages. Some also come with a "notes" area so you can write interesting facts about each picture. You can put your photos in these first, and then pull out special shots as needed to put in frames or add to children's scrapbooks.

Slip-in photo albums are a quick and easy way to organize photos.

Corkboard wall. I have a good friend who loves to look at her pictures every day, so she put up corkboard on a wall in her kitchen from floor to ceiling and pinned her favorite pictures there. This is a great place to display holiday picture cards of family and friends. If you fill this area up quick, you'll have to remember to update it seasonally.

Collages. If you find that a lot of your pictures are not centered or close enough to the subject, you can cut out only the important people and important sites from a particular occasion and put them in a collage. It doesn't have to be fancy. Use a glue stick and glue them to the paper that comes with the frame. If you have a large blank wall in a family room, you can hang collages as you make them. Each frame will represent a different time or event in your life. They are fun to look at and they save a lot of space.

Photo boxes. Many stores carry these decorative boxes now. If you choose to use them, decide how you want to keep them: all family pictures chronologically or separated by each child? Make sure you label each box accordingly. Some of these boxes are so pretty you can leave them out on a bookshelf for easy access. I recommend putting the pictures in order and using cards to label and separate like you would a recipe file.

Use index cards to label and separate categories in your photo boxes.

Scrapbooks. This has become a favorite pastime for many mothers. The end result is beautiful and meaningful, especially when you "journal" or write little stories about what was happening during a particular event. The downside is that scrapbooks take a lot of time and creativity to put together, and it is a big project—not an everyday process. Even if you are great about keeping up with scrapbooks for your family, you need a staging area for the photos and memorabilia that will go into the scrapbooks. For this, I suggest simple household items like manila envelopes, plastic bins or shoeboxes. If your child collects pictures and pamphlets throughout the school year, drop them in the envelope or box and use the summertime to work on his or her scrapbook together. One of the best times for scrapbooking is a rainy summer day. I've even brought our scrapbook materials on vacation. When children are out of their normal environment, they look for different things to do, and scrapbooking can be a fun and creative outlet for them. Give yourself the whole summer. Take your time, create your scrapbook, and have an empty box ready to fill in September.

On your computer. If you have a digital camera, set up files of pictures on your computer. Here are some tips for organizing and using your digital photos:

- Give your files simple names. If you upload pictures from your camera once a month, name the file with the month and year (MAY13). If you upload less frequently, name the files by season and year (WINTER13). Or name them more specifically by event (VACATION13).
- Create digital photo albums on Web sites that you use for developing. This stores photos remotely and protects against a hard drive crash on your computer. The albums also store the photos in chronological order.
- Save your photos on a CD-R or DVD disk, which also protects them from anything that might happen to your computer. CD-Rs or DVDs take up a lot less physical space than photo albums but the photos are not as accessible to look at.
- E-mail digital copies of your pictures to family and friends rather than mailing them prints.
- Create a unique "slide show" screensaver on your computer with your personal pictures, and update it frequently.

START YOUR SYSTEM TODAY

Once you have decided how you want to store or display your photos, buy the items needed to carry out your plan and start with current photos. Purchase your storage boxes or photo album or corkboard now, and then you'll have a process for storing all the pictures you develop from now on. If you only develop between thirty and fifty pictures at a time, it should take you about ten to fifteen minutes to put them in an album or to hang them. If you typically get double prints, divide them up right away and put them in envelopes for the people you give them to. These envelopes can go right in your TO DO file. Once that process is in place, you can then address the old photos that are sitting around your house.

Gather Your Backlog of Photos

To begin organizing old photographs, I recommend you gather them all in one place. If you have an area where you can spread them out, or at least store a box of photos until your project is done, then move them into that area.

Categorize and Purge. Use the C.P.R. process (Categorize, Purge and Rearrange) and start categorizing the photos. There is no right or wrong way to do this. Group them by child, or time of year, or era. As you sort through, purge any pictures that are ruined or dark or blurry. Only keep the good ones!

Absolute of Organizing: Keep only what you use.

Arrange or Rearrange your photos. Finally, it's time to get your photographs where you want them. If you created a pile of photos for framing, start framing! If you decided you want them in an album, take a stack and start putting them in albums. Your children or your husband can help when you're all watching TV. If you want to make it really fun, give each child a stack of photos and a page or an album and see who can get their pictures in first.

If you want your photos accessible to the whole family and visitors, keep them on the bottom shelf of a bookshelf or console table in your family room or living room. I usually have six big albums on my bookshelf at all times. I often refer to them when I'm talking to my children about a trip we took, or someone they don't see too often. They really get a kick out of it. As the albums get older and more "beat up," I tuck them away in my memory box. "What's a 'memory box' and how do I get one?" you might ask. Read on to find out the answer!

7. I Keep Everything, but Treasure Nothing

THE PROBLEM

The first problem I often see when dealing with memorabilia is simply identifying exactly what in your house is "memorabilia." This may be new terminology for you. Ask yourself, "Why am I saving this?" If your answer is, "just because my kids did it" or "it brings back good memories," then that is MEMORABILIA. As mothers, we want to save every precious art project and little card or note that our children have written, but that's just not practical.

THE STORY

Before I had my first child, I went through a serious "nesting" time. One of the best things I did was to go through my "memory box." It was a steamer trunk that I took with me to college, then used as a night table in my apartment when I was single. It had slowly become the place where I kept all those little knickknacks that you don't know what to do with but you don't want to throw away. It also held old letters that my husband had sent me while we were dating. I sat on the bed and read letters, leafed through my college and high school yearbooks, and looked at old photo albums. I picked up buttons and books of matches that

I had saved from special events, and looked at trophies that had once lined a shelf in my childhood bedroom. It was like I had found my own personal treasure box. I laughed, I cried, and I threw away what was stupid. But the emotions and memories it brought back were wonderful and in a way, it prepared me for the new stage of life ahead. I thought to myself, *Everyone should have a treasure box like this.* Years of memories were in one box and I knew where it was if I ever wanted to reminisce again.

THE SOLUTION

You must gather your memorabilia in one place to see the magnitude of your problem, if there is one. For some, this might be an overwhelming thought. I suggest tackling the accumulation of memories in the same way we tackled the overload of paperwork.

TREAT IT LIKE A SCAVENGER HUNT

Go from room to room in your house looking for things that you're hanging on to just because they remind you of a happy time. Once you've found your memorabilia, gather it into one room. If you can't physically fit everything in one room or on one table, start with one room at a time. You may have baby keepsakes for each child in their individual rooms. It makes sense to go through their items one room at a time. You may have the most memorabilia saved, and it may be stored in several places (your closet, the family room, the attic) in several containers. If this is the case, you may need to sort one box at a time.

Make a project plan. Decide how much time you will need to go through your memorabilia based on the amount of items you have collected. If you are doing one room, a two- or three-hour chunk of time in the evening may be enough. If you have several dozen boxes filled with memorabilia and you want to do it all at once, you're looking at a full day project. You need time to go through everything and purge what you don't want and group it into smaller categories. Once you know how much time it will take, put it on your calendar and TO DO list. You may need to ask your husband or a friend to help.

Begin to purge. Using my C.P.R. method, we have already "categorized" in the broad sense of the word, so now it's time to "purge." Purging memories is hard for many people but the process can be emotional in a good way, too. When was the last time you looked at your high school yearbook? Or read a card your husband gave you when you were dating? This is the reason you saved this stuff, right? Take your pile or box, look at everything—but don't dwell too long—and decide: KEEP IT or TRASH IT. If the KEEP IT pile is huge, it can be subdivided into categories such as: children, husband, high school, college, wedding, trips, or other special events.

Absolute of Organizing: Keep purging simple with Yes and No piles.

Take a closer look. Here's the hard part. You have categorized and purged. If your memorabilia still fills a room...you've got to purge again. Be realistic and ask yourself these questions:

- Have I broken down the items into small enough categories?
- Do I really need to save all of these or can I pick a few representative pieces that are my favorites (such as greeting cards or children's art)?
- Will I ever look at this again?
- Does this item give me a good feeling when I look at it?
- Do I have the room to keep all of this in my house?

DISPLAY YOUR TREASURES

If you've really purged all you can, decide if anything you've discovered today is something you want out on display in your house. Put those items aside. Then decide if you have a place to display them now, or if you need to purchase something like a shelf or frame. When deciding where to display items, group like items together and put up a simple display shelf in the room that makes sense for those items. For example, plates or cups that your children have made or decorated could go in the kitchen.

Absolute of Organizing: Put like things together.

Select the Best Storage Container

Items you don't plan to display will go in a memory box. Think about where you want to keep your memory box and what kind of container you would like. You may already have something appropriate in your home now. If you do not have the right kind of storage, place the items in a regular cardboard box labeled "memories" and put them in a safe place. Now you can go shopping for your own treasure box! This chart offers suggestions on containers that will keep your memories in good shape.

Maintain Your Memory Box

Now that you have a logical place for all your memorabilia, you have to keep up with it. Make sure the containers you have chosen are bigger than what you need right now because you will be adding to them. You can "subtract" from

LOCATION	CONTAINER	FIND IT AT
Bedroom closet	Plastic storage container with a lid	Any home store
Bedroom or family room	Wicker chest	Home décor catalog
	Decorative steamer trunks	Some arts and craft stores
	Wooden hope chest	Furniture store or consignment shop
Basement or attic	Plastic storage container with a lid (be careful of things that will melt in the attic)	Any home store
	Cedar-lined steamer trunk	Any home store

Steamer trunks (right) and stacking storage bins (below) are two options for storing memorabilia.

them each year as well. A great time to go through your memory trunk or box is during a transition time in your life. For my children, I sort their memory boxes at the beginning of every summer. (They are transitioning from one grade to the next.) As for my husband and me, we went through our memory boxes when we moved, when we had a new child, and any time we shifted the function of rooms in our house. You can also go through the box whenever it starts to get over-packed! (I call this the "full barrel" method. You clear it out when it's about to spill over.) Going through it means using the C.P.R. process again. But each time, it's easier and quicker because you have already begun the process of paring down what you want to keep. There are things that mean a lot to you now, but in five years you may wonder, *Why did I ever save this?* Then it's time to throw it out and make room for new memories.

Absolute of Organizing: Subtract before you add.

8. My Collections Are Buried in Boxes

THE PROBLEM

Collections take up a lot of space and collect dust, and they are constantly growing. So how do you organize a collection? You may have a collection and not even realize it. If you buy a refrigerator magnet every time you take a trip, you are a collector. You may think these magnets are practical mementos, and they are, up to a point. But after you have more than ten or so, they are not simply tools, they are a collection.

THE STORY

While working with a client in her kitchen, I discovered a large number of both cookbooks and coffee mugs. She lived alone so I suggested that she keep just a few mugs and only the cookbooks that she regularly used. "Oh no!" she said, "I'm not getting rid of any cookbooks or mugs. I collect them." What I thought was a very practical step became an emotional issue.

People are very passionate about their collections, and as a professional organizer, I have to take that into consideration when coming up with a solution for the clutter.

Practical Collections

I USED TO COLLECT MATCHBOOKS from the restaurants I went to when I traveled. I keep them in my memory box because I don't want to use them and I certainly don't want my kids getting into them. When I decide I no longer want them as a memory, I can put them with my candles and simply put them to good use. They'll go from memorabilia to practical tools.

THE SOLUTION

There are probably as many solutions as there are types of collections. And the solutions for how to keep your collections range from utilitarian to decorative. In order to formulate guidelines for setting up your collections, it will help to answer the following questions for yourself.

What do I collect?

As you sort through your things you may find a collection that you had started a long time ago. Or you may discover you have many similar items and you have become a collector by default. Like the items in your "memory box," it's hard to part with these things and seeing them brings back good memories. If these items are not all together right now, gather them up, box and label until you find a permanent home for them. Whether they are T-shirts, postcards or china figurines, you have to decide what to do with them.

Absolute of Organizing: Keep like things together.

Who do I want to look at this collection?

Think about whether your collection is something your family and friends will enjoy seeing, or if it's something that only you can appreciate.

My matchbook collection helps me remember fun travels I had in my twenties, so I keep it in a private place. If you have something that everyone can enjoy, then it should be on display.

Is my collection practical or ornamental?

The refrigerator magnets and coffee cups are a good example of practical collections. You may want to keep them where you use them—in the kitchen. But if space is an issue, you'll have to keep only a few of these out and store the rest, or perhaps create some kind of display area for them. For example, the coffee cups could be displayed on a simple shelf or in a glass-front cupboard in the kitchen. The magnets could go on their own magnetic board instead of cluttering the front of the refrigerator.

If you need to store a portion of the collection, remember to rotate the items on display to keep the display fresh. Ornamental collections should be out on display. If they are packed away in a box, what's the point of having them?

If you need to store a portion of the collection, remember to rotate the items on display to keep the display fresh.

If it won't be used or displayed, why am I keeping it?

If the answer is that you are saving it to pass down to your children or you'll put it out one day when your children are grown, that's okay. Safely pack it away and label it clearly so it's not forgotten. If your answer is, "I have no idea," then consider selling it or giving it away.

Absolute of Organizing: Keep only what you use.

Where is an appropriate display area?

The answer to this question depends on your home's décor. A seashell collection makes sense in a room that has a nautical flair, or in a bathroom decorated in an ocean or shell theme. Fancy china figurines or plates make sense in a formal dining room or living room. And things like German beer steins would look great displayed behind a bar. Maybe you have a collection that has been packed away for a while because it just doesn't match anything in your home. If you really want to display it, you could consider redecorating a room to match a collection. I had some beautiful Delftware I purchased on a trip to Holland, but I really didn't have a room that matched. When I moved into my new house, I made the living room blue and white and bought an inexpensive white display shelf to hang on the wall. Now the Delftware has a home and I enjoy looking at it every day.

The right case or shelf will help you display your collections.

Take stock, consider future additions. If your collection is finite, then it's a lot easier to pick a place to display it. I'm done collecting matchbooks, so a simple box to fit what I have is fine. If you are still adding to the collection, then you should use a display system that can grow. This is not unlike what you do with your photos. More are coming so you have to plan for them. It may mean purchasing a display shelf that has room left in it, or buying something that you can easily purchase another of as the collection grows.

> *If you are still adding to the collection, then you should use a display system that can grow.*

FIND THE RIGHT DISPLAY CASE, CONTAINER OR SHELVING

Have your collection in front of you in the room where it will be displayed. Now look at the size of it and the colors in it. Whether it's formal or casual, monochromatic or colorful, think about what case or shelving would complement it. I always suggest looking around at what you already own first. If there is nothing that would fit, second-hand shops are a good place to start. Then there's always Internet shopping. If you've got a collection that other people might have too, chances are you'll find some sort of display case online. Simple display shelves that hang on the wall are very popular and can be found in almost any home store. Remember, if you don't like the color of the shelf, you can always paint it!

Custom-made display. If you or someone you know is creative, sketch out what you'd like and see if you can easily make it. My son started to collect mini football helmets a few years ago. Being the way I am, I didn't want them all over his room or crushed in a toy box. So I searched for a display shelf. Finally, I decided to measure their sizes, and figure out how many he would have when his collection was complete. Then my husband put together a simple wooden shelf that I painted and nailed to the wall. Sometimes custom-made is cheaper and easier!

9. The Toys Have Taken Over

THE PROBLEM

If you're a mom, you have children. If you have children, you have toys. And if you come from a large family that gives gifts, you have lots of toys. These toys migrate. They move from basements to family rooms to bedrooms to outside—anywhere your children go.

THE STORY

In our first house, when my husband and I had one child, we had a toy area in the corner of our "breakfast room." Some simple, white, plastic shelving held all of our little girl's toys. Then we had two more children. Once, while we were eating dinner, a basketball went flying across the table. "Maybe we need to rethink the toy area," we both said. So we turned the 8' × 10' (2.4m × 3m) mudroom into the toy room. We decorated it with jungle animals, put up some bigger shelves and added a wooden toy box. It was not large, but it was cute. The older children primarily used it as a place to store their toys. When I was home with the baby, we would lay out a blanket and play on the floor in there. The best feature was a locking door, so when we had company over, we could lock certain toys in and pull out the toys we didn't mind the children using. Now, in our second home, my children have an entire playroom, complete with a sofa, toy bins and a TV. As your family grows, you'll need to adapt your home to your changing needs. You also must be creative with the space and the resources you have.

THE SOLUTION

First, decide where you are going to keep toys in your house. Then decide how you are going to keep them. Finally, develop the habit of doing toy clean-outs at different times of the year. Let's look at each of these three steps and discuss some options in hopes that you will find one that suits your family and your home.

STEP 1—WHERE ARE YOU GOING TO KEEP THE TOYS?

When deciding where to keep the toys, consider the set up of your house and the age of your children, as well as their personalities and play styles. Include your husband and children as you designate your "toy room" or "toy area." If your children are old enough, let them help you arrange and decorate the toy room or area so they feel like they own it. They will be more inclined to help you straighten it up when necessary. It makes them feel "big" and responsible to have their own place. Here are some options to consider when selecting a storage area:

Consider the set up of your house and the age of your children, as well as their personalities and play styles. Include your husband and children as you designate your toy room or area.

Toy room. If you are lucky enough to have a finished basement or an extra room on the main floor of your house, you can designate this as a toy room. It will be the room that your children gravitate to during most of the day. Many mothers say they have a basement that they'd like to use as the toy room, but their children are young and they don't want to be alone there while Mommy is upstairs. In that case I say switch your plan. Maybe the basement can be used as the adults' recreation room or home office and the children can have a room upstairs for play. Also, realize that as they get older, your children may want to be downstairs with the door closed. You can rearrange the rooms at that time. The great thing about having one toy room is that even if it has toys all over the floor, you can write it off as "that's the kids' room" and the rest of your house can still look nice.

Children's bedrooms. If you don't have an extra room to devote to toys and playtime, then you may have to use your children's bedroom as the toy area. In this case you will have to be very conscious of limiting toys and keeping them in proper containers, leaving room for a bed and dresser. Luckily, most children do not have many clothes that need to be hung up so you can devote at least a portion of closet space for toys.

Family room. If the bedrooms are tiny and there are no extra rooms in your house, you may have to use part of your family room to keep toys. This may not be your first preference, but it is a reality for many people. How you arrange the room and what containers you use will be key in keeping this room from looking sloppy or cluttered.

A large closet. You could always use a large closet for storing toys. The children can take out what they want to play with, use it in any room of the house, and when it's time to straighten up, put it back in the closet. Again, with this option the containers you choose and the use of space in the closet will be key to keeping it functional.

Combination of options. If you choose to keep toys in more than one of these areas of your house, I recommend you still use the idea of "keeping like things together" and break down all toys into subcategories. Games could go in the family room, action figures in the bedrooms, stuffed animals in the bedroom and arts and craft supplies in a closet. The last thing you want is to have all types of toys in several rooms of your house. Then it is hard to put things away and keep track of what toys you have.

Absolute of Organizing: Keep like things together.

STEP 2—WHAT WILL YOU USE TO KEEP THE TOYS ORGANIZED?

Once you have designated where you will keep the toys, bring all the toys to that spot. This will help you see how much you need to get rid of to make it all fit. Use the C.P.R. (Category, Purge and Rearrange) process and categorize the toys into smaller groups such as: action figures, stuffed animals, games, puzzles, arts and crafts, kits with small pieces (e.g., building blocks, train sets, etc.) and sports equipment. Once you have categorized, decide what can be purged. Anything that is broken or dangerous should be trashed and anything that your children do not play with anymore can be given away. Now look at what's left and begin to consider what containers you can use to store them. Here are some storage container options to consider:

Wooden toy boxes offer easy storage and are easy to access. A toy box with wheels can easily be moved out of sight when you entertain guests.

Wooden toy box. The good old-fashioned toy box is great for big toys that you want out in the open and accessible for the children. They look fine in a bedroom or living room. If you want your living room to have a more sophisticated look when you entertain guests, a toy box on wheels makes it easy to hide the toys in another room for an evening. Be careful not to overfill these, or toys will get broken. These are not great options for little pieces, which tend to fall to the bottom. The benefit—having one box for general toys makes for easy clean-up.

Wooden bookshelf. Bookshelves are great for play sets such as farms or doll houses, which have small pieces inside. They also are great for boxes and puzzles or games, which can be stacked. If your children are climbers, you must make sure these shelves are secured to a wall. The shelves can be used out in the open or tucked into a closet for storage. And if you find one at a second-hand shop, you can always paint it to match your décor.

Toy shelves with plastic bins are great for storing small toys your children frequently play with.

Metal utility shelf. Metal utility shelves are nice and sturdy and usually wider than a typical bookshelf. Use these in a basement or a room that's not a common area in your home because they're not the most attractive storage option. But like the wooden shelves, these can hold play sets, puzzles, games and smaller bins full of toys. Also make sure these are secure for young climbers.

Toy shelf with small plastic bins. Many companies make toy shelves with small, plastic bins that come in pastels or bright primary colors. These shelves are good for small toys that you want your children to access. It is difficult to keep the categories straight, but you can always try to teach your children what toys go in which bins. Labeling the bins with pictures and then words as the children get older is one way to help. Bins are a great option for a toy room or child's bedroom but I wouldn't recommend them for a family room, unless they can be tucked away in a corner.

Large plastic container with lid. When your child has a collection of character or brand-related toys, large containers come in handy. If the containers are clear, children can easily see what's inside. If they're not clear, label the containers with the logo for that toy. You'd be amazed at how early a child can recognize logos for their toys! These bins are typically used for storage and a closet or cabinet is the best place to keep them. But if you must have them out in the open, consider decorating the sides with acrylic paint from an art store.

Large plastic tub. If you have many toys in one specific category such as stuffed animals, an open plastic tub works well. My children always liked cleaning up with tubs because it was like a basketball game. Since tubs are plastic and colorful, I recommend using them in a child's bedroom or out of sight.

Baskets. Like the big open tubs, large baskets can store a lot of one type of toy. However, the baskets are a little more decorative, and they don't look bad in a family room. Small baskets can be used to hold hand-held toys, like the ones found in children's meals at fast-food restaurants. I have a basket in my basement near the back door. When we go for a car ride or to church, I tell the children they can take one or two hand-held toys with them. The toys are usually inexpensive, so if we leave them somewhere it's not a problem. Also, I clean this basket out whenever it gets full. These are the types of toys children rarely miss.

Stuffed animal hammock. These can be found at most toy stores and they are a great option if you want to use the stuffed animals (or any soft toys) as a decoration in a bedroom or toy room.

Clear plastic stackable bins. These bins work well on a shelf or in a closet. They are great for holding smaller toys or arts and craft supplies. If you want the small pieces out of reach for little children, put these bins on top of the shelf or closet so only you can take them down. And if you're catching on to my trend here, I would never leave these out in the open in a family room!

Under-the-bed plastic container. When space is at a premium, you have to use all available options. Under the bed is one of them. Most children use that option anyway, although not in an organized fashion.

There are some nice under-the-bed rolling containers that you can find at home stores or in home improvement catalogs. Limit each under-the-bed box to housing one category of toys and make sure your child knows what is stored in each.

Decorated cookie or popcorn tins. Here's an option for recycling something you may already have—tins. The tins are nice for keeping collections of little pieces together. Make labels for the outside of the tins so your children can identify the toys inside. Depending on how decorative they are, you can keep these out on a shelf or in a closet or cabinet in any room.

Steamer trunk. I love the steamer trunk as a storage option because it can always double as a coffee table. If your children have "dress-up" clothes, this is a great place to store them. However, I have one friend who is a real minimalist and all of her children's toys fit into one steamer trunk. So it could be used in place of a general "toy box." A steamer trunk can be used in any room of the house as long as it doesn't look out of place.

Over-the-door or over-the-closet-bar shoe racks. Shoe racks can be found in home stores or home improvement catalogs. Some toy companies actually make them for dolls or action figures. They are great for special toys that you want to keep nice and don't want thrown into just any container. These racks work well in a child's bedroom or a toy room.

STEP 3—HOW DO I KEEP ALL THESE TOYS STRAIGHT?

In Part I, I wrote about taking a little time each day to get things back to the right place. Involve your children in this process as early as you can. After they're done playing with a group of toys and they're on to the next thing, ask them to help you put the toys back in the right bin. This might be more realistic if your children are small and you are the one supervising their playtime. Once your children are playing independently, you can do a clean-up at the end of the day before bedtime. Ask them to get the toys back to the toy room or toy area. For some that is enough. If you really want to get organized at the end of the day, ask each child to put one type of toy away, so one child would put all the blocks in a bin, another child can put the balls in a tub and another child can help you put away the paper and crayons. Children usually respond better to specific instructions like this rather than a general, "Clean up the toy room!"

Even though you may be cleaning *up* the toys on a regular basis, there comes a time to clean *out* the toys. Here are some options for how and when to make that happen:

Go Through the Toys with Your Children

If you clean out toys with your child, two weeks from now when he or she asks, "Where's my...?" you can say, "Remember, we gave it away to your cousin because you're too big for that now." Or, "Remember it was broken so we threw it out. But now you have a nice, new toy instead."

If the child is involved, I try to make it a simple decision by asking, "Do you play with this anymore?" Then we make a "Yes" and "No" pile. The "Yes" pile goes back in the toy box, on the shelf, etc. Then I deal with the "No" pile on my own. Sometimes I have a specific person I can give a toy to, sometimes there's a charity that I know will take it, and sometimes it's wise to trash it.

Absolute of Organizing: Keep purging simple with "Yes" and "No" piles.

The other good thing about the toy clean out is finding toys you forgot you had. It's like when Woody says in *Toy Story 2*, "Remember to rotate the toys at the bottom of the toy box." For children, it's as good as getting a new toy. If you have more than one child and they each have separate toy areas or toy boxes, I recommend sorting the toys with one child at a time. That way you avoid debates among them over what to keep.

Go Through the Toys Without the Children Around

Most of us will agree that this method is much faster and we'll get rid of a lot more if we just do it ourselves. However, there are often consequences to pay. If you do the clean out and are getting rid of some toys, I would recommend putting them in a holding zone. A "holding zone" can be a black bag or box where you will keep the toys that are going away unbeknownst to the children. You will hold onto them for about two weeks just in case someone is looking for a missing toy. If they absolutely insist on finding that toy, you discretely take it out. Whatever they don't ask for in two weeks should be safe for removal.

MAINTAINING YOUR TOY SYSTEM

If things have gotten out of hand and there are toys all over the house, it's time to "bring it all in." I call this the "Great Toy Clean Out." I bring all toys into one large, open room and begin to categorize, purge and rearrange once again.

When to Maintain

- Before a child's birthday
- Before Christmas/Hanukkah
- Before a change in season like winter or summer—especially for outside toys or toys that may be kept in the garage or shed
- When you are redecorating or rearranging a room with toys in it
- Before a move
- When it all seems out of control!

10. So Many Clothes, but Nothing to Wear!

THE PROBLEM

With clothes there are a variety of problems that might prevent you from keeping them organized. I find most people say space is an issue. Either the closet space is too small, or the dressers are too small. I have even worked with people who have no dressers in their bedroom. Then there's the chore of putting summer and winter clothes away when they are out of season. Add children's clothes into the mix and you've got the problems of random growth spurts, hand-me-downs, and clothes they simply won't wear. And your husband...well, hopefully he's someone who can take care of his own clothes. If not, treat him like one of the children when it comes to organizing solutions.

THE STORY

I recently read a newspaper article about the rising need for junk dealers—the people who come to your house and haul out the big items you want to get rid of but can't throw in the trash. A woman called one company because she literally had clothes piled from floor to ceiling in every room. The only place she had to sit was a portion of her living room sofa! She finally called for help because she

Having Trouble Deciding?

IF YOU FIND YOURSELF NOT ABLE TO PART WITH CERTAIN CLOTHES, think about your goal or motivation for getting organized. Think practically. There are so many charities that take clothing. Why are clothes sitting in your drawers or hanging in your closets if you don't wear them? Ask yourself, "Am I ever going to wear this again?" Honestly answer that question and put it in the right pile.

In giving advice about simplifying your wardrobe, Sarah Ban Breathnach poses this question in her book *Simple Abundance*, "What if everything hanging in your closet were something you loved—something that made you look beautiful or made you feel wonderful when you put it on? Think of how good you would feel every day."

didn't have anywhere to live in her house. I hope that your clothes are not taking over your home, but if they are on their way, let's talk about some solutions.

THE SOLUTION

The best solution to the clothing problem is for you and your husband to set a good example for your children. Start by organizing your own clothes, first.

Organize Mom and Dad's Clothes First

1. Gather all of your clothes on your bed. This includes emptying your dresser and bringing in any plastic bins from the attic. Now you can use the space around your bed for stacking or making piles. Put a clean sheet

on the floor so your clothes won't get lint on them. I suggest you start with folded clothes, then deal with the hanging clothes.

2. Make two piles—"Yes, I Wear It" and "No, I Don't Wear It." Go through every piece of clothing on your bed and make a quick decision.

Absolute of Organizing: Keep purging simple with Yes and No piles.

---

3. Now go through this process of making Yes and No piles with all of your hanging clothes and with your shoes.

4. Once you have decided what you're not keeping, bag it or box it up and get it out of your bedroom. Put it in a place in your house where you will remember to call to have it picked up, or put it in your car so you will remember to drop it off at a clothing collection center.

5. Now you are left with all the clothes that make you look great and/or feel wonderful! It's time to break down the categories even further. You can make nice folded piles back on your bed. Here are some possible clothing categories:

- T-shirts
- Short-sleeved tops
- Long-sleeved tops
- Shorts
- Skirts
- Blazers

- Suits
- Sweaters
- Exercise wear
- Dress pants
- Blouses
- Pajamas

Absolute of Organizing: Organize from big to small.

---

6. Take a look at the piles and see if you have way too much of one category. Ask yourself, "Do I really need all these?" If not, purge some more.

7. Decide whether you can keep all of these clothes in your current dresser and/or closet. If not, put the out-of-season clothes in a plastic bin with a lid. Label the bin and find a storage area where it will fit.

8. If you need to update your bedroom with more appropriate clothing storage, see *Options For Storing Clothes* on page 105.

9. To reward yourself after all this hard work, put on a newly-discovered outfit and go out. Just don't go shopping for clothes!

Organize Your Children's Clothes

1. Start with the oldest child's clothes because they typically don't have any hand-me-downs. Have the child with you to try things on or at least hold them up to see if they still fit.

2. Bring all the clothes into the child's bedroom if you have the clothes stored in other places. Take the clothes and shoes out of the drawers, bins or closets and begin making these piles:

   - *Yes*. The clothes fit, are in good shape and are worn regularly.
   - *Hand-Me-Downs*. These clothes no longer fit, but they are in good condition and will be handed down to a younger sibling or friend of the family.
   - *Donations/Charity*. These clothes can be given away. They must be in fairly good condition and no longer fit your children.
   - *Trash*. These are clothes that are so badly stained or worn that they should not be given to charity.
   - *Memory clothes*. I know this sounds like an odd category for clothes, but I know several mothers who save special clothes or accessories. An example might be a child's Christening dress/outfit or the outfit they came home from the hospital in, or a special bib that was handmade by an aunt. Call these what they are: memorabilia. You want to save them but you're not going to use them again. So package them up nicely and put them with the child's other memorabilia. Just make sure you are not saving too much and try to limit it to really special garments.

3. Put the trash pile in the trash. Bag or box up the hand-me-downs and move them to the other child's room. If they fit now, put them in with

current clothing. If they will fit later, label the box or bin with the size and season of clothes and tuck it in the closet. Next take the donations and move them to your car for delivery later.

4. Take the Yes pile and separate these into smaller piles such as:

• Hanging clothes	• Pants
• Underwear	• Pajamas
• Socks	• Shoes
• Short-sleeved shirts	• Sweat pants
• Long-sleeved shirts	• Sweat shirts
• Shorts	• Sweaters

5. Now look at the dresser and closet and decide if all the clothes will fit. Make a decision about whether you need a larger dresser, or a closet organizing system. Look at the number of shoes and decide where they will be kept as well.

OPTIONS FOR STORING CLOTHES

Dresser. My first option is always a dresser. If you need a new one and have limited funds, second-hand shops are great. You can buy a dresser there and paint it whatever color you want. If you can afford it, buy a good quality dresser that you or your children can use for many years. It's a worthwhile investment.

Basic closet. If you decide to store all the clothes in the closet, first see if you can use what you have, which is typically a hanging bar and a shelf. If you need more hanging space, purchase a double hanging bar, which hangs from the upper bar and increases your hanging capacity by 50 to 100 percent depending on how wide it is. For the children, you could always hang out-of-season clothes up top and current clothing on the bottom bar.

Custom-made closet. There are a number of options for closet organizers. You can purchase anything from a $20 rack system at a home store to custom-made shelving from companies that specialize in closets only. Before you spend too much on a custom closet, remember that children's clothing sizes change quickly, so the configuration should be flexible enough to accommodate larger clothing.

Also, look at what you have to put into the closet first (i.e., the stacks you just made) to determine what you need to store them. If you only need one simple shelf, consider putting it up yourself to save time and money. Don't make the common mistake of letting someone else design the closet while you try to make your clothes fit in.

Shoe Racks. Look at the number of shoes you have and find a floor rack or hanging rack that will work. You can purchase back-of-door hanging racks, wide floor racks, shoe carousels, under-the-bed rolling bins or fabric shoe racks that hang in the closet.

Short shoe racks work well inside a closet.

WHEN TO DO THE CLOTHES CLEAN OUT

Obviously this is a project that does not happen weekly or even monthly. Children don't grow at the same time every year so you need to be flexible. Here are some suggested times of the year to clean out your clothes:

- At the change of a season. Figure out who needs bathing suits, flip-flops and sandals before summer starts. See who needs new school clothes in the fall. And who needs boots, coats or snow pants before the first snowfall.
- Whenever you or your child is consistently having trouble finding something that fits.
- When you or your husband start a new job that requires a wardrobe change.
- When you feel like your drawers or closets are overflowing or so jammed you can't close them.
- When you are moving to a new house.

When closet space is tight, under-the-bed containers keep shoes dust free and easy to reach.

11. Where to Put All Those Odds and Ends?

THE PROBLEM

We've talked about all the major categories of things in your house, from clothing to toys to paperwork, but what about those annoying little things that can really clutter a room? Sometimes those odds and ends can accumulate and we just don't know where to put them!

THE STORY

While I was helping a client organize her family room, we needed to vacuum the rug. The vacuum was upstairs in one of the bedrooms. When we finished vacuuming I asked, "Where do you keep this?" Her answer was a blank stare. The vacuum had no home. It just remained in the room where it was last used. We quickly rearranged the family room closet and made a space for the vacuum. The closet was logical because it was a central location in the house.

THE SOLUTION

In order to truly have a "place for everything," you must identify those items in your house that don't have a permanent home. To do this, take a walk through your house and play the game of "one of these things is not like the others." This will help you identify what doesn't really belong, like a sewing needle and thread in the kitchen, or a vacuum in the bedroom, or gifts that need to be wrapped on the office floor. Gather those items together and think about the most logical place to keep them. Here are some examples of mini-categories you might encounter and some options for where to keep them.

Wrapping Paper/ Ribbons

Most moms have wrapping paper and ribbons on hand at all times because you never know when someone will need to go to a birthday party. There are several wrapping paper organizers available ranging from hard plastic stand-up bins to soft vinyl totes. You also could create an organizer for yourself out of a box from a liquor store. These boxes have dividers for bottles that work just as well for large rolls of wrapping paper. You can remove some of the dividers to make space for ribbons, scissors and tape.

Assemble and contain your wrapping materials and find a home for them. Think about where you usually do the wrapping. Is it in the den, your bedroom or in the living room? Find a closet in or near that room that has enough space for the container you choose. Make the decision to keep wrapping paper there and let the whole family know where it belongs.

In order to truly have a "place for everything," you must identify those items in your house that don't have a permanent home.

Extra Gifts

If you have the luxury of a completely empty closet or empty shelf in your home, you can shop in advance for gifts on hand, ready to be wrapped. One of my clients devoted an entire custom closet in her office for just this purpose. Another client used one shelf in her linen closet for extra gifts. With this category, you really need to adapt to your living space. No extra room in the house means no extra presents. However, it is a good idea to look at your monthly calendar and consolidate your gift shopping for the month. If you only have a handful of presents to buy, you could probably find a place to stash them. With little children in the house, it's best to keep these out of sight so curious hands don't open the gift prematurely! Like any of the big categories, have all the gifts in one place so you remember what you have! Decide where this will be: your linen closet, an empty closet, your bedroom closet or in the attic (if it's climate controlled) and don't tell the family! Let this one be your little secret.

Adapt to your living space. No extra room in the house means no extra presents. However, look at your calendar and consolidate your gift shopping for the month!

Totes are a simple, space-saving way to organize and store your wrapping paper and ribbon.

Items That Need to Leave the House

This category could include mail, donations, things that are going to a friend, or items you want to return to a store. Store your outgoing items:

1. *In your car.* There's nothing like going right to the finish line. Put the items on your passenger seat so you see them every time you get into the car. Visual reminders are great.

2. *On a table near your door.* Put the items you need to send out in a place you walk by every day. Let them stick out like a sore thumb so you'll return them soon. If you tuck them away, you're more likely to forget about them.

3. *In your bedroom.* Put the items in a place where you will see them every day when you wake up. One of these days you'll remember to write "do returns" in your planner, and then you can have the satisfaction of checking it off your list.

Items That Need to be Fixed

If you leave a broken item exactly where it sits, you might never fix it. You may have a craft table in your home or a work bench in the garage where you do your "fix its." If your fix-it area is crowded, plan some time in your day to do these little projects. You'll be amazed at how quickly some can be done. Include toys and gadgets that need batteries in this area. Keep the supply of batteries close at hand as well as a container for battery recycling. If you don't know where to recycle your batteries, try your township or city's department of public works.

Put together a little box of tools you use most often, such as: masking tape, a hammer, nails, a Phillips head screwdriver, a flat screwdriver, glue, and scissors.

If something needs to be taken out of the house for repair, put it in the "going out" area mentioned previously.

Limit Your Returns

AFTER SEEING MANY CLIENTS OF VARIOUS INCOME LEVELS, I have come to this conclusion: the more you shop, the more you return. I experienced this myself after we moved into our new house. Right after the move, I did a lot of shopping for home items. Before that, I didn't consider myself a big shopper. I mostly bought what I needed and avoided the mall like the plague. The more I picked up, however, the more returns I had. A pile started to grow in my garage, my car and my bedroom. Now that we're settled, the piles have vanished.

So if you are a frequent shopper, you probably have a number of things in your home that need to be returned. Your returns also show you how detailed a shopper you are. If you are returning household things for size, make sure you measure next time. If you return things for color, take a sample of what you are trying to match. If you are returning a lot of clothes, make note of the new size you or your children need. A little planning can save you a lot of time on returns! If you think you may need to take something back, be sure to keep the receipt with it until the decision is made.

Tools You Use All the Time

There are certain tools we moms seem to use all the time. It makes sense to have a small household toolbox easily accessible especially if most of your tools are in the garage, shed or basement. Put together a little box of what you use most often, such as: masking tape, hammer, nails, Phillips head screwdriver, flat screwdriver, glue and scissors. Then find a convenient place for your toolbox; possibilities include a kitchen drawer or closet, the linen closet or a hall table. I use an old lingerie dresser that has several little drawers. It's in the hallway on the second floor and it holds tools, batteries, extension cords and light bulbs.

Cleaning Products

I learned early in motherhood that cleaning products should be kept up high, out of the reach of little children, yet I still go into many homes where cleaning products are kept under the kitchen sink. Even with safety latches, this is dangerous. Save yourself the trouble of installing latches and simply switch your cabinets around. No matter how small your house, there's a high cabinet or shelf where you can keep cleaning products. If you want cleaning supplies in your kitchen, try putting pots and pans or plastic ware under the kitchen sink because these are items that children can play with and then move the cleaners up to high shelves. Another option is in a laundry room or linen closet on a high shelf. Limit the number of cleaners you have so they don't take up as much room. If you want to separate the cleaning products, keep laundry cleaners in the laundry room, household cleaners in a central closet (like the linen closet) and kitchen cleaners in the pantry or a kitchen cabinet.

You can really spruce up a room by simply changing the pictures on the walls and the items on the shelves.

Pictures and Display Items

If you feel as if the pictures or display items in a room are mismatched, take them all down. Now look at what you have and group like things. You might group by color scheme or frame color or theme. My daughter's room became cluttered with all her accumulated knickknacks, so we decided to organize them. We found that she had a lot of blue items and pink items. So we decided to put the blue items on a new, wooden display shelf and the pink items on top of her bureau. Another time she chose to put ocean objects on her display shelf for the summer. The fun thing about knickknacks and display items is that you can change them whenever you want. The items you don't display can be tucked away and brought out at another time. You can organize pictures and display items room by room, or if you want a dramatic change, do your whole house at once. You can really spruce up a room by simply changing the pictures on the walls and the items on the shelves.

Gift Certificates and Gift Cards

One of my pet peeves is people who never use their gift certificates. Why don't they use them? Usually because they can't find the certificate or they don't make a plan to use it. If you think of gift cards as money, put them right in your wallet. When you're at that store and you open your wallet to pay, you'll see the gift card and use it. Or you can keep gift cards and certificates in a special place such as your top desk drawer or your planner as a "to do." Make a note in your monthly list area to go a certain store or make an appointment to use the gift certificate. Keep track of any gift certificates your children receive by keeping the certificates in one location.

Children's Artwork

Here's a category that seems to have a life of its own. Depending on how creative you and your children are, you can accumulate one to five pieces of kiddy art per day for each child. No mother wants to trash her child's creation but then again not many moms have room for all that creativity. The key is balancing sensitivity and realism. You want to treasure your child's creation but you must be realistic about how long to keep each piece. Here are some options:

Display it ...

- On the refrigerator, but limit it to one creation per child. Make it an art gallery that gets updated on a regular basis.
- On a cork board or bulletin board in the play area or a child's bedroom.

- In a plastic box frame if it's a really good drawing or painting.
- On a display shelf if it's a sculpture or chunky piece of art.

Stash it...

- In a desk drawer or in a plastic container under the child's bed if there's no room to display it. When the drawer or container is full, or at the end of the school year, sort through the artwork and decide what to keep and what to trash.
- In a portfolio labeled with the child's name and year.
- In a memory box if it's a piece of art that was done a while ago but is "a keeper."

Trash it...

- Once it has had its time on display.
- If it's a sculpture that has deteriorated or gone bad (like a macaroni necklace).
- If you have multiple versions of the same drawing, painting or art piece.
- After the child has decided he or she no longer likes it or wants it.

Take One Step at a Time

No matter where the paperwork, photos, collections, toys and clothes are in your house, you can begin to shrink the clutter and confusion by tackling one category at a time.

REMEMBER

- Use the C.P.R. method: Categorize, Purge and Rearrange.
- Create a filing system for paperwork you will reference.
- Sort mail and papers every day. Divide it into three categories: TO DO, TO READ and TO FILE. All else is trash.
- Decide how you want to keep your photos and start using that system from this point forward.
- Gather all your memorabilia and find a home for it that allows you to reminisce whenever you want.
- Put your collections on display.
- Decide where toys will be kept in your house and choose storage containers that match your home décor.
- Go through toys and clothes several times a year and weed out what you and your children don't use.
- Once the big categories have a home, find a place to keep the little things that can clutter your house.

Now that your belongings are organized and under control, you can turn your attention to each room of your house. Read on for more ideas on how to create an organized home.

Part III: Organize Your Home

THE COMFORTS OF HOME. A mother's touch is what makes a house a home. I believe part of a mother's job is to organize the home into comfortable, functional rooms. We don't have to do it all by ourselves, but we moms do have to orchestrate and maintain the organization. If you have your time management skills honed, and you have pared down your possessions to what you need, use and love, it's time to tackle the organization of your entire home!

All organizing starts with a decision. To organize the rooms in your house, you have to decide the function of each room first. Once you know the function, you can decide what belongs in or out of that room. Then you can begin to arrange each room to create a functional and relaxing environment for your entire family.

"We shape our dwellings, and afterwards our dwellings shape us."

—WINSTON CHURCHILL

12. Where Do I Start?

THE PROBLEM

The whole house is in disarray, and you've made a decision to get organized this year. There are many reasons to organize the entire home: moving into a new house; welcoming a new resident (new baby, aging parents, a homeless sibling); selling your home; or wanting a fresh start from the years of accumulating clutter. Organizing the entire place can be overwhelming. The disorganization took years to accumulate, so how can you turn it around in just a few months?

THE STORY

My family moved about two years ago. We had lived in our previous house for twelve years, so to say I was comfortable and functional where I was living is an understatement. Moving is a time of great change and upheaval that can send even the most organized mom into a tizzy. After two years in our new home, I can see a big difference between our house and the houses of friends who also moved that year. We chose the "room-by-room" approach while others went with the "all-at-once" approach. We like to balance our schedule with house projects and downtime. Some people are always working on their houses, every evening and weekend. Some husbands end up writing checks to contractors while the wife orders the products and services. My husband and I have a "Home Projects Plan" that we often refer to. We look at costs, juggle priorities and schedule the projects before we jump into them.

THE SOLUTION

The first thing you'll need is a plan. If you don't know where to start, go through every room in the house with your spouse (and maybe even the children). Discuss how your family will use each room. In other words, identify the three most important functions of each room. If you add more than three functions, the room may become chaotic and crowded. Some functions are more obvious than others—bedrooms are for sleeping and the kitchen is for eating and cooking. But think about your day-to-day life and be realistic. You might like to watch TV in your bedroom or have the children do homework in the kitchen. These details will affect what is contained in each room and how you will organize it.

As you walk through the house, take notes on what you need to do in each room. Create a "Home Projects Plan" book using a simple notebook. Have a separate page for each room and write down everything you want to change in that room. The plan should include both organizational projects and home improvements. Write it all down, from adding an electrical outlet to buying new window treatments. If you browse catalogs or home improvement magazines, cut out pictures of what you like and put these alongside your "to do" items. This book is a centralized plan of what needs to happen so you can have your dream home.

Where there's a will, there's a way and where there's not, there are excuses.

You may not have any ideas for a certain room right now, other than "clean it out." That's okay. Sometimes when you clear away the clutter, it's easier to envision a room updated and decorated. You may be able to work with what you have in your home and just rearrange. If not, you may need to purchase furniture or hire contractors to really get your home in shape. It all depends on how far you want to take it.

Absolute of Organizing: Start with a good list.

Estimate Your Costs

After you've written down all of your plans, estimate the costs. This may be as easy as pricing something in a catalog. For contracted services like plumbing and electricity, you will want to get at least three quotes. My husband and I tend to go with the middle range of costs unless one of the contractors is significantly better than the others in terms of quality or customer service. Many times you just have to choose whomever you feel more comfortable with. Consider purchasing items yourself such as lighting and plumbing fixtures and then hiring someone to install them. This can often save you money. Once you have all your quotes, you can ballpark the cost of completing each room. It will come in handy when you are prioritizing which room to do first.

Know Your Budget

Budgeting is a step that many couples skip. If you're lucky enough that cost doesn't matter, then you can keep going until your whole house is done. But most families have to work within a budget. You don't want to be in the middle of a big project and suddenly find you are out of money. When we moved into our new house, we knew there were some immediate fixes to be done. We looked at our annual income and expenses and figured out how much we could put aside for home improvements. When the money was gone, we had to stop. We were realistic about how much we could do in that first year.

Another option might be to take out a loan. Whatever your situation, it's important that you and your husband are in agreement with how much money can be spent in getting your home organized and updated. Decide on the total amount you can spend and then prioritize your projects.

Prioritize

The other purpose of the Home Projects Plan is to help you prioritize. There are different ways to prioritize, and no way is right or wrong. Some common ways to choose which room should be first are by using superlatives such as:

- the worst room in the house
- the most used room
- the most visible room
- the easiest room
- the least or most expensive room to do

Much depends on your personality. Doing the worst room first has its benefits because all else will seem easy. Doing the easiest room first might build your confidence to continue on with other projects. Doing the most used or most visible room first may help you feel that you will at least look organized when you have visitors. Whatever your motivation, choose the first room and stick with it until you've done everything you planned and that you can afford. Roughly plan out the order in which you would like your rooms to be finished. Of course this may change along the way, but it's better to have a plan of where you are going than to have no plan at all!

Absolute of Organizing: Finish one thing before you start another.

Scheduling

Keep the House Projects Plan book in a central location where you and your husband can easily access it. As you plan out your week together, you can refer to this book if your schedule allows a home improvement project. Don't leave all the work for the weekend. Sometimes a project may only take two hours and you could get it done together on a weeknight. Or sometimes a big Saturday project may take some prep work that could be done on Thursday or Friday evening. If you are going to paint the living room on Saturday, you could move furniture, bring in the drop clothes, and put up the painter's tape on Friday night after the children are asleep. Then you can jump right into painting Saturday morning.

When scheduling projects, think about what the children will be doing at that time. If one parent can tackle a job, then the other parent can help by taking the children out of the house. If you both want to do a project, take the children to a friend's house or a grandparent's house. If possible, plan projects for a weekday if all your children are in school and your husband can take a day off. Sometimes you have to be creative if you want to get these projects done.

When your children are old enough, you can involve them in the projects. My four-year-old recently picked up a roller and helped me paint an outside wall! Planning ahead and thinking a project through is often half the battle. Including your children in the process is important because you want everyone in the family vested in the outcome. Use incentives when necessary like, "If you all help clean out the garage on Saturday, we can go out for dinner and a movie that night."

How long will this all take?

Now that you have a good idea of what you want to do, how much it will cost and what services it will involve, you can take a look at the big picture. Many people talk about home improvements and say, "Oh, it never ends!" I disagree. It ends when your comprehensive list is finished and your house is as you wanted it. Sure, circumstances will change, and a new project may be born. If you look at each project as finite then there will be a time when you can sit back and say, "We're done."

If the task of organizing your entire home seems overwhelming, count the rooms in your house. If you can organize one room a day, that's how many days it will take to finish the project. An average size house has ten to twelve rooms. At one room a day, you can finish in two weeks. Or, let's say each room will require a week to organize. Then you'll be finished in three months. If your rooms each require a lot of work, let's say one month per room. You still can estimate that in one year you will have your home exactly as you want it. Not bad when you consider how many years it took to get it the way you didn't want it!

13. I Need a Home Office!

THE PROBLEM

You may be thinking you don't need a home office because you don't work from home. Wrong. Papers are coming at you faster than you can read them. Every one of your children has three phone lists for all their activities. You're making doctor's appointments, paying bills and filling out forms on a weekly basis, and your daughter has just asked you to be her Brownie leader! How are you going to keep it all organized? Every mom needs some sort of home office. No matter the size, the home office is where Mom can get it all together.

THE STORY

Several of my clients have the same problem. They have already set up a home office. For some, it's in their basement. Others have a spare bedroom, others just have a desk in a living room. Once that area becomes cluttered and frustrating to work at, they branch out instead of using C.P.R. (Categorize, Purge and Rearrange) to stay organized. Milk crates with files appear in the dining room, and tabletops start to accumulate piles of papers. These moms assume they need a new piece of furniture or a bigger room to hold it all. What they really need to do is get back to basics.

THE SOLUTION

Whether you need to create a home office from scratch or you have an office that is disorganized, you can follow my Room Organizing Worksheet (page 370) to create your own "Mom Command Center." Start by asking yourself these questions and write down the answers:

What is the function of my home office? Is the purpose of your office to pay bills, send letters, keep files, and hold the family computer? Or will you also be running a home business? Will the children be allowed to use your desk and computer? All these questions have to be answered before you can set up your office in the most efficient manner. Make your decision and write down how you are going to use your office. This will help you focus on what you will need in your office.

What do I like about my current home office? Is it convenient because your office is in the main area of the house so you can work when the children are around? Or is it tucked away so it's nice and quiet? Is it light and cheerful? Does it have beautiful furniture in it? Whatever the case, note the positive points of your office so they remain during your reorganization!

Note the positive points of your office so they remain during your reorganization!

What don't I like about my office right now? Maybe it's that you can't see the top of your desk, or that you lose things easily, or that there are piles of paper on the floor. Be honest and identify the problem areas.

What is in my office now? This is really the "Categorize" step of my C.P.R. process. If things in your office are not categorized, you need to physically move them into piles to identify what is there. If they are already in categories, then take a look around and jot down everything you see. Your categories may include: mailing supplies, bills, computer equipment, family paperwork, and photos. When you make a list of categories, it's easy to identify what doesn't belong.

What do I want to keep in the office? Include in this list not only the categories of items but also the furniture or storage containers that are working well for you.

What, if anything, needs to be added? Do I need to hire someone? Sometimes the answers to these questions are obvious. You may need more file cabinets or a better desk chair. But sometimes you won't know what needs to be added until you dig out from all the clutter. It's okay to leave these two answers blank and come back to them. If you need a contractor to make some improvements to your office, make sure you get three estimates for each service required.

Purge. By process of elimination you have determined what does not belong in your office area. Box these items up if necessary and move them out! This is the "Purge" step of C.P.R. Big items can be stored in the garage or basement until you can get rid of them, or you may need to move things to the appropriate room in your house.

Absolute of Organizing: Subtract before you add.

PUTTING IT ALL TOGETHER

Basic Supplies: A typical home office should include a file cabinet, a desk, a phone, a computer and a printer. Some supplies might be: stamps, a phone book, checkbook, envelopes, tape, stapler, scissors and paper. If you will be running your own business from this office, you may also need to bring in your inventory, reference material, forms, catalogs or shipping materials.

Furniture: Many home businesses involve using reference materials like directories, catalogs or other books. If you need those close at hand, make sure you have a wall shelf or a standing bookshelf. Also make sure you have adequate file cabinets and desktop space for what you do at your desk. If you are going to do scrapbooking or crafts in your office, make sure you have a clear tabletop as well as a desk.

Containers: You may need bins for paper or storage bins for things like crafting supplies. If you are using the desk for your In Box, Bills-to-Pay bin and File bin, make sure you have space for all of them. Stand-up bins or wall-mounted bins are a great way to keep these papers visible and orderly without taking up too much desk space.

Work Within Your Budget

IF YOU DON'T HAVE A DESK, there are options at various price levels:

- You can purchase a new one, custom fit to your needs.
- You can find one in a second-hand shop and fix it up to your liking.
- You can make your own desk from a folding table with file cabinets underneath.

I have one friend who was really creative and made a desk from an old, wooden door and two sawhorses!

If your home business involves inventory that you take with you to clients, it makes sense to have the items in containers that travel well, such as a suitcase on wheels or lightweight plastic bins. If you ship items from your home and don't need to carry them out, you can arrange them on a shelf or in a closet with the shipping materials.

Once you've decided what you need for your office, go shopping online or at an office supply store and bring those containers to your office. Once you're sure you have everything, bring it together and assess the situation. Do you need an entire room or will a portion of a larger room suffice?

WHERE WILL THE OFFICE BE?

A typical home has many options for creating a home office area: a spare bedroom, the corner of your family room or living room, or an area in the basement. Even a spare closet can be turned into an office. I've also noticed that many new homes incorporate a desk right into the kitchen counter space. If this is the case in your house, make sure the kitchen desk area is big enough to meet your needs. Maybe it's just big enough to keep your bills, or it's where your child can do his or her homework. Decide on its purpose and make sure it's equipped for its function.

Wherever you decide to put your office, make sure it's in a convenient place where you will use it. Several clients I know have a desk set up in a basement but then tell me they just don't feel like spending time there. An office area that you don't utilize every day is really of no use.

Think about your habits before you decide if you want your office in the main area of your house or in a tucked away spot where you can retreat to do your work.

HOW WILL YOU SET UP YOUR OFFICE?

To arrange or rearrange your office, think in categories. If your office has multiple functions, create zones for each function. If you are using your office area for managing your household files and running a home business, you need to have separate file drawers or file cabinets for each function. You may even want to have two desks, one for personal and one for business.

If you have a computer and several pieces of electronic equipment, make sure you set them up near a grounded outlet and use a surge protector. Also make sure the computer is in a position that will not have glare from the sun if there are windows in your office.

Think about the flow of paper in your office and set the area up in an assembly line fashion. If yours is an office for managing your home, you could set it up like this:

To do bin → Open space on desk → Printer → Shredder/trash can → "Going out" table

If you are also using your office to manage a home-based business, your set up may be more complicated. Many home-based businesses involve taking orders, collecting money, and filling and shipping orders. You can set up stations for each step in the process. Have order forms by the phone or computer, wherever they come in. Then spread them out on a table for filling orders. Keep a record of who has paid and who has not. You could use a letter holder on the table or two bins accurately marked. Have your packaging materials either under the table or in a closet in your office. Once the packages are ready to deliver or mail, have a "Going Out" bin by the door of the office. Your straight-line process might look like this:

Take orders → *Record payment* → *Fill orders* → *Package* → *Send out product*

Having your business set up in this way will avoid confusion about where a certain order is, and who has paid. It also helps you see exactly what part of the process you need to focus on at any given time.

Put on the Finishing Touches

Once your office is set up functionally, make sure it also is aesthetically pleasing. When you feel at ease and have a clear space to work, you will have a clear and focused mind to do your work.

- If you like visual reminders and motivators, put up a bulletin board. Post pictures of loved ones, pictures of prizes you are working towards, or simple notes. Bulletin boards do have potential for clutter so make sure you keep them current. Don't cover old notes with new ones.
- If your office is in a corner of a larger room in your house, make sure it blends. You wouldn't want a metal desk in a French Country living room. Try to match the wood tones of the furniture.

- If your file cabinets are visible in your office, also make sure they are wood. Metal or plastic bins should be tucked away in a closet and not out in the open.
- If you have clients come to your office, make sure you have a comfortable place for them to sit, and a clear table for them to use.
- Add something pretty like a vase of flowers, a beautiful picture, or a great smelling candle.

USING AND MAINTAINING YOUR OFFICE

Don't let the children touch. If your home office is going to be used by your children because there is only one computer in the house, make sure your work and important papers are filed away or even locked up when you are finished working. This is a great motivator for keeping your desktop clear! When the children use the computer or materials there, make sure they only have access to what they are allowed to use.

Set a schedule for working your home-based business. If you're lucky enough to have your own office with a door, it's easier to be disciplined about your starting and ending time. When you finish for the day, place everything you need to do tomorrow in your TO DO file and write it in your daily planner, then close the door. If you don't set up boundaries and routines when working at home, it is easy to let your work time spill into family time. If you work while the children are home, communicate with them that you are working and what's expected of them. You may want them to play by themselves or watch a movie, or you may have a baby-sitter there to attend to their needs.

Set time in your schedule to manage the family. For the day-to-day management of a family, it's best to do it every day so it doesn't pile up on you.

- Paying bills is a top priority so it's worth the effort to schedule the time and write it in your planner. You can write it down as soon as you receive a bill, such as "send Visa bill" on the 10th if it's due on the 17th. If you handle all the household bills, set a specific day of the week when you pay them.

You can do this weekly, bi-monthly or monthly if you coordinate the due dates with your utilities and credit cards.

- Phone calls can take up a lot of a mother's time in any given week. Instead of just calling someone when you think of it, make a list on a daily or weekly basis of whom you need to call. Then you can be efficient about your time and call when the house is quiet, perhaps after the children go to school or when the baby is taking a nap. You'd be amazed how many calls you can make in a half hour when you have focused time. Even if you're just leaving messages, you can get your calls out there. If you're in the middle of doing something else, use caller ID or the answering machine to screen your incoming calls. Only answer if you have the time to talk.

The secret to maintaining an organized office is to keep all your office materials IN while keeping toys, food, and extraneous stuff OUT!

- Filing is something you can do in about five minutes per day. If you don't receive a lot of papers to file you may be able to do it once a week. The other method to use is the "full barrel" method, which means when your "To File" bin is full, it's time to file.
- Reading may be another function that can take place in your office area. You can read periodicals for your business or information from school or children's activities. Again, make room in your schedule to read your incoming papers every day and it will only take five to ten minutes. If you let it pile up, not only does it take longer, you'll also be less likely to want to tackle the pile.
- Use your daily planner to keep track of special projects. Try to work on one project per day if possible. You may be shopping for new car insurance, planning a birthday party or decorating a bedroom. Create an action file for each project and pull that file out when you're working on it, then put it away when you're finished for the day.

End of the year clean out. Clearing out your office from year to year keeps it under control. Here are some suggestions for items to clear out:

- Pull out your tax-related information. Total up expenses and income for both personal and business tax forms.
- Review your "Charitable Contributions" folder and total up all those receipts.
- If you're someone who likes to have an idea of where the money went this year, take credit card statements and your checkbook log and categorize your expenses in a simple spreadsheet.
- If you use Quicken or similar software for your banking, create an end-of-the-year report for your budget totals.
- For all reference files, take a look through each one and toss what is outdated or unnecessary.
- Clear out your children's school files at the end of the school year.
- If you have a business that requires you to keep inventory, tally up the cost of that inventory for your taxes. In some cases you may want to have an end-of-the-year sale to clear the shelf.

The secret to maintaining an organized office is to keep all your office materials *in* while keeping toys, food, and extraneous stuff *out*! Do this on a daily or weekly basis so it doesn't pile up, and you will have a functional home business—even if that business is simply managing your home and family.

14. Never Enough Closets or Storage

THE PROBLEM

So many moms tell me they don't have enough closet or storage space. If you have an old home, your closets are probably small and few. You know why? Because they had less stuff in the old days! If you have a newly built home, you may have larger closets and more of them to work with. There are pros and cons to closets in each type of house. While the old houses may have sturdy wooden shelves, closets in the new homes usually have wire racks. Some people have so many closets they can't decide what to put in them and each closet becomes a catchall.

THE STORY

One of my clients has a small house where she and her husband raised six children. Family gatherings were pretty tight at their house after their children were married and had their own children. They built an additional family room with an average-sized closet in it. The original idea for the closet was to hold the coats for guests because the front hall closet was packed. But the new closet actually became a place to put odds and ends that didn't have an obvious place in the house. So after a few years, the closet contained shopping bags, the vacuum, games, extra blankets, children's chairs, and small appliances that were only used a few times a year. There also were bags of miscellaneous papers that had been cleared off the dining room table when company came. One of their daughters bought them a closet organizer to help them out. A year later, it was still in the box, buried under the stuff in their closet. Their son opened the door one day and jokingly said, "See, we put the closet organizer in there but it doesn't work."

> *The first step in organizing a room is organizing its closet.*

THE SOLUTION

To truly organize your closets and storage, you've got to determine what storage you have, the functions of each closet or area, what needs to be stored, and what if any additional storage options you need. Use your Home Projects Plan book to help tackle this problem.

To assess your storage areas, take a walk through your house. Is there a usable attic, basement, or crawl space? How about a shed or garage? What about shelves or built-in cabinets in your home? Maybe you have an armoire, an old trunk or tall bookcase that you aren't using. All of these things are potential storage.

Functions of Closets

After you have cleared out the clutter in your house and decided on the function of each room, it should be easy to decide the function of the closets. The first step in organizing a room is organizing its closet. An organized closet allows you to maximize what you store so you can better arrange what is left out displayed. Remember to keep like things together and limit the function of the closet to two or three categories. For instance, a bedroom closet may hold clothes, shoes, and extra linens. A family room closet may hold games, throw blankets, and candles. A closet in the front entrance may hold outerwear, umbrellas, and backpacks for school. This helps prevent the overloaded and overstuffed closet where everything is shoved in and piled high. Even if your closet is bigger than you need, limit the use of it. There's nothing wrong with having space to spare!

....
Absolute of Organizing: Keep like things together.
....

What Needs to be Stored?

When we talk about storage, we typically use it for items that we don't need every day, or large items that can't be kept in an average room in the house, such as golf clubs, large "outside" toys, gardening tools, the vacuum, holiday decorations, out-of-season clothes, memory boxes, and camping gear. You may also have unique things to store like inventory for your business, a collection that you haven't decided what to do with, or items that you sell online. Write these items down on your list and then treat it like a matching test, drawing lines from the "What needs to be stored" column to the "Storage Area" column. This chart should address the big categories of things you have as well as those odds and ends that don't seem to fit into any category.

SAMPLE STORAGE CHART:

STORAGE AREA	CONTENTS
Attic	• Holiday decorations • Mom's and Dad's memory boxes • Camping equipment
Cedar closet	• Mom's and Dad's out-of-season clothes • Formal dresses • Wrapping paper and supplies • Sewing fabric

continued on next page

STORAGE AREA	CONTENTS
Basement	• Tool bench • Painting supplies • Large toys • Arts and craft supplies • Laundry detergents • Dry food and bulk items
Front hall closet	• Hats, gloves, coats • Umbrellas, boots • Video camera • Portable TV for car
Linen closet	• Blankets and sheets • Cleaning supplies • Vacuum • Extra sundries and refills
Garage	• Bikes • Sports equipment • Decorative flags • Pool supplies • Folding chairs • Outside toys • Stroller • Ladders

continued on next page

STORAGE AREA	CONTENTS
Kitchen closet	• Kitchen cleaning supplies • Broom, dry mop • Plastic wrap, foil, sandwich bags • Cookbooks • Lunch boxes and water bottles
Shed	• Lawn mower • Gardening supplies • Wading pool • Wagon • Extra lumber

PUTTING IT ALL TOGETHER

When you start reorganizing a closet, you've got to take everything out. Use the C.P.R. (Categorize, Purge and Rearrange) process and remember that in this case "purging" may just mean moving something to a different closet. Before you rearrange, take a good look at the space you have. Be sure to use it efficiently before placing any items inside. In some cases you may need to temporarily put a category in a cardboard box or bag until you purchase the container or shelf that you want for your closet.

Additional Storage Options

Now that you've decided what's going into a closet or storage area, consider how to fit it all in so that it's accessible. There's always the option of hiring a closet organizer company to come in and custom build shelves and racks. But sometimes it's just as easy (and less expensive) to work with the shelving you have and make minor changes. Here are some quick tips for efficiently using the space in your closets:

Example Layout of a Child's Closet

Memory Box

Sheets and blankets

Clothes to grow into

Shoe organizer

Laundry basket

Toys

Art portfolio

- Put in a second hanging bar that hangs below the one you have for more hanger space.
- Use hanger holders that can fit four or five pairs of pants or shirts, if your horizontal space is tight.
- Use a shelf topper on the top of your closet if you've got extra "head room."
- Use a vacuum-sealed storage bag for bulky items such as comforters and sweaters.
- Modify the wooden shelves you have in a closet to suit your needs. Make a shelf taller or longer by relocating shelves or adding them. You can do this with plywood and a 2' × 4' (61cm × 122m) board or the brace.

If you simply don't have enough closets, then consider furniture that has built in storage. Many companies make pieces of furniture that offer additional storage. If you don't have a front hall closet, you could use a coat rack or a storage bench. If you don't have a garage, then you can use a shed or basement for storing outdoor equipment.

15. The Kitchen Is the Family's Hub

THE PROBLEM

Kitchens come in all shapes and sizes, but their function is basically the same. This is where you cook and eat and entertain guests. And more often than not, this is where you talk on the phone, take messages, help your children with art projects and homework and play scheduling secretary for the family. Given all those functions, there is a lot of "stuff" that can end up in the kitchen by the end of the day.

THE STORY

One of my first clients hired me to organize her kitchen. Like many of the older homes in my neighborhood, hers was not an "eat-in" kitchen but instead had an area for cooking and a separate dining room where the family ate. She told me that the dining room table was usually filled with children's toys and art projects by the end of the day and in order to eat, they moved the clutter onto the floor or pushed it to the center of the table. Her story is not uncommon, especially among stay-at-home moms with pre-schoolers. I wanted to help her create a more serene table for the family meals without cramping her family's easy-going style. The dining room was fairly large so we were able to create zones for the room's many functions. We added a nice activity table for her children to use. We also used shelves in a corner to store the toys. With the dining room table cleared of debris, we dressed it up with a nice tablecloth and vase of flowers. When we finished, the room finally looked more like a grown-up dining room than a playroom.

THE SOLUTION

Determine all the functions your kitchen serves by using my Room Organizing Worksheet (see page 370) to answer these questions:

What do I like about my kitchen? It might be that you like the cabinets or the set up or the size of your kitchen. If so, these are things that you won't have to worry about changing. I believe it helps to focus on the positive so you know it's not a lost cause!

What don't I like about my kitchen? A common concern I hear from my clients is that the counter space is cluttered or the cabinets are so full, things fall out every time they're opened. Or they say there simply isn't enough space in their kitchen. Sometimes that changes just by paring down to what they need, use and love in their kitchen. Decide what it is that you don't like and let that be the focus of your reorganizing efforts.

What is in my kitchen now? You can jot down the categories of stuff in your kitchen just by opening the cabinets. And sometimes one category is the biggest problem and it doesn't even belong in the kitchen! I had one client whose kitchen table was filled with paperwork for a class she was taking. When I asked her where it belonged, she said, "In the office." So we boxed it up and moved it to the office. Kitchen problem solved. Now it was an office issue. It's okay to push these off because when you finish organizing the kitchen, you can handle the office.

Absolute of Organizing: Finish one thing before you start another.

What do I want to keep in the kitchen? Make sure your answer to this question agrees with the functions you've established. And consider this: Even if you use the kitchen table for projects because it's the biggest table in the house, you don't have to store all those materials in the kitchen. Your children can still do their homework at the kitchen table, but keep their pencils, scissors, and glue in a desk somewhere else. When the schoolwork is done, have them put it back where it belongs. Even if you like to sit at the kitchen table to do bills and read the paper, you don't have to keep them there. Clear it off when you're finished so the kitchen can go back to its original purpose: a place to cook and eat.

What, if anything needs to be added to the kitchen? And do I need to hire some-one? If there are any obvious changes like a new floor or counter, jot those down now. You can come back to this question on the worksheet once you have categorized and purged. Perhaps you don't have enough room for all your necessities and a new closet or cabinets are needed.

Categorize

Begin this step by pulling everything out of the cabinets so you can see how much of each category you have. This also allows you to take a new look at the empty space in your cabinets; clean them out and start fresh with a new system.

Purge

There may be items that have been buried for years that you didn't even realize you had. You may find broken items. Or you may realize that your Crockpot has been used only as a place to dump odds and ends! If you have three sets of dishes and two are from the 1960s, maybe it's time to part with them. Find yourself a complete set of matching dishes for everyday. Decide how many are reasonable for your family. If you've still got sippy cups and your youngest is in high school, there's another item you can purge. Create a box for trash and one for donations, and then move these boxes out of the kitchen and dispose of them once the kitchen is organized.

Find Convenient Locations

Now that you have what you want to keep in your kitchen and it's categorized, think about how to rearrange these items back into your cabinets and drawers. Start with the items that you use every day. Other items like serving dishes, appliances that are rarely used, and entertaining items like a punch bowl may need to be kept in storage if your kitchen is too small. Leave that decision until the end. If you buy food or paper products in bulk, you will probably need a storage shelf somewhere else in the house to keep those items. Below is a list with suggested locations for the various categories:

- *Everyday dishes*: Place above dishwasher for easy unloading.
- *Glasses*: Keep near the fridge since that's where you use them.
- *Serving dishes*: Keep up high in cabinets as they're not used every day.
- *Bakeware*: Keep where used—near oven or in drawer underneath oven.
- *Pots and pans*: Keep in low cupboards for easy access. These are okay for kids to play with.
- *Kids' plastic dishes and cups*: Keep in low cabinet or drawer so kids can reach them.
- *Baby bottles and baby food*: Keep in high cabinets near stove so kids can't get into them.
- *Dry food and canned goods*: Keep like things together in the pantry or on a lazy Susan. It will be easier to find what you need.
- *Plastic containers*: Keep them where you use them—in a drawer or cabinet near the fridge or under the sink. Take off the lids so you can stack them or buy collapsible ones.
- *Cookbooks*: If used often and in good condition, keep them out in view. If not keep them on a shelf in the pantry or cabinet.
- *Paper products/foil/wraps:* Keep up high in pantry or cabinet to keep the kids out.
- *Lunch boxes/water bottles*: Keep in the pantry or a low drawer or cabinet so the kids can reach them easily.
- *Small appliances*: Keep in low cabinets or pull out drawers for easy access.
- *Entertaining pieces*: Keep in out-of-reach cabinet or in storage since these are only used a few times each year.

Of course you have to consider the age of your children and your family habits when determining what's right for you.

- As your children get older you may want them to be able to get their own snacks and drinks, but when they are young you might want to keep those items out of reach.
- When determining a low or high shelf, think about the weight of objects and what's most comfortable for you to reach.
- If you have a child with food allergies, it's a good idea to put the "bad" foods up high and create a drawer or shelf for his or her special food. This makes it easier for baby-sitters and other family members to know what your child can eat.

MAXIMIZE YOUR SPACE

If cabinet space is a problem, make sure you are making the most of yours. There are several products on the market that can help maximize the space you have. Collapsible or stackable plastic storage containers are a great idea. If you have a lot of "head" room in one cabinet you may want to add an under-the-shelf basket to double up the space.

If you can't reach your mugs, you can install a pull-out mug rack with hooks. A simple wire rack can help you store small plates on top of larger ones in your cabinet. Before you purchase these items, make sure you know which cabinets they are going into and make a list that includes the measurements of the cabinets so you're sure they will fit.

Counter Tops: The golden rule about counter tops is to only have out what you use every day. There's no sense in having a coffee maker on the counter if you don't make coffee every day.

If you're not a cook, then the cooking utensils can go away in a drawer instead of in a crock on the counter. Also, if you've got the space to stash it, then do so. Tuck that dish rack under the sink and put away the toaster oven if you really need the counter space.

Absolute of Organizing: Finish one thing before you start another.

An Organized Fridge Is a Healthy Fridge

This may sound crazy but I even categorize the food in my refrigerator. If you think about it, that's how refrigerators are designed. There's a shelf for drinks, a bin for fruit, a bin for vegetables, a drawer for meats, a shelf for leftovers, a shelf for dairy items and door shelves for condiments. Separating the food this way serves two purposes:

1. You see what you have and therefore what you need.
2. It's easier for you and your children to pull foods from the various food groups when preparing a meal.

If the food is all over the place, items will get buried in the back. Before you know it, you're buying something unnecessarily or opening a new jar of something that's already in the refrigerator. I once cleaned out a refrigerator that had ten half-eaten loaves of bread, five jars of pickles and seven half-gallons of ice cream. In that household, new foods were opened before the old ones were finished. The refrigerator was packed and it was hard to see what was in there. If your refrigerator is so packed you can't fit anything new in, don't go food shopping until you can see some space.

MEAL PLANNING

One way to avoid the over-stuffed, unorganized refrigerator is to look at your leftovers when planning a meal. That's not to say that every night is a "leftover" night (children hate that word). Think of it as a "leftover make over." Look at the pasta, rice or vegetables you have and think about a new sauce to put over them or how you can toss them into a casserole or soup. It's a chance to be creative with your cooking. Once you've chosen your make over item, also make something new to round out the meal. This will keep the meal fresh. Avoid the habit of making a new full meal every night and then having a refrigerator full of leftovers by the end of the week. If you find you have many leftovers no one eats, you may need to make smaller portions for the next meal.

Another way to handle leftovers is to have a "whatever you want" dinner. Pull out what's in the refrigerator and place it on the counter in categories. Then let everyone choose one meat or protein, one starch and one fruit or vegetable.

Snacks: Many nutritionists recommend having healthy "ready snacks" like yogurt, carrots, celery sticks or apple slices placed at the children's level so they can grab them on their own. If you let them know what shelf is theirs, they can decide what food to eat. It only takes a little planning ahead and some categorizing to really have a healthy refrigerator.

Snacks for guests: I have to admit, one of the reasons I like keeping my house organized is that it's never a problem to have visitors. I love the challenge of finding a snack I can whip up from the food on hand. And if I find I don't have a lot of one snack, I use a three-tiered dessert stand or a divided serving tray and just put out a little of each snack. You could use three different types of cookies, chips, crackers, fruit, nuts or candy. If you have half a tray of brownies left from the other day, cut them, arrange them on a plate and sprinkle with confectioner's sugar to make them look just-baked. There's no need to run to the store every time someone comes over to visit. Think about what snacks you like to make and always have those ingredients on-hand.

MAINTAINING YOUR KITCHEN

Once you have set up your kitchen efficiently, you'll need to maintain the organization.

Daily Clean-up Routine

It's easy to spend a lot of time in your kitchen, especially if you have three meals a day at home with the children. To cut back on this time, I have a clean-up routine after each meal. I only hand-wash dishes and sweep the floor after dinner, unless

Stay Organized During a Renovation

RENOVATING YOUR KITCHEN CAN BE VERY DISRUPTIVE to daily living. I recommend that before the contractors come in, you organize what's in your kitchen as mentioned in this chapter. Then you will have a clear picture of what additional storage or counter space you need before you redesign it. Once the contractors are scheduled, take out things that you use every day like utensils, a few plates, mugs and glasses, coffee maker, etc. Place these items in a box or two and mark them "Everyday items." Likewise, take out everything else in your cabinets and put them into labeled boxes. This should be easy to do once your kitchen is organized into categories. After your kitchen is renovated, you can easily take one category at a time and put it back into the correct drawer or cabinet.

there is an exceptional amount of dirt on the floor or dishes in the sink before then. Here's my clean-up routine:

- Have the kids clear their own plates
- Rinse dishes and load the dishwasher
- Put all the food away
- Wipe the table and counter tops
- Run the dishwasher after dinner
- Put clean dishes away in the morning

Once a week, I wipe down the counters and appliances with a disinfectant. During my weekly house cleaning I mop the kitchen floor.

Papers

When it comes to the kitchen, just say no to papers. The only papers you should have in the kitchen are:

- Take-out menus
- Coupons (in a coupon caddy)
- Recipes (in a recipe file)
- A family calendar
- A note pad by the phone
- A perpetual food list on the refrigerator

All other papers should be kept in your home office area.

Refrigerator Art

Keep refrigerator art to a minimum. If you must have photos on the fridge, use a magnetic plastic frame to keep the grease and grime off them. If you hang children's art, use a clip to keep it from flying off with every slam of the door. I also recommend displaying one piece or art per child and rotating it from time to time. If your refrigerator looks like a scrapbook , it's time to start a scrapbook!

16. I Can't Even Walk in the Kids' Rooms

THE PROBLEM

Your child's bedroom was in perfect order when he or she was a baby. You neatly put away his or her clothes every night and picked up any toys and books and placed them on the correct shelf. Before the child arrived you had carefully decorated the nursery to your liking. The curtains, bedding and pictures all matched and it was a peaceful, beautiful room. Then your child grew up. Toys and knick-knacks accumulated, posters and unrecognizable artwork appeared on the walls, shoes and socks are forever strewn, and you can't see the rug through all the toys that lie there. Now you just want to close the door and forget about that room!

THE STORY

When I think of really difficult children's rooms, there are a few that come to mind. I hate to say it, but it's the smart, creative children who are the hardest to organize. So take heart: If your child's room is a mess, chalk it up to creativity and intelligence! One room I can think of belongs to a boy whose parents did not own a TV. In his spare time, this child made art projects, read books, did puzzles and played games. (All the wonderful, mind-stimulating stuff our children

> *Your child's bedroom is a place for him or her to sleep, but it may also be the playroom, the art room and the reading room.*

should be doing!) To make matters worse, their house did not have a playroom, so any organizing solutions had to be implemented in his small bedroom.

THE SOLUTION

Think about what activities take place in your child's bedroom. It's a place for him or her to sleep, but it may be more. Like the child in my story, it may also be the playroom, the art room and the reading room. As your child grows older it is a place where he or she can display his or her personality. Once you have the functions, use my Room Organizing Worksheet (page 370) to answer the following questions.

What do you like about the room currently? You may like the furniture and décor in the room but you just can't appreciate it through all the mess. Perhaps you like the size of the room or closet, or maybe there's a particular feature of the room that you like, for instance a window seat. Make sure you keep or enhance the positive aspects of this room as you organize.

What don't you like about the room currently? Most clients I have worked with point to the amount of stuff that fills their child's room, or to the fact that everything is out and nothing gets put away. Whatever it is that you don't like about this bedroom, make it the focus of your reorganization efforts.

What's in the room now? Here's where we get into categories again. If everything is everywhere, begin to make piles on the floor or bed so you can assess what's in this room. Take heart, it will all get put away as part of your organizing project! Some typical categories are:

- Toys
- Puzzles
- Dress clothes
- Art supplies
- Games
- Stuffed animals
- Finished artwork
- Books

- Knickknacks
- Clothes
- Trophies and medals
- Collections
- Finished schoolwork
- Memorabilia

Purge: Look at the categories and pull out anything your child doesn't use or wear anymore. These items can be donated to a charity or handed down to another child. Also get rid of anything that is broken and clothes that are not wearable. Box up these "purged" items and move them out of the room. Then look at your remaining piles. Is there too much of one category? Reason with the child to let go of some things, or decide what the child won't miss and purge it. Refer back to the chapters in Part II for more details regarding clothes, toys, paperwork, memorabilia and collections.

Absolute of Organizing: Keep purging simple with "Yes" and "No" piles.

Rearrange: I recommend organizing from big to small. Now that you have categorized and purged, take a step back and look at the big picture of your child's room. You may even want to use boxes to remove everything to see the whole room without the clutter. Now you can assess your furniture situation.

What, if anything, needs to be added to the room? Do you need to hire someone?

- Does the child have a good-sized dresser for all of his or her clothes?
- Is the closet set up for what it needs to contain?
- Is there a desk in the room so he or she can make art projects, store art supplies and do homework?
- Is the bed the right size for the child? Are there storage possibilities under or around the bed?
- Are there any shelves on the walls for display items (like knick-knacks, collections or trophies)?
- Is there a bulletin board, magnetic strip or plastic frames for displaying artwork?
- Is there a toy box, shelf or bins for all the toys in the room?

Now comes the fun part—you get to go shopping! There are so many options with the Internet, catalogs, second-hand shops and home stores that it doesn't have to be an expensive trip. I believe it's best to know exactly what you're looking for before you go shopping. If your child's room has white furniture and you need to add a desk with some drawers, shop for a white desk with drawers. It's also good to think long-term. If you invest in a full-sized dresser now instead of a tiny baby dresser, you won't have to buy new furniture in five years. And if you purchase a big bookcase now, you can use it for books and stuffed animals. As the child grows he or she can add more books and perhaps keep trophies on top.

The fact is, your child is going to grow and change but the room will stay the same size. Maximize the storage possibilities now so you will have room for the big items later.

Your child is going to grow and change but the room will stay the same size. Maximize the storage possibilities now so you will have room for the big items later.

PUTTING IT ALL TOGETHER

Now that you have identified the categories of what stays in the room, and you have the furniture and containers that are necessary, it's time to put the pieces of the puzzle together. Take the most important categories—the things your child uses every day—and find a convenient home for them. Things that are not used every day can go on higher shelves in the closet or tucked away in bins with lids. Display items that should be seen and not played with can be placed on a wall shelf.

As you arrange the furniture and containers in the room, remember to keep some open space so the child can stretch out on the floor to read or play. A little open space is good for the mind. If he can't move freely in his bedroom, the child

Children's Bedroom

Display Shelf

Desk with
bulletin board

Toy box

Open play
area

Dresser

Closet

Bed

Two-tier book-
shelf with lamp

Entrance

may feel frustrated or stifled. If it's a room that is that full of stuff, you really need to think about what you can move out. You may even consider renovations to create more space.

Even little children can have a hand in keeping their rooms straight. The children can pick up their clothes and make their beds in the morning, and then put their toys away in the evening.

Put Limits on What They Keep

By purchasing containers you are limiting how much stuff your child keeps. If you give him or her a shelf for display items, then once that shelf is full, that's it! Don't fall into the habit of simply buying new display shelves whenever the old ones are full. Instead use the "full-barrel" method—once it's full, clean it off. If your child accumulates little figurines or pieces of nature frequently, you may want to help him or her change the display shelf on a seasonal basis. Just like changing the artwork on your refrigerator door, you have to keep it fresh so it doesn't get cluttered.

Absolute of Organizing: Subtract before you add.

Keep Clean-up Simple

Once your child's room is organized, someone will have to keep up with it. Hopefully that someone is not always you, Mom. Even little children can have a hand in keeping their rooms straight. Remember the daily routines we established in the time management section of this book? The children can pick up their clothes and make their beds in the morning, and then put their toys away in the evening before bed. The simpler the clean-up instructions, the better they are. Every morning, I can be heard saying, "Clean clothes in the drawers, dirty clothes in the hamper." Likewise I say every evening, "Put your books on the book shelf and toys in the toy box." Now doesn't that sound simple? Even a three-year-old can follow simple instructions. Avoid saying things like, "Clean up this room," especially to young children. It's overwhelming to them and they might just fight back or think, "I can't do that." Giving specific instructions that sound easy to do will help them say, "I can do that!"

17. Our Main Bathroom Is Embarrassing

THE PROBLEM

If you have one main bathroom that is used by both your children and anyone who comes to your house, you probably struggle on a daily basis to keep it presentable.

Children leave toys around the tub, gobs of toothpaste on the counter, dirty towels anywhere but on the towel rack, and little boys often "miss" the toilet. (If you know what I mean!)

THE STORY

One of my clients had only one full bathroom in her house. It was used by her daughter as a place to play, which is fine, but I thought about how a visitor would feel taking a shower in a tub filled with toys. I've been in that situation, and before you step foot in the shower, you have to clean up other children's toys. Not something you want to do while visiting another person's home. When I looked at this client's linen closet, which was right outside the bathroom door, there was plenty of room to store the bath toys. We just had to start by cleaning out the linen closet.

THE SOLUTION

When considering how to organize your bathroom, you have to take into account what type of linen closet space you have. I suggest you store every bath item you can in your linen closet and only keep the bare essentials in the bathroom.

Store every bath item you can in your linen closet and only keep the bare essentials in the bathroom.

Take a look at some simple solutions to common bathroom problems by using my Room Organizing Worksheet (page 370).

How do you use your bathroom? While it may seem obvious, the function of your bathroom depends on the number of bathrooms in your house, the size of the bathroom, its location and its storage capabilities. Think about who uses this bathroom and what they use it for. If there is too much going on in your bathroom, maybe some functions like doing hair and makeup can be moved to the bedrooms.

What do you like and don't like about your bathroom? If you have no closet in the bathroom, then you may want to add storage cabinets under the sink. If your medicine cabinet is too small, then consider purchasing a bigger one from a home store. If your bathroom looks too juvenile and you want to redecorate, think about a design that the whole family will be happy with. If your bathroom gets too steamy, you may need to install an exhaust fan. This is the time to get to the root cause of your bathroom disorganization. It may be that you have the organizing tools, but no one uses them. In that case, you need to establish a better clean-up routine for your whole family to adopt.

What's in your bathroom now? Pull everything out of the cabinets. Take things out of the tub or shower area and begin to categorize them. Then do the same thing to your linen closet. Write down all the categories on your room organizing sheet to see if there is anything that should not be in the bathroom area. Combine categories that are in both the bathroom and the linen closet.

What do you want to keep in the bathroom? Some essential bathroom items you'll want to keep are:

- Two rolls of toilet paper (one on the holder plus one extra)
- Toothbrushes and toothpaste (one or two tubes maximum)
- Hand soap
- Shampoo and conditioner
- Body wash or soap for the bath/shower
- Washcloths, a hand towel, and a bath towel for each person
- Cosmetics (if you put them on in the bathroom)
- Hair supplies (if you do your hair in the bathroom)
- Step stool or potty seat for small children
- Bath toys in a container (if they can't be kept in the linen closet)

Look at the piles of categories you have created and decide what can be tossed. Here are some obvious ones: moldy bathroom toys, towels that are thread bare, medicines that have expired, old toothbrushes, and bath mats that are shedding. Don't fret too much about getting rid of these items. Most of them are inexpensive and can easily be replaced.

If you are really tight for space in the linen closet, keep extra sheets in the bedroom closets.

Purge: If you find you have too much of one category, pare it down. Some categories that tend to accumulate in bathrooms and linen closets are: medicines, cosmetics, travel size lotions and shampoos, towels, bath toys, nail polishes, perfumed bath salts and beads that you receive as presents, and cleaning products. Consider what you really need and use. If some sundries are still good, but you don't use them, try to find a shelter or nursing home to donate them to. Box up the donations and move them out of the bathroom along with the trash.

Rearrange: Look at what you will be keeping in your bathroom and where it will go. If you have cabinet space under the sink or in a medicine cabinet, begin to put your essential items in them. If you have a plastic bin with holes in it or a mesh bag for bath toys, it's okay to keep them in the bath because they are contained. If you've got too many bath toys to keep in one container, store some in another bin and keep it in the linen closet or under the sink. As you put everything back in, you will probably notice where you need containers or bins. If you are really tight for space in the linen closet, you could keep extra sheets in the bedroom closets or extra blankets in another area of the house. My grandmother taught me this trick for keeping a set of sheets together: Place the folded fitted and top sheets inside the pillowcase. Space bags, which allow you to store several comforters, blankets and sheets in a smaller container by vacuuming out the air, are also a great way to make room in a linen closet.

What needs to be added to this room? Jot down what types of organizers you need and then go shopping! Make sure you have the measurements of the cabinets or drawers to buy the right size. In the meantime you can store your bath items in boxes that are labeled with the category until you can transfer them into your new organizers. Whatever you want to change about the bathroom, write it down and price out what the changes will cost. Organize what you have before you take on any major remodeling. Like the kitchen, it's easier to see what improvements you need when a bathroom is cleared out. It will also be much easier to put things back in the bathroom when they are categorized and contained.

To keep a set of sheets together, place the folded fitted and top sheets inside the pillow case.

MAINTAINING YOUR BATHROOM

Once you have reorganized your bathroom, give your family a tour. Show the children where bathroom toys will be kept, and make sure everyone knows which towel set and toothbrush are theirs. If you have several people using one bathroom, it's a good idea to color code the towels. Demonstrate for your family how and where a wet towel is hung. Make it fun, but make sure everyone knows how to clean up after themselves. Let's face it, you're still going to pick up after the little ones in the bathroom but maybe they can help you put the bath toys away. Ask the older children to hang up their towels and wipe off the counters and sink after they brush their teeth.

If you have several people using one bathroom, it's a good idea to color code the towels.

Before guests visit, I always check our main bath to make sure the toilet is flushed, there's toilet paper on the holder, towels are on the rack, the sink is toothpaste-free, and toys are in the bin. Then I light a candle and breathe a sigh of relief.

18. Everything Ends Up in the Family Room

THE PROBLEM

If you've only got one room to call the "family room," it can become quite cluttered. Most people use this room to watch television, which means that DVDs and videos are kept nearby. If your children are small, this may also be where toys, books, games and puzzles are kept. And if you have any social interaction, this is where guests gather when they visit.

Gone are the days of the formal "parlor" and the "children's nursery," when we could keep things separated. Now we have "great rooms" and "all-purpose" rooms. With so much happening there and so much stuff to store, these rooms can fill up fast.

THE STORY

I have a friend who has a small living room (about 13' × 16'; 4m × 5m). Her family of four uses this room to watch TV, read, play with toys and do the family paperwork. Because she is so organized, she has created zones and only keeps what she uses. As a result, her family room always appears cozy and not cluttered. Here is how she accomplishes it:

1. There are two tall bookcases that hold only the parent's books and framed photos.
2. There is a small desk where the mail goes to be sorted, and bills are paid.
3. There is a small TV on a table with storage underneath for videos.
4. There is a small shelf under the window that holds baskets of children's toys and puzzles.
5. The coffee table has a shelf underneath for children's games.
6. Bigger toys are kept in decorative floor baskets, and the remaining toys are stored in the basement.
7. The sofa and love seat are arranged in an "L" position along the walls, facing the TV and the big window, leaving an open area in the middle of the room.

Everything has a place in this room and there is adequate storage, which makes for easy clean up. It's a great example of making the best of a small living room.

THE SOLUTION

Recall the functions of your family room. Then use the Room Organizing Worksheet (page 370) to plan how you will organize your family room.

Remember to think positive and keep favorable aspects of the room intact.

What do you like about the room currently? Is it cozy? Is it wide open? Does it have a lot of natural light? Remember to think positive and keep those aspects of the room intact.

What don't you like about the room currently? Maybe the room doesn't have a lot of light. Maybe there's no style to the room because you've been adding furniture without an overall plan to decorate. Maybe there's too much going on in this room and it's cluttered. Whatever the case, decide what you want to change about the room as you organize.

What is in the room now? Make a list of the categories of items as well as the furniture. If objects are scattered all over the room, pile like things together so you can assess your situation. If you haven't already, pare down your possessions in this room. Refer back to the chapters in Part II of this book to organize things such as photos, memorabilia, paperwork and toys. Any of those items that do not belong should be boxed up and moved to the correct room.

Absolute of Organizing: Keep like things together.

What do you want to keep in this room? It should be the bare essentials of what you like and the things you need to make this room functional. This list will be your starting point for rearranging.

The trickiest living rooms are those with two focal points, like a fireplace and a TV.

What, if anything, needs to be added to this room, and do you need to hire someone? If you know at this point that you would like a contractor to come in, continue to organize the room as best you can before you call for quotes or go shopping. If you don't know what needs to be added at this point, simply skip this question and come back to it after you have categorized, purged and rearranged.

Absolute of Organizing: Use the C.P.R. process: Categorize, Purge and Rearrange.

PUTTING IT ALL TOGETHER

Once you are left with what stays in the family room, set up zones for different activities.

Two focal points. The trickiest living rooms are those with two focal points, like a fireplace and a TV. You want to have the seating facing the TV for obvious reasons, but it's also nice to have a conversation area where people can sit and enjoy the fire and actually talk to each other. To do this, you have a few options.

1. Put the TV along the same wall as the fireplace, combining your focal points.
2. Put the TV on the opposite wall and partition the room into two areas, one for sitting by the fire, and one for watching TV.
3. Put the TV on an adjacent wall to the fireplace and keep the furniture in an open angle where you could look at either one from the same sitting area.

Areas that flow. If you choose the third option above, you are creating areas that flow. Going along with this idea, you really don't need to divide your room in any way. If you like the idea of one big room for children to play, people to read or sit by a fire, and a place to watch television, then you can have a family room with a wide-open middle area and furniture along the walls. However, when it comes to storage, you still want to have zones. For instance, you can store your books and CDs along one wall, then have a box or basket for toys along another. If there are games and puzzles in this room, keep them all in one cabinet or on one shelf. This type of set up works well in a small area and is almost a necessity when you have limited space.

Distinctive zones. If you've got a large, square family room or one that is long and narrow, you may want to partition your room into distinctive areas. Some possible areas might be a recreation zone (for TV, music, and playing), a quiet reading area, or an office area. You can create these zones with area rugs by putting one in the middle of the recreation zone and one in the quiet reading area or the office zone. Or you can choose to leave one area without a rug. You can also partition with furniture by placing a chair or a sofa with its back to one area, and then set up everything behind that piece of furniture for a different purpose. If you have a studio apartment or a large basement

Use rugs or furniture to create distinctive areas within a large, open room.

Family Room

Shelves for books, CDs and videos

Reading chair and ottoman

Shelves for books, games and puzzles

Fireplace

Child's chair

Basket for small toys

Tall lamp

Newspaper bin

Toy trunk

TV and stereo

Coffee table

Couch, chair and end tables in the shape of an L

for your family room and you want to divide a room without putting up a wall, you can use standing screens, a large curtain or shelving units to create a more "movable" wall. Just remember the larger the room, the more zones you can have, but I still recommend only using each room for two to three functions. Any more than that and you will have a room that feels chopped up.

Even though your family room may be the place where everything happens in your home, you don't have to keep everything there.

Hidden treasures. When space is at a premium in your house, you've got to start looking for hidden treasures. I mean little improvements or storage options that will have a big impact on the organization of a room. One hidden treasure that I found when we moved from our old house to our current one is built-in bookshelves and cabinets. We have one wall in the family room that has seven bookshelves, two small cabinets and four large cabinets that run the length of the wall. I am amazed at all the stuff this wall system holds! It holds our massive video and DVD collection, and eight storage bins of toys underneath. The two small cabinets hold all of our family's games and puzzles. I once considered built-ins a luxury item that I couldn't afford. But if you add up the shelving and storage bins you buy over time, investing that money in custom cabinets could be a simple solution to your family's storage issues. This type of storage is also flexible for families of all ages. I can envision our children's movies and toy bins being replaced with trophies and sports equipment as my children get older.

Other hidden treasures could be furniture with storage. Consider an ottoman in which you can store toys or blankets. Always opt for end tables and coffee tables with a drawer or a shelf underneath. Have a TV stand or entertainment center that will hold all of your electronic equipment and your CDs, DVDs and videos if possible. Decorative trunks or floor baskets are great places to store your family room items to keep it looking stylish.

Also remember that even though your family room may be the place where everything happens in your home, you don't have to keep everything there. Use storage options around your house and bring the toys or projects in and out as necessary.

19. I'm Living Out of My Minivan!

THE PROBLEM

You are a mom, and therefore a chauffeur as well. Some of us drive from day care to work and back again every day. Others drive to doctor's appointments, preschool and the supermarket. In the afternoon, we drive to ballet, music lessons and soccer. We also know children do not travel light, especially when they are young. There are diaper bags, snacks, and sports equipment to remember. For safety reasons you want to have your car or minivan well equipped for anything that might happen during your travels. Inevitably someone is screaming for something you don't have as you set out for the day's errands and appointments.

THE STORY

A few years ago, I made the mistake of letting my husband pack our car for vacation. We had only been on the road half an hour when my youngest asked for a drink. "The cooler is in the back," my husband said. So I had to instruct my daughter how to climb in the back of the station wagon, move a few items and dig out a drink. Not only was this unsafe, but it was messy. When the next child asked for a snack, I told him to look in the grocery bag by his feet, but unfortunately there were only canned goods, bread and cereal in the sack. I knew instinctively what the children would want during our two-hour drive, but my husband figured if the children wanted something, they could either wait until we got there or they would bring it themselves. He was just happy that we got everything in one car! From then on, my husband has let me pack the car for any long trips, and I have fine-tuned the art of strategically packing a car for three children.

THE SOLUTION

Be prepared and have your car packed with essentials for both you and your children. Look at the items listed below and then take a notebook with you as you drive around for a week. Write down anything the children ask for that you don't have, as well as anything you wish you had. This will become your personal wish list for your car.

Safety Items

- Gas container and funnel
- Jumper cables
- Cell phone charger for car
- Fix-a-flat
- Spare tire and jack
- Road flares
- Cell phone
- Ice scraper
- Maintenance book for your car

Convenience Items

- Deposit slips for the bank—make it easier to use the drive-thru
- Maps of places you travel to often
- Directions and phone numbers of out-of-town friends you visit
- Baby wipes—great for spills on clothing, seats and console areas
- Loose change—if you need to pay tolls
- A snack, gum or mints
- A change of clothes or coveralls—in case you have to change a flat tire
- Sun shield for the side windows and the windshield
- Pen and paper

Baby Needs

- Pacifier
- Diapers and wipes
- Change of clothes
- Teething gel
- Little toys
- Little blanket
- Baby food or bottle
- Acetaminophen or ibuprofen

Toddler Needs

- Snacks
- Little toys
- Diapers
- Books
- Change of clothes
- Baby wipes
- A towel—to wipe off playground equipment after it rains

Grade Schooler's Needs

- Drink or snack
- Hand-held toy
- Book
- A big blanket

Teenager's Needs

- Portable music player
- Book

Absolute of Organizing: Start with a good list.

PUTTING IT ALL TOGETHER

Now that you have a list of everything you want to keep in your car, start to assemble these items. Categorize them according to where they need to be in the car. Your items should be kept up front. Items the children need should be within reach in the second seat. Any safety items can be stored in the trunk or back of the car. Find appropriate containers for each area such as the glove compartment or side door pockets in the front seat, a back-of-the-seat organizer for the children's things, or a small diaper bag to leave in the car for the baby. The tools and car care equipment can fit in a tool box or a plastic milk crate in the trunk or back of the car.

Road trips. When taking car trips that are two hours or longer, we pack the portable TV in between the two front seats and let the children watch a movie. I also make sure that everyone is as comfortable as possible, with shoes off, pillows and blankets and everything they could ask for within reach, before we leave our driveway! Before a long trip, I also visit the dollar store to buy inexpensive toys for the children. Each hour I'll hand out something new to keep them occupied.

Everyday errands. For short jaunts to the store or school, put the child who needs to be buckled in right behind the driver's seat. Older children who can buckle themselves can go on the other side of the back seat. This will save you from having to run around your car or climb in the back of your minivan every time you go out.

Your purse and diaper bag. If you don't want to feel bogged down with baggage every time you leave the house, consolidate your purse and the baby's diaper bag. First, take a look at what you bring with you for every trip in the car. See if you have one bag that can accommodate all those things, and leave it by the door. I love to use backpacks of all sizes because they allow your hands to be free to carry a baby or to hold a child's hand when crossing a parking lot. If you use a basic backpack instead of a standard "diaper bag," even Dad won't mind carrying it. If there's anything you can leave in the car, pack a small bag and leave it there. These items might include a baby's change of clothes, spit up pads, diapers and wipes, a pacifier, some snacks for the children, and little toys. For yourself, you may like to have tissues, a small makeup case, a brush and some gum or mints. If these items are always in the car, then all you have to grab when you leave is your wallet, keys and cell phone. Several women I know often leave their entire handbag in the car. No matter where you live or how safe you think your car is, *this is a bad idea*! It's too easy for keys to get locked in or for your wallet to be stolen. Instead, consolidate your daily travel items, chose a nice, easy bag to carry and either leave it in the car without your valuables, or leave it by the door in your home.

Absolutely Organized

Congratulations! If you followed every chapter in this section, you should now have a completely organized home. At the very least, you should have a plan to attain that goal.

REMEMBER

- Create a Home Projects Plan that gives you a vision of what you want to do in each room of your house.
- Work on one room at a time.
- Use the "Room Organizing Worksheet" (page 370) to plan how you will organize each room.
- Decide the functions of each room first.
- A home office can be as simple as a desk and file cabinet.
- Plan what needs to be stored in your home and what purpose each storage area will serve.
- Kitchen or bathroom counters should hold only what you use every day.
- An organized refrigerator is a healthy one.
- Limit your children's toys, knickknacks and artwork with practically sized containers.
- Maximize your closet space so more items can be put away.
- Designate zones for different functions in your family room.
- Equip your vehicle with everything you need to travel with kids.
- Teach your family how to maintain the beautifully organized home you have created!

Part IV: Race Against Time

IN OUR FAST-PACED WORLD, parents and children may feel like every day is a footrace. We wake up, get dressed, sometimes grab a bite for breakfast, and then go from one thing to the next: work, school, gym, store, ball fields.

Parents often feel like a relay team. "You take her. I'll take him. See you back here at 7. I'll do the dishes, you do the pickups. I'll do the homework, you do the baths." Sound familiar?

We teach our children to tell time when they are young. I suggest we teach them how to manage their time as well. If we teach time management, maybe some things will get done completely and thoroughly without a rush to the finish line, and maybe our children will have some white space on their calendars and some downtime in their days to just enjoy being kids. Instead of passing on our stress, we can pass on our calm, forward-planning skills to our children.

"Let our advance worrying become advance thinking and planning."

—WINSTON CHURCHILL

20. At the Starting Line…Organizing Starts with the Parents

THE PROBLEM

Sometimes that which drives you crazy about your kids is the one thing you see in yourself, if you take a close look. How often have you said, "I can't believe you waited until the last minute to do that paper!" and, "You've got to plan ahead" to your children? And yet, aren't you guilty of the same offenses? If you expect your children to be organized at home, in school, and with their time, then you've got to first look at yourself and see if you are setting a good example.

THE STORY

I have a son who is always in motion. From the moment he wakes up until the time he crashes into bed, he is moving. We joke that he only has two gears: high and off. Sometimes, when we want to have a quiet, easy morning or just want to do nothing, it's aggravating that he is in our faces asking for something every five minutes. Then I look back to my typical day. I am constantly in motion, too! And the family joke is that I usually "hit the wall" at ten at night, when I finally sit down on the couch to watch TV. Many times, I just go to sleep. Being active isn't a bad thing. For me it's a means to be and to feel productive. For my son, who has a lot of natural energy, it's simply how he is made. The challenge for us as parents is to channel that energy to a point where we are all happy and no one is antsy or annoyed. The other thing we can do is show him that it's OK to have downtime or quiet time during the day. We don't always have to be going on to the next thing and then the next thing. Sometimes it's OK to just be.

Absolute of Organizing Your Family: If you lead, they will follow.

So what does this have to do with organizing your kids? Well, if you have a child who is a procrastinator, or one who is not proactive but rather reactive, then maybe he learned it from you! So, before you yell, "Clean up that room!" take a good look at your own room.

I always say there is no right or wrong way to organize. There is only what works and what doesn't work. And you, as parents, know when your system is working. Bills get paid on time, appointments are made and kept. Everyone has what they need for school and work. And you certainly know when it's not working, because the opposite is true. Try taking this test to see how well you are organized in your own life:

ORGANIZING SELF CHECKLIST

Do you pay your bills on time?	Yes	No
Do you make appointments on time?	Yes	No
Do you sit down to a family dinner more than three times a week?	Yes	No
Is your morning routine efficient and stress-free?	Yes	No
Do you RSVP to invitations and return phone calls in a timely manner?	Yes	No
Do you get a chance to see your friends at least once a month?	Yes	No
Do you have downtime in your week?	Yes	No
Are there clear tabletops in your home?	Yes	No
Can you easily find what you need?	Yes	No

Can your spouse and children easily find what they need in your home?	Yes	No
Do your children have responsibilities at home?	Yes	No
Are all your clothes either hung up or in drawers?	Yes	No
Could you say right now what categories of things are stored in your attic, basement, or garage?	Yes	No

If you answered yes to most of these questions, then in my opinion, you are an organized person. Regardless of how your house looks at any given time, you are a functioning adult. And I'm betting that there is a general feeling of calm in your home.

If you answered no to most of these, you probably need some help with time management, organizing your things, and/or organizing your home. In this case, I would bet your home life feels stressful.

There really is a trickle-down effect when you are organized.

THE SOLUTION

If doing this self test proved to you that you are not organized, but you still want your child to be organized, then you've got two choices. One is to get yourself organized first, then go on to teach your child. The other choice is to accept the fact that you have shortcomings in this area, admit this to your child, and learn together to get things under control.

Set Your Goals

I always recommend to my new clients that they start their organizing processes by finishing this statement: "If I were more organized, I could…" Finish this statement yourself and write down your answer. Then ask your child to do the same. Post your statements on the refrigerator or a bulletin board to motivate both of you. By finishing this simple statement you have set a goal. Maybe you've decided that if you were more organized you could have more free time, save money, pay your bills on time, or take up a hobby. Maybe your child decided if he was more organized he wouldn't have to fight with his parents, or he would get better grades, or he would have more playtime. There really is a trickle-down effect when you are organized. Let's take a look at two real-life scenarios.

Scenario 1

An organized person keeps excellent tax files. He has a file for charitable contributions, business expenses, and deductible medical expenses. When the first of the year comes, he can clear out each file, total up the costs, and accurately record them on his tax form, getting the maximum amount of deductions that he is allowed. He compiles the papers and hands them off to a tax professional so he knows he is filing in accordance with any new tax laws. It is done well before April 15 and his refund is in hand before the spring.

Being organized doesn't just mean putting your things away. It means being efficient, organized with your time, getting your priorities straight, and creating balance in your life.

Scenario 2

An unorganized person has bags of papers, not files. As he starts to receive his W2 forms in the mail, panic sets in as he realizes it's tax time again. He spends several nights riffling through piles of papers that contain all kinds of receipts, some tax-related, some not. At some point he *thinks* he has it all together so he tries to fill out the tax forms on his own. However, there are receipts still lying on the bottom of a bag somewhere that may have given him more deductions. It's April 14 and the clock is ticking. He makes it to the post office just in time for the deadline. However, he wasn't aware of some new tax laws so he made mistakes, gets audited, and the whole process starts again as he tries to find proof for exemptions that he claimed. Clearly, the unorganized person has cost himself time, stress, and money. And so the cycle continues.

Being organized doesn't just mean putting your things away, although that is part of it. It means being efficient, organized with your time, getting your priorities straight, and creating balance in your life. It is not an end goal, it is a means to an end. What that goal is depends on you and your children. As we go through the process of organizing we will talk about the goals for each area of your children's lives. When the goal is clear to you and your children, it's a lot easier to motivate them.

Categories of Organizing

My first book, *Absolutely Organized*, walks you through the process of organizing the three main areas of your life: your time, your belongings, and your home. When you keep these areas of your life organized and balanced, you set a good example for your children.

Time management leads to less stress and more balance between what you must do and what you want to do.

Time management skills are essential to being organized. When you successfully manage your time, you know how long things will take, and you can plan accordingly. Likewise, you can decide how much you can do in one day and you know when to say no to too many commitments. People who are not good time managers often try to do too many things and end up running late or completely missing appointments, or they leave things to the last minute. Either way the result is the same: stress. Time management leads to less stress and more balance between what you must do and what you want to do.

Our houses, our offices, and our cars are filled with our belongings—from furniture to toys to paperwork to clothes to personal mementos. Keeping everything under control is a constant battle for some people. A few basic principles can help you organize all of your belongings so they are easy to find and to use. We've all heard of the idea to keep like things together to make them easier to manage and find. If the idea of organizing your entire house is overwhelming, it may be easier for you to deal with one category of belongings at a time. To do

> *When it comes to organizing your home, it's best to start with a written plan.*

this, you may need to gather it all into one clear room and follow my process.

If you want to take the room-by-room approach when it comes to organizing your home, then it's best to start with a written plan. Like a builder who walks through a new home and makes a punch list, you too need to walk through each room and write down what you want to do with it. This could include clearing out the clutter, painting, or undertaking a bigger construction or repair job. When you have the whole house plan, you can then get quotes for big jobs, budget, and plan when you can get it all done. Even if it's going to take years, you have a plan! When you start, focus on one room at a time until it is finished. Then move on to your next priority.

These are the major areas of organizing. To get these areas organized, I believe there are certain rules, or absolutes, that organized people follow in all aspects of their lives. As a review, here is a list of my 10 Absolutes of Organization taken from *Absolutely Organized*. Use these principles to organize your own affairs first so you set a good example for your children.

Absolutes of Organizing

1. *The method to use is CPR:* Categorize, Purge, and Rearrange. This can be used to organize any room in your home or category of items you have. Start by sorting everything into categories as general as you can make them (papers, clothes, home decorations, etc.). Then purge whatever you don't want or need or use. Finally you can put everything back together by rearranging things into logical places and containers if necessary.

2. *Keep purging simple with "yes" and "no" piles.* As you go through one category of items, don't get caught up in too many ways to sort. The "yes" pile means you love it, need it, or use it. The "no" pile is what you don't need or want anymore.

3. *Keep only what you use.* This sounds logical, but many people keep things because of emotional attachment, or because they might use the items someday. If you only keep what you use, your life will be clutter-free.

4. *If you don't plan it, it won't happen.* Many times we fill our minds and little pieces of paper with things we mean to do, like cleaning out a closet or fixing a broken item. Planning it means making the phone call, scheduling the appointment, and putting it on your calendar—even if the appointment is with yourself.

5. *Keep like things together.* Again, this sounds so obvious, but how many times do we find that toys or paperwork or books are located all over our houses? If like things are kept together, it's easier to see what you have, what you need, and what you don't. A classic example of this is with food. How many times have you bought something you thought you were out of but later found it hiding at the back of a cabinet?

If like things are kept together, it's easier to see what you have, what you need, and what you don't. How many times have you bought something you thought you were out of but later found it hiding in a cabinet?

6. *Start with a good list.* Whenever you go shopping, plan a house project, or plan your day, you have to start with a good list. Once the list is complete you just have to stick to it to be efficient.

7. *Subtract before you add.* Before you go shopping for anything, make sure you are taking something out of your house first. This could be with clothes or furniture. In the case of organizing your files, before you start making new files, make sure you've cleared out whatever old files you can get rid of.

8. *Finish one thing before you start another.* This applies to projects that you

start and products that you use. How many toothpaste tubes or ketchup bottles do you have open at once?

9. *Organize from big to small.* When you are doing my CPR process, make general categories first, then if one category is too big to handle, chunk it down into smaller piles. For instance, if you have a room full of books to organize, you can break them down into business and pleasure. Then you can break pleasure down into classics, paperback novels, self-help, etc. Many people make the mistake of starting to organize with a small area like a drawer in a desk, but they don't see the bigger picture. When using the big-to-small method, organize the room first, then the desk, then the drawer.

10. *Daily routines are a must.* So many people get organized but have trouble staying that way. I believe the only way to keep up is to develop routines, like straightening up daily, cleaning weekly, and cleaning out on an annual basis.

This basic review of your own organizing skills will help you as you begin to help and teach your children to organize their time, their belongings, and their spaces. The basic principles are the same, but there are certain nuisances to teaching your children how to be organized. If you push too hard or demand too much, they may fight back. If you are too laid-back and give them too much freedom, then chaos may become a way of life in your home. Show them a good example, help them make choices and plan ahead, and you will lead your children into adulthood with valuable life skills.

The Odd Couple Syndrome

By now you might be saying, "I'm organized, but it's my spouse who's not on board." Believe me, in my years as an organizer, I have often felt like a marriage counselor. Sometimes it's the husband and sometimes it's the wife who is the neatnik. Like all other conflicts in marriage, you have to resolve this one with compromise. And bullying your spouse rarely works. Neither does buying a container, sticking it in a room, and hoping your spouse will use it! I think a written organizing plan and a walk-through of the home is the best place to start discussing organizing in a nonthreatening way. Talk about what your family would like to do with a certain room. Or talk about your family's goals for getting organized. For instance, if your husband's old stuff is taking up too much space in the basement, say something like, "What do you think about making this the playroom? Let's see what we would have to clear out in order to do that." Or if the wife's papers are all over the kitchen, you can ask, "How would you like a desk in the family room so you could do all your paperwork there?" Focus on the positive solution instead of the problem you have with your spouse.

Show them a good example, help them make choices and plan ahead, and you will lead your children into adulthood with valuable life skills.

THREE STEPS TO BEING AN ORGANIZED PARENT

1. Make sure that you, the parents, are setting an organized example. Review my ten Absolutes of Organizing.
2. If you need to work on some areas, learn with your child and practice what you preach.
3. Set goals with your family and compromise where necessary.

21. Time Trials . . . Where Does Their Time Go?

THE PROBLEM

I firmly believe that all good organizing starts with time management. If you are constantly running in several directions, and you never know what tomorrow will bring, then how can you possibly plan to get your life in order? The same is true for children. Today, so many children are overscheduled with music lessons, sports, and other extracurricular activities. Is it any wonder that sports equipment, books, and clothing get thrown on the floor as children come home and head out for the next things on their schedules?

THE STORY

Michael is the youngest of five children in a very active household. He plays multiple sports including baseball, basketball, and soccer. He also is involved in Boy Scouts. One day his mother (or chauffeur, as she often feels) picked him up from school, and as many mothers do, she rattled off what had to happen that afternoon. "When we get home you've got to do your homework, eat dinner, and get changed for your game," she told him. So Michael did as he was told, but after running up to his room he discovered he needed a little more information. He yelled downstairs, "Mom! What uniform do I put on?" His schedule was so full that he didn't know which game he was going to!

THE SOLUTION

If you don't want your children to be stressed out and always rushing, you have to take control of their schedules when they are young so they can do this for themselves as they grow into adulthood.

How Do They Spend Their Time Now?

To begin the process of organizing your child's schedule, let's take a snapshot of how she spends her time now. Page 197 has a sample of a weekly time sheet. A blank template is available on page 374.

There are no right or wrong answers on the time sheet. Your goal is to accurately capture how your children spend their time.

It's beneficial to complete this chart with your child. If you are trying to organize more than one child at the same time, give each child his or her own chart and individually fill out the chart with each child.

In the column marked morning, jot down anything your child does before school starts. Some possibilities are: practicing an instrument, physical therapy, going to the gym with Mom or Dad, getting dropped off at a neighbor's house, and walking the dog. Write it down whether it's something they have to do or something they just like to do. It all depends on your family situation. Children with learning disabilities may do rhythmic writing to prepare them for the school day ahead, and children who live on a farm may do their chores before school. Many children just get up and get ready for school.

In the midday slot you will most likely fill in "school," but again there may be special cases where your child is not in school every day. You also need to account for their time on the weekend. Do they have athletic events on the weekend? Do they attend religious services with the family?

	MORNING	MIDDAY	AFTER SCHOOL	EVENING
Monday	Watched TV 8–8:30	School 8:30–4	Karate 5–6	Homework 6:30–7:30 Watched TV 7:30–8:30
Tuesday	Watched TV 8–8:30	School 8:30–4	Played outside until 5	Homework 6:30–7:30 Watched TV 7:30–9
Wednesday	Played outside 8–8:30	School 8:30–4	Karate 5–6	Homework 7-8
Thursday	Video games 8–8:30	School 8:30–4	Watched TV 4-5	Homework 6:30–7:30
Friday		School 8:30–4	Went to friends until 6	Out to dinner with family until 8
Saturday	Watched TV 9-10 Cleaned room 10-11	Walked the dog	Played with friends 1-5	Watched a movie 7–9
Sunday	Church 10-11	Played inside 12-2	School project 2-4	Watched TV 7-8:30

Next fill in all after-school activities, whether they are planned or not. If your child does not have scheduled after-school activities, then just write down what she did in the last week to get an idea of a typical week.

The evening slot is for anything that happens between dinner and bedtime. Again, if nothing is scheduled at that time, just write down whether your child is doing homework, watching TV, playing with friends, etc.

Remember, there are no right or wrong answers here. You just want to get an accurate picture of how your child spends her time. If you think that your child may be opposed to this idea, you may want to play detective and just observe for a week, making your own notes on the time sheet. Make sure that you don't encourage your child to change what she is doing during this week. If she is watching TV, don't say, "Why don't you practice your violin?" That would be distorting the picture. Just write it down, and bite your tongue.

Ask your children how they would like to spend their time, and assure them that you will consider their interests when coming up with an ideal schedule.

Sitting down to look at a weekly time sheet can be an eye-opening experience for both children and adults. Even if you're not working on your own time management skills, it might be a good idea to do a time sheet for yourself and share that with your child. Just look at it and talk about whether there are any surprises. Talk about what's missing from the time sheet. No chores? No outside play? Too much time on video games or the Internet? Noticing these things will give you ideas for how you and your child might make better use of your time.

How Would They Like to Spend Their Time?

Now switch your focus away from how your child is spending her time now, to how she would like to spend her time. You can do this by simply asking her, What do you like to do first thing in the morning before school? After school? In the evening? At the bottom of the weekly time sheet or on small sticky notes, write down what your child says. With younger children it may come out in this way,

How Much Time Is Necessary for Homework?

IN ORDER TO ANSWER THIS QUESTION, parents need a clear explanation of the expected workload from their child's teacher or teachers. Many educational experts use the ten-minutes-per-grade formula, so if your child is in sixth grade, you can expect sixty minutes of homework. If your child is spending much more or less time than the teacher expects on a regular basis, you might want to investigate further.

To help your child budget her time, ask her to estimate how much time she will spend on each subject for a given night's homework and write those estimates in her assignment book. Then clock exactly how much time is spent on each subject. Were her estimates close? Do this for a week to get a real feel for how long it takes to do one page of math, one page of language arts, or to study for a chapter test, for example. Then, going forward, you and your child can really know if homework is going to take half an hour, an hour, or more, and you can plan accordingly. This is best done at the beginning of a school year to set a routine for homework.

"I never get to play with my friends after school." Or an older child might say, "I'd like to get a part-time job so I can afford a car." Or they might say, "My friend takes ballet, I wish I could do that." Assure them that you will consider their interests when coming up with an ideal schedule, but you also have to consider the rest of the family. If they have free time, then this is a lot easier. If they are booked, then ask these questions: What activities do you want to continue doing? What activities can we drop or postpone? Of course there may be some activities that are non-negotiable like religious instruction or tutoring, for example. Let your child know what these activities are so they are not up for discussion. Right now you are just brainstorming and making a list of how she would like to spend her time.

What Do They Need to Do?

Make another list of activities the child needs to be doing if these activities did not appear on her time sheet. Again, you may want to put each activity on a sticky note or jot it at the bottom of the time sheet. Is the child spending enough time on schoolwork? Is regular homework completed on time, and is she prepared for class every day? Does she spend a lot of time studying, but her grades don't reflect her work? Maybe she needs a tutor or additional help from a specialist.

Chores teach children responsibility and make them feel like integral parts of the family.

If your child is taking music lessons, is she spending an appropriate amount of time practicing the music? If she never practices or plays the instrument, maybe it's time to give up the lessons. Have this discussion with your child. Ask her if she still enjoys playing the instrument. Her interests may have changed, and she may be ready to move on to something else. Let her know that if she wants to continue on with the instrument, she must commit to practicing every day or on a regular schedule that you both agree on.

Absolute of Organizing Your Family: Give your children a few options that you can live with, and let them choose.

Has the child been assigned chores, but she does not do them? Write down the specific chores. If you have never assigned your kids household chores, maybe this is the time for you to think about it. Giving children chores teaches them responsibility and makes them feel like integral parts of the family.

These areas of homework, musical or sports practice, and chores are just general areas that you should consider when you think about what your child should be doing with her time. When you finish this part of the time management exercise, you should have three pieces of written information:

1. A time planning worksheet that shows you how your child is spending her time.
2. A list of how your child would like to spend her free time.
3. A list of what she needs to be doing but is not.

Armed with this information, you can now proceed to plan out an ideal schedule for your child, one that will make both you and your child happy. You'll want to reassure her that with a little time management, you can fit in a lot of things, but maybe not everything at once.

THREE STEPS TO MONITORING YOUR CHILD'S TIME

1. Fill in a weekly time sheet of how she spends time now.
2. Identify what's missing and what is too much.
3. Talk with your child about what she needs to be doing and what she wants to be doing with her time.

22. Choose Your Events . . . Evaluate Seasonal Activities

THE PROBLEM

Most parents I meet agree that many kids today are overscheduled. There are so many resources for extracurricular activities, and sometimes we parents want our children to have it all and do it all. We want them to be musicians, exceptional athletes, and academic geniuses. Of course we want them to have it better than we did, it's only natural. But at what expense? Often, the same parents who enroll their kids in extended sport seasons and multiple activities are the ones who are stressed out and complaining that they are always running and never have time to relax. How do you think the kids feel?

Absolute of Organizing Your Family: You can't overload your children's schedules and complain that you're too busy or they're too cranky.

THE STORY

I started to notice this overscheduling when my first child was still in diapers. Looking to meet some other stay-at-home moms, and looking for something to pass the days with my new little daughter, I signed up for a Gymboree class at a local church. When I got there, it seemed like a lot of the moms already knew each other. As I started to meet them and talk to them, I soon found out that they were involved in similar activities every day of the week! They did swim lessons, music circle, dance class, art class, and Gymboree. And most of these kids were only two or three years old! I wondered whether this was more for the moms or the kids?

Fast forward to our first summer in our new house. My kids were ages three, six and nine. It was difficult to find friends whom they could invite over to the house because most of their friends were at summer camp for three to six weeks, or they were on swim teams that practiced every day or they were taking academic enrichment classes. Whatever happened to having the summers off? My kids just wanted to sleep late, explore the creek behind our house, and ride their bikes. I was willing to have other kids over to keep my own children occupied, but it took us a while to find friends who were available to simply play!

THE SOLUTION

Slow down and think it through using the information you compiled in the last chapter about what your children want to do and what they must do. Consider your options and your lifestyle before setting the schedule in stone.

Talk to Other Parents

When your children are young, or if you move to a new area, it's a good idea to talk to other parents about available activities. Find out which ones have convenient times for you and your family, which ones are reasonably priced, and which ones will give you a free trial class! There's nothing worse than enrolling your child in a new activity, paying for six months, and finding out on the first day that he hates it! It's also best to match the activity with your child's personality. You wouldn't put a shy child in an acting class unless he showed some interest in it first. Talking to other parents and asking them about their child's personality is a great way to see if your child will fit in. It's also a way to set up carpools if the transportation to and from the activity is a hassle. And, the children will be more inclined to go to an activity if there is a friend going with them.

Extracurriculars Can Help Focus

WHEN I FIRST STARTED TAKING my youngest child to karate classes, I stayed in the waiting room and spoke with the other parents. I really began to feel that I was in the right place as I learned about the other children in the class and their personalities. Most of the other parents described their children as extremely active and easily distracted. Some of them had cognitive difficulties like autism, ADD and sensory integration problems. My son has not been diagnosed with any of those, but he does display similar characteristics. All the parents agreed that the discipline of karate was a way to channel their children's energy and quiet their minds. The benefits were twofold for my son: He enjoys and excels at karate, and it's good for his focus.

Consider Appropriate Activities for Your Child's Age

Early Childhood. Many townships now have sports teams for four- and five-year-olds. It's a way of getting kids started in a sport before the competitive spirit kicks in. There are multiple resources for other kinds of activities in the arts and music as well. Think of the younger years (ages four to six) as a time to introduce your child to all sorts of activities. Look for ones with free introductory classes or short-term enrollments so if your child does not take to the activity, you have an easy out. Invariably there will be certain ones that your child loves and wants to keep going back to. But if he doesn't stick to one, don't get discouraged. He's young and can't be expected to master anything at this point. It's a time for experimenting.

Elementary and Middle School. During grade school your child will go through many changes, physically, mentally, and socially. Keeping him involved in something outside of school is a good idea, but look for a middle ground. If your children choose to participate in no extracurricular activities, it could mean that they are watching more TV or playing too many video games. Or, if you're lucky, it means that you have a great neighborhood with a lot of kids who play outside all the time and your children can burn off their energy and socialize with others in their own backyard. Nothing wrong with that! On the other hand, too many activities might mean that they are running every day after school and in the evenings, making home a very stressful environment for everyone. I use the gauge that on three days (or nights) out of the five-day school week children should have no commitments. This gives them time for homework, downtime, and sit-down family meals.

> *A good gauge is that on three days out of the five-day school week a child should have no commitments. This gives him time for homework, downtime, and sit-down family meals.*

Absolute of Organizing Your Family: Kids need downtime. Factor that in.

Between the ages of six and fourteen, your child should start to show some interest in particular activities. He might even limit himself to one sport that he really likes. With childhood obesity on the rise, one sport per season is a great idea to keep your child active all year long. Also, having extracurricular activities will help your child budget his time better. This is the life stage when the child's personality really takes shape. His activities and interests will reflect his budding personality if you, as a parent, expose him to different experiences, give him some options that you can live with, and ask him for his opinion about what he wants to do.

High School. By the time they reach high school your kids should have a pretty good idea of what they want to do in their free time. Are they into sports? Scouting? Martial arts? Theater? Music? These are all questions that you and your child should be able to answer with ease. However, there are typically more options for them as they get older. Student government, language clubs, and community service groups are available in most high schools. These might be things they haven't tried before. Your child also might want to get a part-time job so he can earn and spend his own money. Again, this is a decision that you as parents should make with your child. Do you want the child to have a part-time job? If so, how many hours per week are acceptable for him to work? And how will he get to the job? These are all things you have to consider before committing. Likewise, before he joins a high school sport, make sure you know the time commitment and costs. Typically, high school sports are much more time consuming than sports kids play in younger grades.

> *In high school, kids should have a pretty good idea of what they want to do in their free time. However, there are more new options available to them as they get older.*

Absolute of Organizing Your Family: Give your children a few options that you can live with, and let them choose.

Consider the Other Family Members and Their Commitments

Once you have sat down with each child, no matter what their ages, you as parents need to come to some decisions. Set aside some time to really plan out the extracurricular activities. You should have a list of what each child wants and needs to do (from Chapter 21). You'll also need a month-at-a-glance calendar to plot this all out. Now look at the year as a whole, then break it down into months,

	JAN	FEB	MAR	APR	MAY	JUNE
Child 1	Basketball ————————		Baseball ———————————————————			
Child 2	Ballet ———————————————————————————————————					
	Acting ————————————————					
Child 3	Karate ————————————————————————————————————					Gymnastics

Seasonal Chart. A seasonal chart helps you identify your busiest months at a glance.

weeks, and days. Find out how long the seasons are for your children's sports and other extracurricular activities. You might just take a big piece of paper and make blocks for each month. Write in each sport or activity using a different color for each child. Laying it out this way lets you see where your busy months are, and where you have a fairly light schedule. Now think about your work life and how that interacts with the kids' activities. Does either parent have a busy season or a season where their workload is a little lighter? You've got to balance that out with the kids' activities. Sometimes we don't have all the data to plan out a whole year, but if you have a general idea of what the busy months are, you can make better decisions as new opportunities arise.

Once you've looked at the year from a seasonal perspective, look at just one month. In the example in the chart above, the family has ballet and karate from September to June. January to March is the busiest season, with four activities happening at once.

Then look at which days of the week all the activities fall on. If it turns out that your kids are all active on the same days of the week, consider a carpool. Setting up carpools in the beginning of a season is a real time saver and stress reducer for all families involved. If you know dinnertime is hectic around your

JULY	AUG	SEPT	OCT	NOV	DEC	
	Camp	Soccer ———————————————————				Child 1
	Camp	Ballet ———————————————————				Child 2
———————		Karate ———————————————————				Child 3

house, and you'd rather be out driving at seven or eight P.M., find someone who doesn't mind driving between five and six P.M. When we first moved to our new neighborhood, I set up carpools for each of my children: one for Confraternity of Christian Doctrine (CCD) class, one for preschool, and one for dance class. This was a real time saver and gas saver for our family, and it helped us connect with our new neighbors. In fact, when we considered different options for activities, carpooling was an important factor in our decision-making process.

As a parent, you have to set the priorities and then live with the schedule you've created.

When planning and scheduling your kids' activities, you also may want to consider how your family likes to relax or connect in the evenings and on weekends. Is it better to be running one child per night to an activity, or would you rather have one or two hectic nights where everyone is busy, and then a couple nights with nothing to do? We all have options and we all control our time. You first must decide how you want your schedule to look, and then you can arrange activities so it works according to your plan. If you decide

How to Set Up a Carpool

1. Find out who else from your neighborhood is going to the same activity at the same time as your child. You can do this by talking to people you already know, by looking at the team or class list, or just by introducing yourself to a familiar-looking parent at the class.

2. Start the conversation by simply asking if the other child needs a ride. You could say, "I see your son Tommy is on my son Justin's baseball team. Does he need a ride to practice Thursday night?" Most likely the other parent will ask to reciprocate. If not, you can say something like, "No sense in both of us driving from this neighborhood, would you like to set up a carpool? What works better for you, driving to practice or picking up from practice?" Then find out the details of the other family's schedule.

3. Options for keeping a fair balance: You might establish that it's always easier for you to drive one way and for the other family to do the other leg of the trip. In some cases, you may want to alternate by weeks. For example, this week you drive in the

Friday is family night, then nobody schedules an activity for that evening. If you say Sundays are sacred, then you won't even consider a class or sport that runs on Sunday mornings. Of course, our schedules change from time to time and we have to be flexible, but understand that as the parent, you have to set the priorities and then live with the schedule you've created. Don't be a slave to your children's activities and then be miserable because your life is so hectic. I hear this morning and they drive in the afternoon, then next week you switch. In other cases, you may have to go by the day of the week. Whatever the case, it's best to keep it as simple as possible. Consistent routines make it easier to remember when you have to drive and help the children feel secure in knowing who is taking them and who is picking them up.

4. Information to gather: Make sure you get the other person's cell phone number in case of an emergency. If the children you will be driving are small, find out if they need car seats. Also find out if the children have any allergies or medical conditions that you should be aware of. Today there are so many kids with allergies, you wouldn't want to unknowingly expose them to something that would make them sick.

5. Keep your communication clear and frequent. If anything changes in your schedule or the schedule of the class or activity, call your carpool mate. Better to over-communicate than to assume one thing and be wrong.

from so many moms and dads: "We're running so much with the kids on weekends that it's a pleasure to go back to work on Monday morning!" That's fine if everybody's happy doing what they are doing. But if it feels more like a treadmill that you want to get off, then change something. Set the family priorities and then fill in with the extra activities to enhance your lives, not burden them.

Plan Ahead for What Happens in the Summer

Summertime is a great time for kids. Remember your own summers growing up? Hopefully they are filled with fond memories of outside activities, relaxing times with friends, and family vacations. We all know that times have changed. More moms are working in the summer. Hanging on the streets is not always the safest option. As much as we might dislike it, we have to plan our summers in early spring. Full-time working moms probably know this better than anyone. If you need day care all year round, many times your options change in the summer months. So, like anything else, you've got to plan ahead. Here are some things you'll have to consider:

Certain types of kids thrive on routines and schedules and can be quite lost without them.

1. Are your children old enough to be at home by themselves?
2. Would you like to have an in-home caregiver?
3. Is it better for your kids to be at a camp during the day?
4. Do they need to be driven anywhere during the day?
5. How much would day care cost?
6. Can you change your work schedules so one parent can work from home a few days a week?
7. Is there another family you can swap child care with? (i.e., I watch your kids on Monday and Wednesday, and you watch mine on Tuesday and Thursday.)
8. Even if Mom is home full time or part time, do you want planned activities or camps for your kids?
9. Is a half-day or a full-day camp better?
10. What vacations do you have planned for the summer?
11. Do you want nothing planned at all?

As I said, if both parents work full time all year, this might be a no-brainer. But if Mom works part-time or not at all, or if Dad works from home, you still might want to think about how your house will function differently in the summer. The common denominator here is that all the kids are out of school, so that means change!

Plans for Preschool Children. When kids are young, plan as little as possible. Make sure that they get some outside time and a nice nap in the afternoon. If pools or beaches are part of your summer plans, then make sure your kids can swim. If there's a short summer camp or class they can attend just to break up the monotony of the summer, then go ahead and sign up. But keep their days as open and carefree as you can, whether they are with a parent or a baby-sitter. These easy days will fly by too fast.

That having been said, there are certain types of kids who thrive on routines and schedules, and they can be quite lost without them. So if your child is used to going to preschool two mornings a week, it might be nice to get him in a day camp, swimming lessons, or some other planned activity for two mornings a week. Check your township parks and recreation department or your local library for these types of programs.

Plans for Elementary and Middle School Children. This is the age where children really look forward to being out of school for the summer. But these are usually the kids that begin the "I'm bored" chant around August. Think "balance" when planning the summer for your children from six to fourteen years old. Whatever you plan to do all summer, it's a great idea to take one week (the first week the kids are off from school) and plan to do nothing. I know many moms who do this, whether they have teenagers, little ones, or kids with special needs. Everybody deserves a week off from their jobs. And your kids' jobs are to be students for about nine months a year. So let them sleep late, stay in their pj's, and

> *Everybody deserves a week off from their jobs. So let your children sleep late, stay in their pj's, and play all day until they are tired during their first week of summer break.*

play all day until they are tired. If you are working full time, consider taking some time off to be lazy with your kids. If you get bored, work with your kids on some little clean out projects like their school papers or artwork that has been piling up all year. Or clean out their closets, get rid of what doesn't fit, and make a list of what they will need for the summer. Take your photos and put them in albums—do little projects that have been put on the back burner all year, but don't put too many demands on yourself.

The first thing you should consider is whether there are any academic projects that need to happen over the course of the summer. In my school district, every child is given a reading requirements list, usually with an associated project and a math packet to complete. Additionally, you may have a child who needs help in a certain subject. Summer is a great time to get that extra tutoring and to catch him up for the next school year. If either of these applies to your children, help them plan it out. Some children will want to get it all done in June so they can take the rest of the summer off. Others might want to do a little at a time and take all summer to complete the project. Either way is fine. Just have a plan, write it on a calendar, and make sure the child looks at it every week to stay on track.

Once you have planned your summer, ask yourself these questions: Can you live with what you have planned? Is there a balance of planned activities and free time? Are the kids taken care of?

Once the academic needs are met, you can consider what activities or camps your school-age kids will need and want. Start looking for these in early spring, talk to other parents so you know what your kids' friends are doing in the summer, and then register early. Specialty camps fill up quickly. Think about whether you want to spread out your children's activities and camps or have them all go at the same time. As they get older, the children may want to start earning their own money as baby-sitters or day camp counselors. If you know of these opportunities in your area, help your child make some calls in the spring to secure work for the summer.

Once all these decisions have been made (or at least most of them), look at your two-and-a-half to three month summer calendar. The kids don't need to see everything that's going on—it might just overwhelm them. Just give them a little advance notice on a week-by-week basis so they know what to expect as the summer rolls on. More importantly, ask yourself these questions: Can you live with what you have planned? Is there a balance of planned activities and free time? Are the kids taken care of? Good. Now relax and enjoy!

By planning ahead and balancing out the schedule for your entire family by season, by month, and by week, you can make your children's activities a source of fun, not stress for the family. By including your children in the discussions you will teach them the valuable skill of making choices. In this high-speed world of unlimited options, focusing on one thing at a time is a rare skill we can teach our children.

Once your decisions have been made, post your family calendar with everyone's activities on it in a common area of your home (usually this is the kitchen) so everyone can see what's happening on any given day. If you want to, you can designate a certain color pen for each family member so each person's activities stand out in his own color.

THREE STEPS TO CHOOSING SEASONAL ACTIVITIES

1. Look at an entire year for your entire family by mapping out what activities happen in each month.
2. Talk to your child about his favorite activities and help him choose one for each season.
3. Before joining an activity, know the time commitment and talk to other parents about carpools.

23. Set the Pace…Plan Your Month, Week, and Day

THE PROBLEM

There's a comedian who does a routine about being a clueless student. He's poking fun at himself, but what makes it so funny is that we all can identify with his situation. He talks about the science fair. He had nine months to work on his project and did nothing. On the day the project is due, he wakes up in a panic. "Oh, no! That's today," he thinks. So he quickly runs outside and fills a cup with dirt. That's his science project! The problem is clear. As a young boy, he couldn't plan that far in advance and no one helped him plot out the project. The teacher gave the assignment and the deadline, and that was it. I think we've all lived that nightmare at some point.

THE STORY

In contrast to the comedian's story, I have been very impressed with my children's teachers. They have helped my children learn project–planning skills as early as fourth grade. One September, my son came home talking about his state project assignment. He talked about what state he chose and what he was going to do. His details were a little fuzzy, so I asked for the written instructions for the project.

However, the first piece of paper he came home with on this project was a calendar. *That's a new one*, I thought. The teacher wrote in the due date and asked the parent and student to fill in all his weekday and weekend extracurricular activities. Then she asked us to plot out each step of the project with our children so they could see how to budget their time. This teacher clearly recognized the fact that we all have different family schedules and that each child would have to get the project done in his own time.

With my daughter's science fair project, the teachers gave her interim dates for when the idea was due, when the actual experiment had to be done, when the written report was due, and finally when the project display board was required. By chunking down the overwhelming assignment of a science fair, this teacher made the project much more manageable.

You've got to organize from big to small. This applies to organizing both objects and time.

THE SOLUTION

As I often tell my clients, you've got to organize from big to small. This applies to organizing both objects and time. Think big first. As adults, we may be asked at our place of employment to set goals for the year. They have to be measurable, realistic, and attainable. For children, a year may be too overwhelming to think about and plan out, so let's set the bar a little lower and help them plan for a month at a time. Ask yourself and your child, "What has to happen this month?" For school-aged children, that may mean a project in a particular subject, a big test on a unit in one subject, or midterm exams. If nothing big is going on in school, then think about extracurricular activities. Is there a ballet recital or karate test coming up? Think about what's going on in your family. Maybe there is a trip or a big birthday celebration that you all need to prepare for. Always start with the top priorities first and then you can work in the less important things on your calendar. Once you have your monthly goals, you can begin to break them down by weeks and days.

Project Planning 101

If your children's teachers are not helping them with project planning, then it's up to you as parents to do this with them. This is an essential skill to learn in elementary and middle school so that by high school and college, your children can do this for themselves. If you don't consider yourself a good project planner, it's probably not because it's difficult to do. Most likely it's because you don't take the time to plan ahead, and you're OK with winging it or throwing it together at the last minute. As adults, we can do this, some of us better than others. When it comes to helping your children do well in school, a little planning followed by a weekly check-in to see if they are keeping on target is important for their success as students. Show them how to plan out a project they have now, and next time let them do the planning. You can still help them by asking questions like: When is the project due? What has to happen first? How long will that take? Are you really going to do that after basketball practice? These questions will help them think it through.

When it comes to helping your children do well in school, a little planning followed by a weekly check-in to see if they are keeping on target is important for their success as students.

Start with a Month-at-a-Glance Calendar

Kathy Schlegel of Organized Enough, LLC, is a professional organizer with many clients who are students with ADD. She recommends the desktop or "blotter-style" calendar with big blocks for her students because she says the kids need to "see time." They can see at a quick glance any place they have to be that month, but there's also enough space to write in activities, tests, and projects. That makes a lot of sense, especially for kids who are visual.

Another option for planning your month is a typical wall calendar. The blocks are smaller so you can't write in a lot of details, but like the desktop one, you can see at a glance what major activities or responsibilities you have each day.

Before you settle on one type that will be most effective for your child, you might want to simply draw this month or next month on a white sheet of paper.

On the monthly calendar, have your child write in the due date of the big project or test. She might even want to write this in a bold color so it stands out every time she looks at the calendar. Then have her fill in extracurricular activities, trips, and anything that will fill up her time for a good portion of the day. If you're plotting a project, know how many pieces or steps there are to the project. Is there research, writing, or an oral presentation involved? Allow time to work on each piece. For a big test, know how many chapters are involved. Allow for studying one chapter per night, and then one night for you to quiz your child. Also note the number of chapters for a book report so you can give your child a goal for reading the book and writing the report. Take the due date and work backwards, avoiding all those days where it would be impractical for her to do this extra work. For example, don't plan to write a report the day after a sleepover

March

MONDAY	TUESDAY	WEDNESDAY	THURSDAY	FRIDAY	SATURDAY	SUNDAY
1 Research Topic	2 Karate	3	4 Karate	5	6	7 Write Outline
8 Type Parts 1 & 2	9 Karate	10 Type Parts 3 & 4	11 Karate	12	13 Write Notecards	14
15 Practice Oral Pres.	16 Karate	17 Practice Oral Pres.	18 Karate PROJECT DUE	19	20	21
22	23 Karate	24	25 Karate	26	27	28
29	30 Karate	31				

Month Calendar. This style of calendar lets your child see all of her activities for the month.

Is Your Child a Visual or Verbal Learner?

HOW DO YOU KNOW if your child is a visual or verbal learner? I always like to use the map example. If you need to get from point A to point B, would you rather follow a drawing like a map or read numbered instructions (e.g., Step 1)? You may intuitively know this about your child or you may have to ask or try it out. Another way is to try assembling something such as a Lego structure. Is it better to show you a picture or to tell you how to put it together? If your child prefers the drawings, she is visual. If she likes the written instructions, she is verbal.

party or the afternoon after taking the PSATs. Plan the interim tasks on days that are open, and write in the tasks.

Once you have the big project plotted out, your child will need to do one of two things:

1. Post the calendar in the area where she does homework so she knows which piece of the project to work on each night, or

2. Copy the individual tasks into her homework assignment book. (For example: March 1, "Research Topic," if she has an assignment book with dates.)

Use a Weekly Time Sheet to Map Out a Typical Week for Your Child

Now that you have your child's month planned, you can break it down into each week. Take a clean weekly time sheet (page 374) and fill in her extracurricular activities first. Next, you can use the midday section to fill in any special classes she might have, such as gym, library, or music. Looking at the week, broken down into blocks of time for each portion of her day, will show you and your child how open (or not) her schedule is. Hopefully there are some empty spaces in that

	MONDAY	TUESDAY	WEDNESDAY	THURSDAY	FRIDAY
Marie					
School	Library	Gym			Music
Home	Dog	Dinner	Dog	Dinner	
Extra-curricular		Dance		Chorus	
Charlie					
School	Music	Library			Gym
Home		Dog	Trash	Dog	Dinner
Extra-curricular		CCD		Basketball	
John					
School		Music	Library		Gym
Home	Dinner		Dinner		Dog
Extra-curricular	Karate	CCD	Karate		

Picto-chart. This style of chart works well for young children who are learning to read.

Making Picto-Charts

IF YOUR CHILDREN ARE YOUNGER and need visual cues to remember things, try making colorful picto-charts for them. You can take photos yourself and place them on a chart. Cut photos from magazines or use clip images on your computer. On the chart, place the children's names down the left side and each weekday along the top. Then place the photos of the activities on the corresponding days. See page 222 for an illustration of a completed picto-chart.

week so you can use those days to help your child work on some personal goals. For instance, if she is learning to play an instrument and can't find the time to practice, the goal may be to schedule twenty minutes of practice time each day. To accomplish this, you may have to cut out some TV time, or have her practice before school. Your child may feel like she is going all the time, but putting it on paper can show her how much free time she actually has. On the other hand, you may feel like your child has all the free time in the world, but when you look at her schedule you see that she is booked every day of the week. If you and your spouse have done the seasonal planning exercise, this should not be the case. But if too many activities have been added, seriously consider dropping some of these from your child's schedule.

If extracurricular activities are not overwhelming, then there should be some time in each week for the children in your home to take over some chores.

> *As your children get older, they need to take on more chores around the house so that by the time they are eighteen, they are responsible adults.*

Make Room for Chores

If one of your organizing goals was to help your children do more for themselves and help more around the house, then now is the time to talk about that. Presumably, you've got the schoolwork under control by scheduling out major projects and tests and finding time each day to do homework. If extracurricular activities are not overwhelming, then there should be some time in each week for the children in your home to take over some chores. In my house, my biggest complaint was that the kids were not taking responsibility for the dog that they all begged us for. Because they have school activities, sports, and acting classes, it always fell on me to walk the dog, feed the dog, and clean up the yard. Also, our dinner times had become more hectic, and I felt like I was trying to do everything between the hours of four and six P.M. My kids are ages seven to thirteen so why not get them involved? I had talked to a neighbor whose daughter and son each take a week and either walk the dog or do the dinner dishes. When I heard this, I felt like my kids were getting off easy! So, I created a chore chart for my children, placing their names down the left side and each weekday along the top. I filled in their extracurricular activities and spread out the chores of taking care of the dog and helping with dinner. So on a day when my kids have no activities after school, they are doing one of those two things. In addition to these weekly chores, they each have chores that basically involve taking care of themselves: making their beds, clearing their plates after each meal, and putting their clean clothes away. I started to teach them those basics at about the age of five. Additionally, my thirteen-year-old cleans her room every two weeks and baby-sits for us on occasion, while my ten-year-old takes out the trash once a week. The seven-year-old helps clean up the playroom because he uses this room the most. I believe this is a good balance of chores so that the kids don't feel they are slaving away all the time, but they are definitely learning to take care of themselves and to pitch in and do chores that affect the family as a whole.

As your children get older, they need to take on more chores around the house so that by the time they are eighteen, they are responsible adults. Keep in mind that they are probably still in school, so school is their priority. Also keep in mind that they may be living on their own very soon, especially if they plan to go away to college, so they need to know how to do laundry, how to cook, how to pay bills, and how to clean (at least a bathroom!). Adding a few chores every year is the best way to go when teaching your children to take care of themselves and to help pitch in around the house.

Let Your Child Choose a Calendar or Planner for Herself

As your children get older, the picto-chart may be too simple for them. In middle school and high school, students have more work to do and may need a more

MONTH _____						
SUNDAY	MONDAY	TUESDAY	WEDNESDAY	THURSDAY	FRIDAY	SATURDAY

Month-at-a-Glance Calendar. *This style of calendar can replace wall or desk calendars.*

detailed system. This is a great time to introduce them to a day planner. The best way to choose a calendar or day planner is to take your child with you to an office supply store or to a bookstore where calendars and planners are sold. With so many options out there, you have to see which one works for your child. First, decide where the child is going to use the day planner. If it goes to school with her, choose a thin planner, not a diary-style planner, which would add bulk to the backpack. Also, thinner means bigger pages for writing. Open up the planner and see if there are columns for each day, small blocks, or one page for each day. Some kids like lines to write on and will read from top to bottom for each day. Other kids prefer open blocks and will read left to right, like a book. There's no way for you as the parent to know, unless you show them and ask them which looks the most appealing.

Month-at-a-glance. Some day planners are filled with pages that show you a month at a glance. These are good for replacing a wall or desk calendar, but may not give enough space for details. If the planner has both monthly and daily pages, they can use the month-at-a-glance for where they need to be, and then the individual days for what they need to do.

Day planner. These are good for detail-oriented students who like to write down tasks and then cross them off the list. Some daily pages have lots of lines and some even have time charts. These are usually small enough to fit in a backpack or purse but are only good if your child is going to pull them out and open them up. Many middle schools and high schools provide these to students. The trick is getting your child to use it! It's certainly an effective tool if the teachers remind students to write down assignments, and you ask your child to see it each night before she does homework. If the size or style of pages doesn't work for your child, then find one that does and ask the teacher's permission to use it.

Absolute of Organizing Your Family: Don't be afraid to talk to your child's teacher or principal about organizational help.

Try Out Your New Schedule

At this point you have helped your children plan out their months and weeks. You have even supplied them with weekly and daily planning tools. You all should understand that the daily tasks you have plotted together will help your children achieve their monthly goals, whether that involves completing a school project, getting an A on a test, or finding time to practice guitar. Confident that you have planned well, you can now focus on one day at a time. Make sure you put the weekly calendar in a prominent place where your child will look at it every morning. Some options are: a bulletin board in her bedroom, on her desk, on the door of her bedroom, or on the refrigerator. Even if there is nothing special needed for school that day or nothing to do in the morning, it's good for your child to know what to expect when she comes home from school. You may have to remind her at first, but hopefully checking the schedule will become a habit. At the end of the first week, check in with your child and see how she's doing. Is the plan working, and does she feel like she has balance in her week? Continue doing this until the month is over and/or your child has achieved her goal. (Some projects may span more than one month.) Recognize her achievement with a little celebration so your child gets a feeling of accomplishment. This is her first step towards getting organized, so you want to encourage her to keep going! Make her favorite dessert, let her choose what's for dinner, or just make an announcement with the rest of the family present.

THREE STEPS TO TIME PLANNING

1. Plan out a month with your child. Prioritize school projects first and break them down into smaller tasks. Let her see the month at a glance.
2. Plan out a typical week—including your child's activities, special classes in school, chores, and downtime.
3. Help your middle-school-aged and high-school-aged children choose day planners that make sense to them.

24. Daily Conditioning…Develop Routines

THE PROBLEM

You may feel like you can get organized on your own. When the kids are at school, you straighten up the house, do the wash and the shopping, have dinner planned, and have activities written on a family calendar. Or if you work full time, you may be a model employee, getting your work done efficiently and handling multiple responsibilities with ease. But then the kids come home, papers are dumped, toys come out, clothes are thrown, and the requests for your time and energy are never-ending! Chaos prevails and you wonder what happened to all that organization. At some point it all piles up and overwhelms you until you start thinking, "What's the point?"

THE STORY

A friend of mine has two boys who take swimming lessons once a week after school. While they both love swimming, they always gave their mom a hard time about going to the lessons until they actually got there and got in the water. The problem was the quick transition. The boys got off the school bus, came in the house, wanted a snack, needed to get changed, and had to head out the door again in thirty minutes. Most kids can't switch gears that fast, and doing so will send them into a tizzy. So their mom decided to change the routine. Now she meets them at the bus stop with a snack and their change of clothes all ready to go. When they get to their swimming lessons, they change in the locker room. This is the new routine. The boys know it, their mom plans for it, and everything goes pretty smoothly.

THE SOLUTION

Instead of thinking of routines as boring, think of the serenity they can bring. There certainly is something calming and soothing about our routines.

Even if you as the parent establish the system of organization in your family, you've got to train your children to keep up with the system so it doesn't need an overhaul every week. The best way to do this is to establish routines that keep order in your home. Instead of thinking of routines as boring, think of the serenity they can bring. There certainly is something calming and soothing about our routines. According to the Raising Children Network in Australia[1] and the American Academy of Pediatrics,[2] there are both physical and psychological benefits to having family routines. Some of those benefits are:

1. Living in a predictable environment makes children feel safe and secure.
2. Routines built around family rituals like vacations, or simply reading at bedtime, strengthen the bond between parents and children.
3. Routines help set our body clocks and teach children ways to stay healthy, like brushing their teeth or washing their hands.
4. As children develop daily routines, parents have to nag or remind them less, and daily responsibilities become automatic, not problematic.

It has been my experience that in times of chaos or real family tragedies, our routines bring us comfort and focus. It has also been my experience that routines help children remember little tasks that they need to do each day, and help them to get things done in a reasonable amount of time. Here are some ideas for developing or improving your family's routines.

Morning Routine

Start with the time that each family member needs to be out of the house in the morning and work backwards to establish what time you need to get up. If your child likes to sleep until the last possible minute, then he will only have time every morning to do the essentials such as get dressed, make his bed, have breakfast, brush his teeth, and head out the door. If your child likes to take his time in the morning, then you've got to establish an earlier wake-up time to allow for that. Talk to your children about what they need or want to do each morning and you, as parents, can then estimate the time all that will take.

Once you have a to-do list for the morning, think about the most efficient way for your children to do their tasks. For example, I like to have my children finish upstairs before they come down for breakfast. That means they are dressed, beds are made, and all necessary items are out of their rooms before they come to the kitchen. The one thing they go upstairs to do is brush their teeth after breakfast. If that's a big deal in your house, consider keeping the toothbrushes downstairs in a powder room so your children can brush as the last thing before they get in the car or on the bus. This method uses physical locations in the house to prioritize tasks.

Some kids or families may want to prioritize their mornings by what is most important to them. Do the more important things first.

Some kids or families may want to prioritize their mornings by what is most important to them. If you feel eating breakfast is the most important part of the morning, do that first. Then, after the children eat, they could get dressed, brush their teeth, and pack their schoolbags. If making the bed is not a big deal, leave that chore as the last step in the routine so that if time is running out, that's the one thing that

Delegating Can Improve Routines

ONE OF MY CLIENTS wanted to make school mornings go more smoothly because her kids were constantly missing the bus. When I asked about their usual morning, I found out that the children were up early and dressed but they usually were waiting for their mom to finish making lunches. An easy fix for that family was to either make lunches the night before or to teach the kids to pack their own lunches.

doesn't have to get done. There's no right or wrong here, you just have to decide what works best for your family. You also want to make sure that the wake-up routines happen in a positive, unhurried way.

Once you have established the morning routine, you need to train your children to follow it. Once again, there are several options.

1. Visual reminders. This could be a chart on your child's bedroom door or mirror. Picto-charts are the easiest to use. (See the example on page 233.) Either draw them yourself or download some clip art on your computer. Keep it simple: a bed, clothes, a toothbrush, and a healthy breakfast. That should tell them all the basics. Add other symbols as necessary.

2. Another way to remind them visually is to lay out things such as their clothes, library books, or musical instruments as they need them for school. Put these items in an obvious place so they can't be missed.

3. To remember their "special" classes, such as gym or library, that may only happen once a week, you can post their weekly schedule as I explained in Chapter 23. Get them in the habit of looking at it each day so they know what they need to bring or wear to school.

Morning Routine

Get Dressed

Make Bed

Eat Breakfast

Brush Teeth

4. For a very tactile approach, you can make up index cards for each chore and have the child flip them over or put them in a certain place after they complete each task. For example, the cards can be on their dresser in the morning and then brought downstairs when they complete them.

Finally, when your kids are set to walk out the door, the American Academy of Pediatrics recommends that parents say goodbye to their children with a kiss, a hug, or a wave, and the words "I love you."[2] This gives each child a positive feeling with which to begin the day. For younger children who are reluctant to go to school and to leave their parents, it might also help to tell them where you will be while they are in school. For example, you could say, "Mommy will be food shopping today while you're in school so we can have a special treat when you get home." Or "Daddy will be at work while you're in school, but when I meet you back home, we can play baseball." This helps the child feel connected to you and gives him something to look forward to.

After School/Before Dinner Routine

School-age children have so much going on between the hours of four and eight P.M. that it's often difficult to think of a regular routine that takes place. While each day might be different in your house, you can turn certain processes into routines to give

Telling younger children who are reluctant to go to school where you will be while they are in school can help them feel connected to you.

233

some structure to your family members' lives regardless of where they are running to after school.

Is it any wonder that mudrooms and mudroom furniture are so popular now? This is a much-needed place to dump all our stuff when we come home. If you've got a mudroom, great! If you've got lockers and bins for your children to store their coats, hats, and book bags in, even better. If you don't have these things, you can still establish a routine for when the kids walk in the door. Show them where it is acceptable to put their schoolbags. This could be in a closet, in their bedrooms, or in a designated homework area. Show them where to put papers that you need to see. This could be on a mail table, in a bin on your desk, in a hanging file in the kitchen, or right on the kitchen table—wherever you will see the papers and go through them on a daily basis. See Chapter 36 for more specific instructions on setting up homework areas and landing zones for school papers. Show your children how to empty their lunch bags if they carry their lunches to school.

Designate landing places for schoolbags and papers during the first week of school so your children can establish a quick routine.

All these landing places should be designated during the first week of school so your children can establish a quick routine. It's also a good idea to have your children wash their hands as soon as they come home from school. All of this should take about five minutes once they get it down. Then you can sit down and ask them about their days. Of course I find that boys and girls are different. My daughter does this routine without even thinking about it, and my sons seem to need constant reminders. If visual aids work with your child, you may want to have a sign, index cards, or a whiteboard right where he comes in the door, just like you use for the morning routine. If you feel like you're always verbally reminding him, try the Socratic method and ask questions: Where is the book bag supposed to go? What do you need to do before you have a snack? Where do the papers go? Most

Entryway Organization

Backpack •   Books for •   Coat •
             homework   rack

Bench for shoes •   Mail table •

of the time, they will know the answer. If not, show them again. Use consequences like no TV, no going outside, or no snacks until everything is put away.

So that covers the first five to ten minutes when the kids get home. How about the rest of the afternoon and evening? In the previous chapters, you established an ideal plan for what each child will do after school. This plan includes household chores, after-school activities, and homework. The routines they use to get these things done are a way of fine tuning and making everything easier. The routine might be to unpack, have a snack, and start their homework at four. When they start their homework they might have a routine for that, too. Two brothers that I interviewed had very different styles of doing their homework. When I asked them about their after-school routines, they both said that they like to relax for about an hour after coming home from school. Then they would start their homework. One did the easiest homework first, then continued with the harder homework after dinner. The other liked to do the hard homework first and then do the easier homework after dinner. One also mentioned that he is motivated by what's on TV. On a good TV night, he likes to be finished by 8:30 P.M. and some nights it became a game like race-against-the-clock to get his homework done, shower, and get his pajamas on, and be seated on the sofa by that time. On a not-so-good TV night, he might take a more leisurely approach to homework.

Every child is different. Observe your child and know his tendencies so you can help him develop realistic and non-stressful routines after school.

In any case, he has created his own routine and found his motivation. Every child will be different. Observe your child and know his tendencies so you can help him develop realistic and non-stressful routines after school.

Bedtime Routine

I think we parents all know what should happen at bedtime, it's a matter of making an effort to enforce that routine in our own homes. The American Academy of Pediatrics recommends that all children have a regular bedtime and winding-down routine.[2] For children of different ages, establish a bedtime and make sure they know what it is. This time can fluctuate for different reasons, but as the parent, you need to set limits. For instance, a child's bedtime might be 9:30, but on a night when he has a lot of homework, bedtime might need to be ten. The better plan is to estimate how long the homework will take before he starts. Then

Remember, there is comfort in routine. Doing the same thing every night will help your children wind down and get sleepy.

plan to start earlier—not finish later. You might also have a child go to bed earlier if he is sick or if he has to get up extra early the next morning. On weekends, you may also let the time slide a little bit, but let that be the exception, not the rule. Even if the time slides by half an hour, you should still follow the same routine. So the routine for most school-age children might look like this:

Finish homework

Shower, get into pj's

Have a snack

Watch a little TV

Brush teeth

Read for 20 minutes

Lights out

Remember, there is comfort in routine. Doing the same thing every night will help your children wind down and get sleepy. When you change the routine, you might throw them off and cause conflict. For instance, if your young child is going to bed a little earlier than normal one night, take time to read with him, even if it's for a shorter amount of time, if that's part of your normal routine. Or if he usually watches a little TV before bed and you've been out that evening, let him watch half an hour instead of an hour of TV.

Explain Changes in Schedules

A FRIEND OF MINE has two little boys who are both on the autism spectrum. She knows that her oldest son, who has more severe autism, will actually regress in the summer if there are no academic activities and routines in their plans. To get him ready for the transition from full-day school to their summertime schedule, she creates a story with words and pictures to prepare him for what is about to come. These are called social stories. The story describes what is going to change and why. It also emphasizes the positive aspects of the changes that go on in the summer. The pictures are useful because they make it easier for her son to visualize what will happen. She reviews this story about two weeks before the summer starts. Other plans she makes for the summer include an extended school year as well as half-day camps for a good portion of the summer to keep her boys cognitively and socially engaged. Although these exercises are intended for kids with autism, they also work for children who are averse to change and who need to keep busy.

Summer Routines

"Summer routine" may sound like an oxymoron. The best thing about summer is the lack of routines and schedules, right? Well, to some degree, yes. But there are some kids and parents who thrive on schedules and routines, and suddenly throwing them out the window for two to three months could cause a lot of stress.

To avoid the stress or chaos that can happen in the summer with kids and neighbors running in and out of your house, think about what your family likes to do in the summer and set some parameters. If your house is the place where all the neighbor kids come to play, maybe let the parents of those kids know what hours your house will be "open." I've heard some moms declare that from eleven to five they're OK with friends coming over, but before eleven they like to get some chores done, and after five they need to get ready for dinner. Likewise, if your kids are running around the neighborhood all day, you might want them to check in at a certain time in the afternoon. If my older children are out and about in the neighborhood, I ask them to check in by phone or in person around three. Then I let them know if I need them home or if they can keep playing until dinnertime.

Here are a few summertime routines that other moms have shared:

- One family has time for chores and summer reading in the morning, then they all go to the swim club from noon to five.
- Another mother runs errands in the morning, takes her children to swim club from eleven to two, and is home for the toddler's nap from three to five.
- Another mother works until three, so her children aren't allowed to have friends over until she gets home. Her older son baby-sits the rest of her children during the day.
- One family sends their grade-school children to camp from nine to noon every day. Mom does her errands, chores, and work during that time. After noon, anything goes!

As the summer winds down, try to get your kids back on their school schedules about two weeks before school starts.

Even if your days are unstructured and your kids are going to bed later and waking up later, you can still stick to your morning and bedtime routines throughout the summer. As the summer winds down, try to get your kids back on their school schedules about two weeks before school starts. They're going to fight it at first, but by the second week they should have their body clocks set to school time (early to bed and early to rise), and the first week back to school will be easier for them.

Establishing routines for the transition times of the day—namely morning, after school, and bedtime—will help your children do what they need to do in a timely manner. You'll need to establish the routines with them. Do this with visual reminders as the children are learning the routine, and then verbally remind them as they get older and more accustomed to the routine. The goal is that one day they will get through their routines on their own!

THREE STEPS TO DEVELOPING ROUTINES WITH YOUR FAMILY

1. Have everyone get up at the same time each day. Do everything upstairs before coming down for breakfast. After breakfast, brush teeth and pack bags. Use visual or tactile reminders if necessary.
2. Create an after-school routine that allows time for homework, a family dinner, and getting to activities. Designate a place for the children to put backpacks, coats, and papers.
3. Stick to a nighttime routine that settles the children down and allows everyone to get a good night's sleep. Go to bed at the same time each night.

Make Your Time Work for You

Now you have evaluated and sharpened your own organizing skills. You also have the tools to help you organize your child's time and schedule.

REMEMBER

1. You can't expect your child to be organized if you're not. Set a good example by following your own rules.
2. Plan out big projects or events on a monthly calendar, setting interim due dates for each piece of the project.
3. Make a weekly calendar for your child to follow. Include time for homework, extracurriculars, and chores. Note any special classes at school (gym, music, library, etc.)
4. Choose a daily planner that fits your child's style.
5. Limit your child's extracurricular activities to allow for downtime and family time.
6. Start to plan your family's summer activities (camps, baby-sitters, summer jobs, vacations) as early as March.
7. Establish morning, after-school, and bedtime routines to help children remember what needs to be done.
8. Implement your child's school-year routine (bedtime, wake-up time, morning duties) two weeks before school starts, to help your child's body adjust to the schedule.

An organized schedule will help your children get the most out of the activities they participate in and give them the structure they need to thrive.

Part V: No More Scategories

IF YOU LOOK AT YOUR CHILD'S ROOM, or your whole house, and discover that everything is everywhere, it's time to get rid of the scattered categories or "scategories." Remember the song, "One of these things is not like the other?" We were learning early on from *Sesame Street* how to put like things together. This valuable skill can be used now to organize your children's belongings.

Nothing makes a child more proud than showing off her own stuff. Whether it's their toys, artwork, or special collections, children need to feel that they have something of their own. As parents, we can show them how to organize and respect their possessions so they can have them for a long time and be proud of their things. When you place items together, keep the categories flexible. Put things together by color, by functionality, or by size. I suggest parents set the parameters and let their children make some creative choices.

> "Children in a family are like flowers in a bouquet: There's always one determined to face in an opposite direction from the way the arranger desires."
>
> —MARCELENE COX

25. Contain Your Toys

THE PROBLEM

Toys swarm around kids like mosquitoes at a picnic. You might think you have taken care of the toys, but they keep coming back and multiplying. When children are young, parents can control the toys to some extent with bins, toy boxes, and shelves. But as children get older, the toys change. In some cases, the toys get smaller in size but larger in quantity. Things that we adults wouldn't even consider toys become precious play things to our creative-minded children. And suddenly we don't feel like we have a say in what stays or goes or where it is kept. The *Keep Out* sign might go up and the bedroom door might be locked. Although their tastes in toys might change, children are sometimes unwilling to part with special childhood favorites. So how do we deal with all the change and abundance?

THE STORY

I remember walking into one little girl's bedroom and letting out an appreciative sigh. It looked like a page out of a Pottery Barn catalog. There was a dark wooden crib, one dresser, a little chair, and a couple of shelves on the wall. Not only was the room beautifully decorated in pink gingham, but I noticed that all the toys, right down to the stuffed animals, matched. They were all pink and white! My first thought was, "Now here's a mom who still has control over her daughter's toys." My next thought was, "How long is this going to last?" I thought of my own daughter and son, and I remember thinking how different their play styles were. I knew that there was no way I could control all of their toys to be a specific color that matched our décor!

THE SOLUTION

Because we are dealing with one category of things in your child's life at a time, we can easily use my CPR method of organizing to get it all under control. CPR stands for categorize, purge, and rearrange. I always start with a large category and only break it down into smaller components if it cannot be contained with one container or shelf. When you begin organizing, some categories may already be contained in a box, closet, or cabinet. In this case, start the process of organizing by removing all of the items from their storage areas. Other categories may be scattered all over your house. You will need to gather all the items into one spot. Then you can take the large category and break it down into smaller subcategories. As you are sorting into subcategories, you can purge anything that you don't want or need. Or you can wait until you have all the categories in front of you, and then purge whatever you have in excess. Dispose of broken items, and donate or sell unused or gently used items. Looking at your categories in piles on the floor helps you visualize what room these items can fit into, then what containers you might need. Then you can begin to rearrange these items to make a place for everything. Remember this CPR process whenever you organize a category of items.

> *Start with a large category and break it down into smaller components only if the large category cannot be contained with one container or shelf.*

Set Realistic Expectations

Before you start physically working with your child to organize her toys, you've got to get in the right frame of mind and set realistic expectations of the outcome. If you can remember back to before your child was born, you were probably planning for the perfect nursery: choosing the crib, the blankets, and colors of the room, maybe even a theme. Life was simple for your infant. All she needed was a crib, changing table, a closet, and maybe a little dresser. I'm sure you never thought of how your child would look or act as an adolescent. No one ever dreams of a child's room covered in crayon drawings, clay creatures, and little scenes with plastic guys all over the windowsills, dressers, and nightstands, but that may be what you have now. As children grow and change, so do their tastes in toys. You can't have everything the same color, and any theme you had is out the window. What you can do is keep the toys contained to certain rooms in the house and teach your children where they can put those toys when it's time to straighten up.

> *As children grow and change, so do their tastes in toys. You can't have everything the same color, and any theme you had is out the window.*

The Great Toy Clean Out

To start this process of getting control of your children's toys, set aside a couple of hours with your child to do a toy clean out project. It's up to you if you want to tackle one child's toys at a time or if you want to lump all your children's toys together and do them all at once. I have been doing an annual toy clean out at my house for about ten years, and we make it an event. It really is a fun and rewarding exercise, so sell it like that to your kids! Maybe promise them a treat at the completion of the project. If you know which room you will keep the toys in, clear some floor space in that room. Then all the toys from around the house should be brought to that one location so you can sort them. You can make this part fun by assigning different rooms to each family member and having them gather up the toys in their rooms. After everyone is finished and all the toys are in the designated room, use my CPR method and sort the toys into categories. Your categories can be whatever you want them to be. Some suggestions are: learning toys, outside toys, games, electronic games, building toys, dress-up clothes, arts and crafts, and musical toys. Your family can decide on the categories together, then make piles. As you sort, throw out anything that is broken. Also purge anything obviously not used by your children. These could be toys they have outgrown. Once all the toys are sorted, look at each category and decide if you really need all that is there. If you find a category is too large and you can part with some of the toys in that category, put the toys in a donation bag.

Once you have all of your categories under control, look at the piles and *decide* (and sometimes this is the hardest part of organizing) where each category will be kept. Everyone's house is set up differently, and your volume and type of toys will vary. But one thing parents can decide across the board is where the toys will be kept. Should each child keep her own toys in her own bedroom? Or is there a family room, playroom, or basement in your house that can serve as a central location for all toys? If you're sticking to one room, you may decide to put games on a shelf, outside toys in a bin or toy box, and learning toys in a cabinet. If arts and crafts are something that your kids like to do, you'll need to have a table or some flat surface area that is easy to clean. A drop cloth or tablecloth under the table is a good idea for protecting your floor.

Everyone's house is set up differently, and your volume and type of toys will vary. But one thing parents can decide across the board is where the toys will be kept.

If toys will be in more than one room of the house, decide with your child which categories go where. For instance: stuffed animals in the bedroom, sports toys in the garage, and all other toys in the playroom. Keep the toys where the children use them

When to Clean Out the Toys

SOME GREAT TIMES to have the Great Toy Clean Out is before Christmas, before your child's birthday or at the beginning of summer vacation. This way you will make room for new toys that will be coming into your house. If you have a consignment shop nearby, your children may be motivated to sell their old toys and make some money!

and try to make it logical for your children. After all, the goal is to have the children maintain the system on their own.

CHOOSE YOUR CONTAINERS

Once you have decided where to store the toys, you can work with your child on how they will be stored—in other words, what types of containers you will use. There are many choices. Here are a few with pros and cons listed for each:

Built-in Wall Cabinets and Shelves

Pro: You can customize these to fit your needs. Books, games, and videos can go on the shelves, and bigger toys, small toys in bins, or arts and crafts items can go underneath. These types of containers look like furniture and can be repurposed as the children grow.

Con: They are the most expensive option.

Wooden Toy Boxes or Steamer Trunks

Pro: These are inexpensive but sturdy, and they look nice in a toy room or bedroom. They also make for easy clean up.

Con: Toys get lumped together and are not easily seen by the kids. Toys also get buried at the bottom.

Metal/Wire Industrial Shelving

Pro: Sturdy and inexpensive, these types of shelves can hold large, heavy toys. You can also put certain toys on top shelves if you don't want your young children getting into them.

Con: They don't look nice in a family room or bedroom. (I would recommend them for use in the garage, basement, or in a closet.) Small objects will fall through the wire shelves, so you need bins or a shelf cover.

Open Plastic Tubs

Pro: These are inexpensive, colorful, and easy to move around. You can also use color coding to keep like things together (for example: blocks in the green bin, stuffed animals in the blue bin).

Con: They are always open, so little kids will tend to get into these more. They may not be the prettiest option if you are keeping toys in a family room.

Floor Baskets

Pro: Costs vary depending on size, but baskets work well with all kinds of rooms and décor.

Con: You have to limit the amount of items or types of items in each basket to keep them organized.

Plastic Bins with Lids

Pro: These are inexpensive storage options, great for stacking up in a closet or sliding into a cabinet on the ground. They make for easy clean up, and if they are clear, the kids can see what's in them.

Con: These are not a pretty option for leaving toys out in a room. If the bins are tucked away, sometimes the kids forget what's in them, so you might have to be the one to pull them out from time to time.

Don't Be a Perfectionist

I KNEW A MOTHER WHO WAS VERY NEAT. Her son was three years old, but his toy room was almost always meticulous. The mother made sure every toy was in a specific spot along the wall or on a shelf. One day his grandmother came to baby-sit and noticed that as soon as the mother left, the little boy got a mischievous smile on his face and proceeded to take every little toy and toss it across the room. The grandmom laughed, knowing that the child was enjoying his freedom. When the playing was done and before the mother came back, the grandmother put everything back in its place. And the incident remained their little secret.

While it's important to keep things organized and to teach children how to pick up after themselves, it's unrealistic to expect perfection from them. Perfectionism also limits their ability to cut loose and have fun. They need a space that is all their own, so they can take responsibility for it. Set realistic goals for your children and create a level of organization that they can maintain at their age level. Unrealistic standards can make your child frustrated and she may just give up on organizing and picking up after herself all together if she never meets your standards.

WHAT'S YOUR ONGOING SYSTEM?

Once you have sorted, purged, and contained your toys from all over the house (quite an accomplishment, by the way!), you and your child need to agree on how you will continue to keep the toys organized. As I mentioned before, deciding is often the hardest part of organizing. The second hardest part is *maintaining*. As a general rule, I believe there are two ways to maintain any organizational system that you establish in your home:

Keep your toy organizing system realistic and simple. Delegate responsibility for the toys to your children as soon as you can.

1. Straighten up on a regular basis—either daily or weekly. In other words, get into the habit of putting everything back in the right room, right container.

2. Use the "full barrel" method, which means when a container is spilling over or a room has become overrun with toys, it's time to clean up. Full barrel could also refer to your personal tolerance for clutter or messes. So once you or your child feels like things have gotten out of control, straighten up. Have the whole family help with this process.

Whatever you decide is the right or most realistic option for your family, keep it simple and delegate the tasks to the children as soon as you can. Even three-year-olds can put their books back on a shelf or their toys in a bin. Give them one task to do at a time.

Absolute of Organizing Your Family: Keep it simple.

For instance, you can have each child straighten up the toys in her bedroom every morning and the toys in the family room every night before bedtime. Or you could have the children straighten up once a week, maybe on Sunday night or before the house is cleaned. Remember though, that the longer the time between straightening up sessions, the more work there will be. I prefer doing a little each day instead of a big project every two weeks. Also avoid being too controlling and making your child put away every toy as soon as she's finished playing with it. Kids need to leave stuff out, to experiment with things, and to have freedom in their play. If you are a stickler about neatness, the child might rebel and go to the other extreme.

Absolute of Organizing Your Family: If you push too hard, they'll fight back.

THREE STEPS TO HELPING YOUR CHILDREN ORGANIZE THEIR TOYS

1. Set realistic expectations about where and how the toys will be kept.
2. Do a Great Toy Clean Out a couple times a year to move old stuff out and rearrange as necessary.
3. Make an agreement with your children about when they will get their toys back to where they belong either on a daily or weekly basis.

26. Display Your Child's Collections

THE PROBLEM

Quite simply put, children like to collect things; things they find outside, like rocks, leaves, and cicada shells; things they make, like clay creatures, cat's eyes, and model airplanes; and things they acquire, like medals, trophies, and postcards. They are like mini factories churning out knickknacks faster than we can throw away the toys from the fast-food restaurants! And just when you think you've gotten one collection under control, they start a new one.

THE STORY

My friend's son was an avid card collector. He started with Pokémon cards when he was very young, then moved onto sports cards as he got older. Even though there are many options for organizing these cards, such as boxes and binders, he decided to come up with one on his own. He wanted to carry out his plan on his own, and he did not allow his mother in his bedroom for about three days. She knew he was busy doing some redecorating and agreed not to look until he was ready to reveal what he had done. When he finally opened the door, she found that he had taped every one of his baseball cards side by side on a wall and had created his own "wallpaper." This was a great way for him to admire his collection every day. Friends and neighbors who have seen his handiwork always admire his unique decorating. Sometimes if you give children some room to express themselves, instead of trying to control them, they come up with clever solutions.

THE SOLUTION

I don't believe collections are inherently a problem, rather they are a great way for a child to express interest in a subject and learn something new. For instance, a child who collects dinosaurs may learn more about paleontology than he would in school. And a child who collects objects from outside is developing an appreciation for nature. Collections are also helpful when you are looking for gift ideas for your child. If the child has a collection you can add to each year, then you've got a steady source of gift ideas.

> *Collections can help children increase their knowledge and teach them to appreciate things like nature. They also help parents find gift ideas.*

Using my CPR process (see pages 190 and 246) will help establish categories of collections that your child may have. Then you'll want to purge pieces in the collection that are no longer important to your child or pieces of the collection that are damaged. You can rearrange the collection once you know how big it can possibly get, and once you know if your child wants the collection to be accessible or just visible. Then you can find a room in the house that is appropriate and a container that will hold or display the collection.

Identify Your Collections

If you or a family member helped your child start a collection, then identifying it will be easy. But children also have a way of acquiring collections on their own. What starts as a casual interest may grow into a collection. The best time to identify your children's unannounced collections is when you are working with them to organize their bedrooms (see Chapter 37) or toy room. Most likely, their collections are hidden in there somewhere. They might be lining a bookshelf or windowsill or they might be buried in a drawer or storage box. They might also be shoved in the bottom of the closet or in a clothes drawer. As you organize the child's bedroom and begin to categorize items, you'll discover a collection by noticing a large amount of the same item. You might also notice that your son asks for the same type of thing every year for his birthday and has been collecting something over many years. He might also tend to make the same type of craft every time he is feeling creative, or buy the same type of souvenir when your family takes a vacation. These all are types of collections. Here are some collections I have discovered with both my own children and with my clients' children:

Children also have a way of acquiring unannounced collections. The best time to identify unannounced collections is when you are organizing their bedrooms or toy room.

- Mini football helmets
- Autographed T-shirts and jerseys
- Stuffed animals
- Baseballs
- Trading cards
- Hess trucks
- Seashells
- Rocks
- Wooden treasure boxes

Quantify Your Collections

Once you identify your child's collection, you have to determine if the child is going to continue adding to it. If so, what will be the maximum size of the total collection? In the case of state quarters or college football helmets, there are only so many to collect. But often collections can be endless, and unfortunately the room we have in our homes, and particularly your child's bedroom, is not. So make an estimate based on how much your child adds to the collection each year. Is it one item a year or more like ten? And how much longer do you think he will collect these items? You should have a good feel for whether this is a two-year or ten-year commitment, or somewhere in between. These are all things to consider when you want to quantify how big the collection will become.

If your child has a collection that is taking over the room and causing a lot of clutter (or smell or bugs) you have the right to limit that collection.

If your child has a collection that is taking over the room and causing a lot of clutter (or smell or bugs), you have the right to limit that collection. Ask him to pare it down to a reasonable amount that you can either store or display.

Absolute of Organizing Your Family: To prioritize, use the "fire" rule. Ask your child, "If there were a fire, what five things would you want to save?"

Store Your Collections

There is a storage container or display case on the market for almost every type of collection. You can find them with a simple Internet search. But before you buy that shelf or container, consider if your child's collection is practical (like T-shirts or hats) or playful (like stuffed animals and Matchbox cars) or decorative (like figurines or seashells). How you choose to store or display these items will depend on whether your child wants to take them down and use them or if he just wants to look at the collection.

If your five-year-old collects acorns and pinecones, you can control how much stays in the house with the size of the container you give him. But if your teenager has a collection of trophies and medals from a sport he plays, you have to plan for a bigger display case or shelf that is going to leave some room for more. Many children collect stuffed animals and baseball cards but will eventually outgrow these, so I don't recommend investing in specific storage boxes for these things. Instead, use something versatile like a plastic storage bin or tub for the stuffed animals and a shoe box for the baseball cards. That way the containers can be repurposed when the collection disappears.

For collections that your child likes to play with or use every day, choose containers that organize the items yet leave them accessible. For instance, a collection of Matchbox cars or Legos can be organized in a tackle box that you can find in a hardware store. Trading cards can be kept in a binder with plastic sheets designed to hold baseball cards. With these containers, your child can take the collection with him, and still easily find what he is looking for.

Display Your Collections

If your child's collection is decorative or something he likes to look at on a daily basis, then find a way to display it. In some cases, like the boy in the baseball card story, the child can come up with his own unique way to display what he loves. Sometimes you just have to ask the question, "How would you like to display your collection?" Listen to what he says and don't be shocked if he says, "I want them all over my bedroom wall." If you need ideas to get your creative juices flowing, here are a few simple ones:

- Hooks on the wall can hold hats, purses, and autographed jerseys.
- Bulletin boards are great for pinning up postcards, ticket stubs, or prize ribbons.
- Over-the-door racks can hold stuffed animals, Barbie dolls, belts, hats, purses, and Beanie Babies.
- Bookshelves or display shelves can hold any figurines, trophies, or plaques.
- Racks with pegs or hooks are great for holding medals, dream catchers, and beaded necklaces.
- A low bookshelf is good for nature items so the child can add to the

collection, or remove items after they have been there too long. It's even better if you can have the shelf outside on a porch!

Hand down, donate, or sell collection items after your child loses interest in the collection.

- The top of a child's dresser can hold a few figurines, trophies, or treasure boxes that contain smaller items.
- Glass containers are a decorative way to display sea glass, seashells, or rocks. When the container fills up, you can always buy another. These are nice enough to keep in the family room if you choose.

When to Retire Collections

OK, so you've contained a collection that your child loves. Now how long do you have to keep it? Here are some telltale signs that your child is no longer interested in his collection:

1. He is not adding to the collection.
2. He no longer takes the collection items down and plays with them.
3. He has tucked the collection away in a closet or bin and basically forgets that he has it.
4. He has started collecting something else.

So once your child is finished collecting something, what do you do? Here are some simple options:

1. Hand it down to a younger sibling, friend, or cousin.
2. If the items are valuable, sell the collection on e-Bay or to a collector.
3. Donate it to charity.
4. If it's something you think your child would like to have later on in life (like those record albums his dad saved from *his* childhood), package the items and tuck them away in an attic or storage closet. Clearly label the box and give it to your child when he moves out.

If extended family members regularly contributed to the collection with birthday and Christmas presents, let the family members know your child has stopped the collection so they do not continue to buy for it.

The best way to stay on top of these collections is to keep like things together, to ask your child about what he is collecting so you know if he is passionate or passive about it, and to consider the collections when you help your child with a thorough clean up or clean out of his bedroom or playroom.

THREE STEPS TO ORGANIZING YOUR CHILD'S COLLECTIONS

1. Gather the collection together and pare it down to the most significant pieces.
2. Find an appropriate way to display or contain the collection so it can be appreciated.
3. Retire the collection once your child has lost interest in it.

27. Create an Art Gallery

THE PROBLEM

We want our children to be creative, to express themselves. Preschool and grade-school teachers encourage this creativity, too. But what do you do when your little Picasso or Michelangelo is so prolific that you have no place to put all of those lovely pictures and creations?

THE STORY

One client I went to see had a very "artsy-craftsy" family. She had two young children who loved to draw, glue, and create pictures every day. Because they had a small home, the family used the dining room not only as the place to eat, but also as an art studio. Needless to say, the dining room was cluttered with pictures haphazardly taped to the wall, plastic storage bins and bags filled with art supplies on the floor, and cups filled with markers and pencils on the table. When it was time to eat, the family's solution was to sweep all the arts and crafts onto the floor and then move them back to the table when dinner was cleared.

My solution for this client included a few steps. First, find a new location for the arts and crafts area. A child-sized table and chairs could fit in a corner of their basement and the plastic storage bins could also be kept there to create an arts and crafts zone in a much more out-of-the-way room. Secondly, if they really wanted to display artwork in the dining room, they could use frames with swinging doors so things could be updated easily. The third step was a compromise: If the children really wanted to draw at the dining room table, there would be paper, pencils, and markers in a drawer in the cupboard. But the rule would have to be that once the drawing was finished, it would get hung up or stored in the basement with the other art supplies. To deter the clutter from creeping back onto the table, we put out some placemats and a pretty vase of flowers.

Involve your children in the purging process so they get used to letting go of things.

THE SOLUTION

Using my CPR method of organizing (see pages 190 and 246) you can take the category of artwork and break it down into at least two smaller categories: art on paper and three-dimensional art. Involve your children in the purging process so they get used to letting go of things. The more you purge the artwork, the easier it will become. Rearrange your child's artwork that's hanging up to keep it fresh and seasonal. Take some out of hiding if it's in a bin or drawer. Using CPR on your child's artwork at least once a year will keep the clutter pile down and your child's beautiful creations up and on display.

Gather Your Creations

The first thing you must do to develop your own artwork solution is gather it all in. Find the art projects that are adorning the walls, windowsills, and desk drawers in your child's bedroom. Gather all art projects that are decorating your playroom or basement. Finally, take those pictures off the refrigerator so you can come up with a wonderful solution to your child's artwork clutter.

Sort Your Creations

Once you have all the artwork in one place, begin to sort it by category or by child, if you have more than one child. Make sure that any display options will include artwork from each of them. Make a pile of flat paper drawings and paintings and another pile of bulky artwork like ceramic or clay pieces or beadwork. As you sort, make sure that your child is present so she can make decisions about what she wants to keep or not. If she is the type of child who gets really attached to her artwork, and wants to keep everything, it may help for you to hold the pieces up and ask the child for a "yes" (we keep it) or "no" (we don't keep it) decision. When children are physically detached from the art, they can often make a quicker decision. To keep the process moving, you may want to set a timer and prevent the child from taking too much time on one piece. I have often said to clients, "We're not reminiscing here. We are sorting." The time to reminisce is after you have displayed your artwork so you can fully enjoy and appreciate it.

To keep the sorting process moving, you may want to set a timer and prevent the child from taking too much time on one piece. Remember you are organizing, not reminiscing.

If your child has a special affinity for one type of craft, for instance making lanyards or beaded bracelets, the joy for them is probably in the creating and not really in admiring the finished product. So if you find yourself with a box full of lanyards, beaded bracelets, or whatever your child likes to make, consider giving them away or selling them to raise money for a charity. You could also use them as birthday or holiday gifts.

If you come across something you really want to save and the child wants to let it go, then it goes in with your memorabilia (along with other important mementos from your life such as high school yearbooks and letters from your spouse). Another option is to send certain special pieces to a grandparent. Try to keep these items to a minimum and after you finish categorizing and purging, put the artwork you are giving to a relative directly in an envelope to be mailed or delivered. The goal here is to help the child decide what to keep and what to toss. It's not important to save *everything* she has ever made. A sampling is sufficient.

Absolute of Organizing Your Family: Keep it simple.

Now that you have categorized and purged all artwork in your home, you should have one or two piles for each child: one with flat paper, and one with three-dimensional art. If you have holiday artwork that you would like to keep, store it with similar holiday decorations. Now you need to start thinking about where you are going to display this artwork. This may require another pass for sorting. Flip through the papers and see if you have any recurring themes. Some children like to draw and paint pictures of animals, dinosaurs, or seascapes. Others tend to use the same colors over and over. Look for any themes you have going and start to think about what rooms in the house the pictures would complement. Do the same with any ceramic pieces.

Decide on Your Display Options

First, decide on the room or rooms in your house where you would like to see your children's art. Some good rooms to consider are: bedrooms, bathrooms,

Art on a Clothesline. *You can use string, fishing line, or yarn to create a clothesline.*

Magnetic Strips. *These are great alternatives to displaying art on your refrigerator door. You can hang these strips in your child's bedroom or playroom.*

playrooms, basements, and kitchens. If you happen to have artwork that matches a color scheme or theme of a room, then you just found yourself some inexpensive decorations. For instance, if you have a little one who has a dinosaur bedspread and his big brother comes home with a painting of a T. rex, all you have to do is mat it and frame it with an inexpensive plastic box frame and voilà, instant wall art! Likewise, if you have a bathroom with an ocean theme, you can hang any pictures of the beach or sea creatures in there. Try to find a purpose for the classic pinch pot or ashtray that children make in pottery class; whether it's to hold rings near a sink, paperclips on a desk, or the spoon near the stove. By placing your children's art around the house, the whole family gets to enjoy these pieces of creativity every day. Isn't that so much better than having the art collecting dust in a box shoved under the bed?

Now take the artwork to the appropriate room. Check out the wall space and the shelving where your three-dimensional pieces can go. You may not be able to fit all the artwork you chose, so pare it down again.

Absolute of Organizing Your Family: To prioritize, use the "fire" rule. Ask your child, "If there were a fire, what five things would you want to save?"

If you decide that you want all the kids' artwork in their bedrooms or in a basement playroom, then you can choose display options that will house more than one piece. Here are some simple solutions that work well:

- A large bulletin board
- A clothesline hung from the ceiling
- A magnetic strip that runs across the walls
- Cork tiles covering an entire wall
- Crown-molding shelves
- Bookshelves
- Poster frames

By creating sections of the wall space where art can be hung, you are effectively containing the clutter. You want to keep like things together, but not so many that you can't appreciate the individual pieces. Once that area is full, it's time to take down the old and put up the new. When you take down the old, immediately dispose of any pieces that you and your child are not attached to. If the pieces have been on display for a while, your child will probably be ready to part with them.

Make sure your child understands that everything can't be displayed. You can display some, and preserve the rest by storing them in a drawer, a plastic bin, or a portfolio. Seasons change, room décor changes, and so might the artwork your child displays.

Change your art displays seasonally to keep them fresh and cut down on clutter.

Keep It Fresh

Like most organizing activities in your home, some things need to happen seasonally. You can treat artwork the same way. If most of your child's artwork is being done in school, then use the end of the school year as your cue to go through all her artwork whether it's in storage or on display. Going through it year after year, you will see that your child may easily toss the older pieces and want to keep what's new. The favorites will survive the sort every time.

You can also use the seasons of the year to motivate you or your child to keep your art on display seasonal. Once, when my daughter was going through her display pieces, she found that she had a lot of blue and ocean-themed items. We put up a three-foot display shelf and set up a beach theme for the summer. In September we switched it up to include more scholastic items, and then in December we made a Christmas display. When they weren't out on display, these knickknacks were packed away in a plastic storage container in her closet.

Work with your child to keep up with her artwork. Make sure it is a fun and fast activity. Stand back and admire your results after you have displayed her work. After a while you might find that she is changing the display on her own!

THREE STEPS TO ORGANIZING YOUR CHILD'S ARTWORK

1. With your child, gather all the artwork she has right now. Categorize and purge the artwork.
2. Create an ongoing method of storing or displaying new art pieces.
3. Do a full art clean out at least once a year.

28. Do a Quick Clothes Change

THE PROBLEM

Clothing can be a major problem in closets and bedrooms. The problem I see with most closets and bedrooms that I organize is that people keep way too many clothes—clothes that they may wear someday, clothes that they can't bear to part with for sentimental reasons, clothes that are stained or ripped or that they haven't gotten around to mending, and clothes that they've been meaning to give to someone else. It all takes up space in their closets and on their floors. Keeping track of your children's clothing can be even more chaotic when they don't put their dirty clothes in the wash, and when they outgrow their clothes.

THE STORY

A friend of mine has three children and decided it was time to go through their clothes and weed them out to see what they each needed for the summer season ahead. She started with the oldest child's clothes. She removed all of the clothes from the closet and dresser and began making piles on the floor: clothes to grow into, clothes to give to a cousin, clothes to give to charity, summer clothes, and winter clothes. Unfortunately the mother's time was limited to less than two hours so the project did not get completed and the piles remained on the floor. By the time she got back to the project, the piles were messed up and she had forgotten where each belonged, so she had to start categorizing all over again!

THE SOLUTION

I say, if all your child's clothes can't fit in the closets and dressers that she currently has, you've got two choices:

1. Get a bigger dresser and expand the closet, or
2. Cut down on the amount of clothing that she has.

It's that simple. And it all starts with focused working time and decision making. Plan to spend at least two hours going through your child's clothing (based on the premise that the child has one dresser and one closet). If your child has an exorbitant amount of clothing, allow for a little more time. If your time is limited, plan to clear out only the closet or only the dresser at one time. Don't try to do all of the clothes at once. If you can't work for two straight hours, work for just one hour, sorting one drawer at a time, or break the closet down into sections and tackle one section at a time. But have a bigger plan that takes you through all of your child's clothing in a few days. Using my CPR method (see pages 190 and 246), sort the clothes into a few categories, purge as you go, then rearrange the piles you have made into the most logical places in the dresser or closet. Your child should be with you, making the decisions. You are the facilitator. As you go through the steps listed in this chapter, you will be giving your child options that you both can live with and letting her choose. That way, the system you develop is really designed by your child, and she will be more likely to keep up with it.

If your time is limited, plan to clear out only the closet or only the dresser at one time. Don't try to do all of the clothes at once.

Absolute of Organizing Your Family: Give your children a few options that you can live with, and let them choose.

If you follow the methods outlined in this chapter, you can clear out an average child's closet and a set of drawers in about two hours. If you have a system, and you stay focused on the task at hand with your child helping, you might even beat that time! Try to make it fun so your child stays interested. You can even let her put on music (if you can stand it) to keep up the energy.

Organizing a Closet

1. Put a sheet on the ground to keep the clothes clean as you sort, or use a bed for your sorting area. Have one bag for trash and one for donations. If handing down the clothes to a smaller sibling is an option, have a box for that child in the room, too. If the clothing is name-brand and in excellent condition, consignment may be an option for you. So the total number of sorting possibilities is five: Trash, Donate, Hand Down, Consign, Keep.

   Try to make the organizing fun so your child stays interested. You can even let her put on music to keep up the energy.

2. Now start to take everything out of the closet. I usually start with the top shelf, then the floor, then go to the hanging clothes.

3. Facilitate the decision making by asking your child, "Do you wear this, yes or no?" No's go in the Donate, Consign, or Hand Down pile if they are in good condition. Clothing that is really damaged should be trashed. Yes's go in the Keep pile. If she has a hard time deciding, then ask her, "When was the last time you wore this?" If it was more than a year ago, it's time to go. If she says she doesn't wear it, but wants to keep it for memory's sake, put it in her memory box. If she doesn't have a memory box, see Chapter 31 for more information.

4. Get the Donations and Consignment piles ready to go out the door. You may even want to put them in your car. Make sure that you call the consignment shop where you are taking the clothes to find out hours of operation and what they will and won't take. Most consignment shops will only take clothes for a specific season, so if your clothes are not the right season, give them away. Hanging on to them for another three to six months does not solve your problem.

5. Move the hand-me-downs into the other sibling's room. These can be dealt with as you organize your other child's clothing.

6. Now you can put the Keep pile back into the closet or dresser. Ask your child how she would like to find her clothes. Does she like them folded on a shelf or hanging? You may need to add a shelf or shelf dividers in some cases. If everything will be hung up, and you have the vertical space, an easy way to get more space is to add a double-hanging bar. The lower hanging bar is also handy for small children so they can reach the clothes they wear. The upper level can be used for clothes not frequently worn or for out-of-season clothing. If you need to make changes to the closet, still put the clothes back in for now. Make a list of what you will need to improve the closet and make sure to take measurements before you shop.

If you need to make changes to your child's closet, still put the clothes back in for now. Make a list of what you will need to improve the closet and take measurements before you shop.

7. As your child helps you put the clothing away, ask her: "Do you like to arrange your clothes by style or color?" Style might mean sections for: dressy, casual, exercise clothes, and uniforms. Many children like to arrange by color because it's easy to find what they are looking for (i.e., my favorite pink sweater). Even though you might not think this way, remember to go with your child's preferences.

8. If she has accessories like belts, hats, or scarves, ask your child where she wants those kept. Hooks in the closet or a small drawer are two possible options for these items.

9. If you have a high shelf that your child can't reach, use that space for sheets, out-of-season clothes, or bins that you can easily take down.

10. Stand back and admire your little two-hour project. Make sure your child can reach what she needs.

Organizing a Dresser

If the dresser is overstuffed, then this might be the first place you start to organize clothes. Follow these steps for a quick drawer clean out:

1. Put a sheet on the floor or use a bed to sort the clothing you will pull out of the dresser.

2. Have bags ready for donations and trash, a box for hand-me-downs, and a box or bag for consignment.

3. Take everything out, one drawer at a time, and ask your child, "Do you wear this?" If she answers no, then the piece of clothing goes into the Donate, Consign, Hand Down, or Trash pile. If she says yes, fold the item and make piles on the bed or floor. Keep like things together as you make the piles (e.g., shirts, pants, shorts, socks, underwear, pajamas).

Move out of the room anything you are not keeping in it. Put donation bags in your car or near a door to your home. Move hand-me-downs to the appropriate sibling's room.

4. After you have pulled out all the clothes from the drawers and you have your piles and bags in front of you, move out of the room anything you are not keeping in there. Put the donation and consignment bags in your car or near a door to your home. Move any hand-me-

Putting Clothes Away

I HAVE A SIMPLE SYSTEM for getting my kids to put their clothes away. For starters, I only do laundry once a week. So at the end of laundry day, all their individual baskets are in the family room and we each take our own basket upstairs when getting ready for bed (my husband and myself included). I have my children separate their laundry into piles on their bed: pajamas, shirts, pants, shorts, etc. Then each category goes in the appropriate drawer. My husband or I usually help the youngest one with hanging clothes in his closet. I taught the kids at age six how to do this and now it's just a weekly routine for the whole family. Once the clothes are put away, they can have dessert that night!

downs to the appropriate sibling's room. Tuck any memory clothes (like T-shirts or hats) in a memory box, even if it's a temporary container.

5. Take a look at the piles you are keeping and the empty drawers you have. Put small things (such as socks and underwear) in the smallest drawers. If you have large, deep drawers, you may need drawer dividers. These can be found at many home stores. You can also use shoeboxes or gift boxes without lids as a simple, inexpensive way to divide a large drawer. This is the part of organizing that is like putting together a puzzle. Let your child make the decision about what goes where, so it makes sense to her.

6. As you start to put the clothes back into a drawer, ask your child if she would like to break down the categories any more. For instance, shirts

might be broken down into T-shirts and polos. Or your child might like to put the same colors together. Whatever works for her is OK.

Where to Put the Dirty Clothes

Now that you have established a place for all the clean clothes in your child's room, you have to make sure she keeps the dirty clothes separate from clean! Common sense tells us a laundry basket should solve that problem, right? Well, not for all children. Here are a few options to consider:

1. Keep a laundry basket in the bottom of the closet. This is always my first choice because it keeps dirty clothes out of sight.

2. Use a decorative laundry bin or basket that is out in the bedroom. This is a good option when your closet space is limited. It also works well for kids who have a hard time opening their closet doors by themselves. If you find that your child tends to throw her dirty clothes in a certain corner of the room, then try putting a laundry basket in that space.

3. Use a separated laundry bin. You may have seen these three-section laundry bins that work well for the whole family. There are canvas bins for darks, lights, and whites. These can be strategically placed for the whole family to use so that when it's time to wash, the sorting is already done. It's even better if the bins are color coded or labeled so that the separations are clear.

4. Use a combination approach. If your laundry room has enough space, you can place the separated bin there and still have laundry baskets in each person's bedroom. When your children are ready, you can have them bring their clothes into the laundry area and separate it themselves. Just another life skill that they will need to know before they go off to college!

A basket in the bottom of the closet keeps dirty clothes out of sight.

The Seasonal Switch

The change of seasons is a perfect time to go through clothing, not just for children, but for moms and dads as well. Many people I know do the seasonal switch when there is not enough room in the closet or dressers to fit all their clothing. It's also very common when more than one child is in a bedroom and the closets and dressers are shared. The first thing you need is a place to put the out-of-season clothing. Some options are:

1. In a plastic bin or vacuum-sealed bag, labeled with the size and season. These can be stored in the attic, an extra closet in the house, or (as a last resort) under the bed.
2. In a cedar closet or cedar chest.
3. In the back, bottom, or top of the child's bedroom closet, leaving current clothing more accessible.

Once you know where the out-of-season clothes are going, go through the closet and dresser as described on pages 273–276, even if you have just done this six months ago! Children grow fast, and each time you move clothing around, it's an opportunity to purge clothing that no longer fits or clothes that they no longer wear. You'll probably find that the clothes at the bottom of the drawers are rarely worn and are just taking up space. Every little bit of space helps when you're trying to organize. So categorize and purge as you go, taking out the old season's clothes first. Then bring in the new season's clothes if they have been tucked away. Take a look at each piece before you put it in a drawer or closet. What your child liked last year may be so "yesterday" to them this year. Between seasons, I suggest hanging a shopping bag in your child's closet for any clothes that they outgrow in the meantime. When the bag is full they should tell you, and then

> *Take a look at each piece of clothing before you put it in a drawer or closet. What your child liked last year may be so "yesterday" to them this year.*

you can take it to a donation drop off, a consignment store, or hand it down to someone you know.

THREE STEPS TO ORGANIZING YOUR CHILD'S CLOTHES

1. Set aside the time (at least two hours) to work with your child, going through every piece of clothing. Change of season is the best time to do this. Allow enough time to move out whatever is going and to put back in place whatever stays.
2. Facilitate simple decision making by asking questions like, "When did you last wear this?" Keep it simple: Each item either stays or goes.
3. Let your child decide where and how her clothes go back in the closet or dresser (i.e., folded or hanging, by color, or by style).

29. Manage Your Sports Equipment

THE PROBLEM

We want our children to be active. There are numerous options for them to play on all kinds of sports teams: baseball, softball, football, hockey, basketball, lacrosse, and field hockey just to name a few. But with those sports comes a whole lot of equipment. When you start to multiply the sports teams by the number of children you have, it can be overwhelming how much equipment you have to store, clean, and keep track of. Many parents I speak to have a hard time keeping control of all their sports equipment.

THE STORY

One of my first big assignments as a professional organizer was to do a room makeover on HGTV's *Mission: Organization*. The home was a one-bedroom apartment, and the young homeowners had a sports equipment problem. Namely, the man played ice hockey. If you have children who play ice hockey, you know that the equipment is large, sweaty, and plentiful. This man had chosen to dry the pads and jerseys by laying them on top of his dog's crate in his bedroom. Needless to say, his young wife was not happy with that arrangement. Space was limited, so I had to come up with a creative solution to make both homeowners happy. Together we decided that the right room to store the equipment was the balcony, and the right container was a deck box that had airholes for airing out the equipment and keeping it from getting musty. The hockey player just needed to get into the habit of drying out his equipment on his drying rack, then putting it away in his deck box after it was dry.

THE SOLUTION

Most solutions to organizing challenges come from making some decisions and some changes. In the story above, we see that deciding on the right room, the right container, and the right routine can make all the difference. As you look at your dilemmas with sports equipment, keep those three things in mind. If sports equipment is a big problem for your family, before you find your solution, you need to define your problem. Is there too much equipment that you are not using on a regular basis? If that is the case, maybe you just need to weed out the old stuff and contain what you are keeping. Is equipment littered throughout your house, in the mudroom, the family room, and the kids' bedrooms?

If sports equipment is a big problem for your family, before you find your solution, you need to define your problem.

Maybe you just need to decide on one location for storing the equipment and train your family to keep up with it. Do you have bins or racks somewhere and your children are not using the system? Maybe you need to rethink the location of those bins or work with your children to help them develop the habit of putting away their equipment.

What Is the Right Room?

The answer to this question depends on the setup of your home and your own personal preferences. Think about how your family typically leaves the house when running out to a sporting event or practice. Is it through the front door, back door, or garage? Now think about whether or not you have any storage options in that area. Think about where the equipment usually gets dumped and create a solution around that area. My first choice is always the garage. This way you can keep dirty, smelly, and bulky sports equipment out of your living space. If you often leave your house through the garage, putting the equipment there also is a visual reminder for your child to pick up his equipment on his way to the car. If sports equipment is tucked out of the way, it is more likely to be forgotten. If you don't have a garage, some other options include:

Mudroom. Sometimes this is also the laundry room, so make sure the room is big enough to serve both functions before you designate this as the sports equipment area.

Closet. A closet by the back or front door that can be used only for sports equipment is ideal. You can replace the hanging rack with shelves if necessary.

Area by the back door. If you don't have a specific closet or room for storage when you come into your house, you can always create one with a rack, bins, bench, or shelves.

Back porch. If indoor space is limited, an area just outside your house that is protected from the weather is another option for storing sports equipment. The containers you choose will need to be appropriate for this area as well. They will need to be sturdy and weatherproof.

Basement. Like a garage, a basement is a great place to spread out bulky, sweaty sports equipment. The downside to this location is that it may be out of the way in your normal routine, so you may forget what is down there, or you may forget to dry it, clean it, etc.

> Put the equipment where it can be seen on the way to the car so it is a visual reminder for your child to pick up his equipment. If sports equipment is tucked out of the way, it is more likely to be forgotten.

Take Stock of Your Equipment

After you decide where you will keep your sports equipment, ask your children to help you gather up all of their sports equipment (even equipment that is no longer used) from around the house and deposit it in the designated room. With

Mudroom Storage. *If you have the room, the mudroom (or entryway) is a good place to store sports equipment.*

Find New Uses for Old Equipment

ONE OF MY COLLEGE FRIENDS who is a self-proclaimed "hockey mom" had a clever idea for reusing her son's old hockey sticks. She used them as curtain rods in his bedroom by hanging them from rod brackets.

all the equipment assembled, go through it piece by piece, putting like things together. Decide with your children how you would like it sorted. You can put all equipment for one sport together by making piles for baseball, basketball, hockey, football, etc., or you could sort it by which child it belongs to. You could also put similar items together by making piles for balls, sticks, rackets, pads, shoes, skates, whatever works for your family. As you sort the items, discard anything that is broken and set aside items your children have outgrown or no longer use. If you are looking for someplace to take your sports equipment that is still in good condition, do an Internet search for a sports consignment store in your area. You can also donate these to a school, charity, or someone you know, or you can store them as hand-me-downs for younger siblings. When everything is sorted you'll be able to see just what you have and decide what sort of containers will work for your area and equipment.

What Is the Right Container?

The containers you use should blend with the area you have chosen to store the equipment in. They should also make it easier for your children to put their equipment away. Before you purchase any containers or have racks installed, consult with your children because they will be the ones maintaining the system on an ongoing basis. Find out if they like to have their sticks and bats hung up individually on a wall, or if it's OK to put them all together in a bin. Likewise, ask if it's OK to put basketballs, baseballs, and footballs in one bin they might have to dig around in, or if they like them on a wire rack where they can see each one. Children can be particular; sometimes the way things are put away can really confuse them and make it difficult for them to maintain the system. So ask the right questions until you are sure you have a container that makes it easy for your children to find what they need, and to put it away later. For instance, your child might like to have his own bag packed for each sport so all he has to do is grab it and go. Every child is different, so make sure your system matches his habits and preferences. You might want to flip through a catalog with storage containers or take your children with you when you purchase any storage items so you can make sure the items are easy for your children to use. They need to be able to open and close the storage container on their own and reach all the way to the bottom of it. When you hang racks or shelves, hang them at the appropriate level for your child. You may want to consider racks with adjustable heights so they can grow with your child.

When you hang racks or shelves, hang them at the appropriate level for your child. You may want to consider racks with adjustable heights so they can grow with your child.

Here are some other options for containers in different areas of your home:

Mudroom. If this is a room that you pass through often, it's best to go with storage that is aesthetically pleasing, like a storage bench or a cabinet with doors you can close. Wall cubbies with bins work well here also for the smaller pieces of equipment like caps, gloves, or goggles. Any wet equipment or pads should be dried out first, either in the garage or outside before being stored in the mudroom.

Garage/Basement. Storage in these areas can range from a custom-designed storage system to do-it-yourself wire racks on the wall. You can also use metal trash cans, plastic bins on the floor, and industrial shelving. To make a simple hanging rack, you can start with a piece of wood mounted to the wall, hold up the sticks or bats, and mark where to put in flathead nails or screw-in hooks that will hold them up. You can also hang milk crates from the hooks and make a simple bin for pads and balls. If you've got the classic PegBoard used for tools already in your garage, you can repurpose it for sticks and rackets. A gardening container that is made for rakes and brooms can also hold bats, lacrosse sticks, and tennis rackets. Whatever is big enough for your equipment and sturdy enough to hold it all works well. If you have the money for a custom designed system, many closet makeover companies also design cabinets for the garage. Just make sure your equipment is organized before the consultant designs a

Photo courtesy of The Container Store

Garage Storage. *The garage is an ideal place to store sports equipment. Your child will see his equipment on his way to the car before a practice or a game and be less likely to forget anything.*

system for your family! Also, check online for racks that are specifically designed for your family's favorite sports.

If you have more than one child or more than one sport, then labeling is essential.

Closet. If you've got a designated closet for sports equipment, protect the floor with a plastic runner or mat. Low shoe racks work well for boots or skates. A sturdy cylindrical bin, such as a trash can or an umbrella holder, can hold sticks and bats. Small bins up on a shelf can hold anything from tennis balls to ski gloves. If you need the hanging bar for jerseys and coats, use it. Otherwise, hang hooks on the back wall for things like tennis rackets, ski poles, sports bags, etc. If the closet is big enough, you can stack bins in one corner for the out-of-season or less-used equipment.

Area by the back door. Much like a mudroom, you can create an area by your back door to hold seasonal sports equipment by bringing in a storage bench and a wall shelf with hooks. Because this area is small, any out-of-season equipment will need to be stored elsewhere in the house. I suggest using plastic storage bins and putting them in a basement or garage until they are needed. Make sure to label them clearly!

Back porch. Like the example in my story, sometimes the only storage option is outside your home. If you have a covered porch or balcony, a plastic deck box with airholes can work well for all kinds of pads, balls, and gloves. If you've got football or hockey pads or skates that need to dry out before they are put away, you can use a clothes drying rack, a clothesline, or simply hang the wet items on a hook or nail outside to air-dry them. Just make sure that whatever you keep out there will not be damaged by the weather.

How Do You Keep It Organized?

Once your family makes a decision about where to keep the sports equipment, and you've installed or purchased bins or racks to hold everything, you've got to maintain the system. If you have more than one child or more than one sport, then labeling is essential. Label your sports bags or color-code them for each child. Label the bins with children's names or the name of the sport. Make each child accountable for getting his equipment back to the proper place after every game or practice. Once the season is over, do a clean out of any equipment or clothing that will no longer be used. Pack that sports equipment away until next season and bring out the equipment for the sports your kids are currently playing.

THREE STEPS FOR MANAGING YOUR SPORTS EQUIPMENT

1. Define your problem. Is it the volume, location, or wrong system or container?
2. Decide what room and what containers work best for your family.
3. Get into the habit of putting the equipment away daily, and clean it out and rotate it at the end of a season.

30. Curtail Your Cords

THE PROBLEM

We are a plugged-in society. Never before have children had so many electronic devices that require cords, chargers, and headphones. Add to those the multiple USB cables that digital equipment requires in order to connect our cameras and MP3 players to the computer, plus video game consoles, controls, and games, and we've got a lot of electronic equipment and accessories to keep track of. These devices are not cheap, so it would be beneficial to keep them in a safe place where they can't get damaged or lost.

THE STORY

Our family recently went on a vacation. As with every vacation, I started with a list to help the kids pack their backpacks with toys and activities. The list included: a PSP, Nintendo DS, cell phone, MP3 players, digital camera, a digital video camera and chargers for each. When I looked in my teenager's carry-on bag it looked like she had cleaned up at RadioShack! Luckily she had made quilted bags for each of her small electronics to hold the chargers and headphones and to keep them protected as we traveled.

THE SOLUTION

To help your children keep their electronic devices working properly and to keep them from getting lost or damaged, you can set up a home base and a method of travel for their phones, MP3 players, cameras, and games. The home base will be where they keep and charge the units when they are home. The method of travel will be the case that they use when they have the device with them on the go.

Charging Stations

If you search online, you can find charging stations ranging in price from twenty dollars to two hundred dollars. Most of these hold three electronic devices and are incorporated into a desktop organizer. With that in mind, you can easily find one to match your home office, your kitchen, or your child's bedroom décor. But first decide where the best place is for your children to store their electronics when they are not in their backpacks, purses, or pockets. A charging station is a great way to keep your electronics together and keep the wires out of sight. However, it is best to keep the charging cords unplugged until they are needed. According to the US Department of Energy, appliances continue to draw electricity while the products are turned off, and in the average home nearly seventy-five percent of all electricity used to power electronics is consumed by products that are switched off. You may have noticed that a charger that is plugged into the wall

Charging Station. A charging station lets you charge multiple devices in one location and keeps the cords neatly out of sight.

will be warm even if the device is not plugged in. That is because it is still drawing electricity. Unplugging these cords will also cut down on greenhouse gases. Part of being organized is being efficient, and that includes energy efficient in your home. It's never too early for your children to learn these lessons.

Containing Each Device

If you don't have room for a charging station, you can still keep your electronics organized by having a bag or case for each device. A homemade case can be made with fleece or a soft, quilted material that is sewn into a small rectangle with a drawstring closer. If you want to be really creative, you can sew on a patch or have it embroidered to identify what is in the bag, such as "camera" or "phone." Be sure the container can hold the cord and/or headphones and games that go with the item. Whether it's homemade or store-bought, a case will protect each unit from getting scratched or damaged, especially if the items are being transported in a purse or backpack on a daily basis. Electronic stores usually have cases for each type of game system, but your kids can also use a large pencil case to hold their devices, chargers, and game disks or cartridges. If your child has trouble with losing small things, make a suggestion to keep the game disk in the large plastic case that it comes in. These are about the size of a DVD case and are easier to find, although bulkier to carry. When your child uses the devices at home,

Keep the charging cords unplugged until they are needed. Nearly 75% of all electricity used to power electronics is consumed by products that are switched off.

have one designated spot where she always puts them back. This could be a table in the entrance of your home, a desk or shelf in your child's bedroom, or a bedside table. Have her keep the charger in this location at all times unless she will be traveling and needs to bring the charger with her.

Label the Cords

If you have cords that are being kept separate from the device they belong to, then it is a good idea to label the cords. This can be done simply with a blank, white address label that you wrap around the cord and stick to itself, then write the name of the device on the label. This works well with USB cords that are used to connect cameras or MP3 players to computers. Kids can keep these cords in a desk drawer where the computer is, and just pull them out as needed. To find all sorts of unique ways to wind up and store cords and cables, check out this Web site: www.cableorganizer.com.

Limit the Use and Accessibility

As you go through this process of helping your children organize their electronics and all the accessories that go with them, it's a good time to also talk about the responsible use of these devices. Make sure your children know when they are allowed to use each of these items, and for what length of time. Many times children acquire these gadgets and there is no discussion about how to use them. For instance, you might not want your child talking or texting on a cell phone after a certain hour of the day. Or the school might not allow your child to bring in electronic games or cameras. If you find that your child is using these electronics for an extended period of time, then it's a good idea to establish the home base in a place where you have control over the usage. In other words, if you want your child reading at night before bed and not talking on the phone or playing video games, make sure the devices are "put to bed" first at their docking station in a common area of the home. For children who need to be supervised on their use of electronics, it's not a good idea to keep them in their bedroom. This can change as the child matures.

> *If your child is using her electronics for an extended period of time, establish a home base in a place where you have control over the usage.*

Wrap Up Your Cords

ONE OF THE BEST SOLUTIONS I have come across for keeping your cords under control comes from another professional organizer named Donna Smallin. She suggests taking your cord and folding it back and forth so it is about eight inches long and not more than two inches thick, and pushing it through an empty toilet paper roll. I use this for my hair dryer cord, the VCR cords that are not always plugged in, and extra extension cords that we have in our home. Wrapped up cords take up a lot less space and won't get tangled.

Likewise, if you want your child to use her cell phone only in case of emergency, limit the hours she has to talk on it, and keep it somewhere you can see it until she leaves the house. Get your child in the habit of packing the phone in her backpack in the morning before school, and returning it to the designated drawer, charging station, or table when she returns. You can treat this like any other school supply that gets packed and unpacked each day. If you find it hard to keep track of how long each child spends on each device, you can always make a chart like the one on page 296. List the device, where it can be used, and for what length of time it can be used, along with any other conditions you want to establish.

Home-Based Game Systems

In addition to portable electronic devices, most families have some sort of plug-in gaming device like a PlayStation, an Xbox, or a Wii. These also come with their own arsenals of attachments, wires, and of course, games! The toilet paper roll

CHILD	CELL PHONE	MP3 PLAYER	HANDHELD VIDEO GAME PLAYER
John (eleven years old)	For calling parents only.	Thirty minutes at a time when riding in the car or playing in your room. Not at school.	Thirty minutes at a time, only on weekends. Not at school.
Kathy (sixteen years old)	Up to two hours per month, unlimited texting. Not after 10 P.M. Never while driving.	When riding in a car, no headphones while driving. In your room after homework is complete.	Thirty minutes at a time after homework is complete.

Electronic Usage Chart. This simple chart lets your children know when and where they can use their electronic devices.

method described on page 295 works well to contain the power cords when the device is not plugged into the TV and to wrap up cords to the attachments. It's best not to wrap the cord tightly around the device because this pulls at the connection of the cord and could possibly tear it. Depending on how many attachments (paddles, joy sticks, controllers) you have, you can store them in a nice wicker basket on a shelf or in a cabinet by the TV. If you've got a lot, maybe keep the most used items out and store the other peripherals in a box in a closet or cabinet. Because the games come in containers very much like DVDs, my family stores them in the same way—on a bookshelf by the TV. The games are kept separate from the videos by a bookend. Again, depending on how many you own, a wicker basket or decorative box that can be found at any home store will also work well for keeping video

Games, controllers, and other attachments can be stored in baskets or other containers near the game console.

games organized. As with any organizing task, compile what you have, get rid of any that are broken or you are not using, and find a nice container that is big enough for keeping all your controls and games in one spot.

THREE STEPS TO CURTAILING YOUR CORDS

1. Designate a home base for your electronics in an appropriate room with the appropriate container.
2. Use cases to protect your device and keep cords and headphones together while you are out and about.
3. Wrap up and label your cords.

31. Savor Childhood Memories

THE PROBLEM

All good parents want to savor the precious moments of their children's lives, but everyone does this to varying degrees. If you are the type of parent who saves every birthday card, every toy car, and every cicada shell your child ever picked up, you're going to have a problem. By the time that child is fifteen you won't have room for all of his memorabilia. And, quite frankly, you may have some yucky stuff hiding in boxes! If you save everything when your child is young, then when you hand the responsibility over, he may go one of two ways, either he will want to save everything, or he'll want to save nothing. The solution lies in finding a happy medium.

THE STORY

One of the first calls I received when I was starting out as a new professional organizer was from one of my neighbors who wanted me to organize her husband's belongings. She told me that he had so much old stuff from his childhood that it was cluttering up their bedroom and home office. Apparently his mother had saved *everything* from his childhood and then passed it on to him when he got married. At one point in the conversation my neighbor said, "I mean, he still has his teeth!" Her husband was only about forty years old, so I thought this was an odd statement. I would hope he still had all his teeth at that age. "No," she said, "I mean he still has all his baby teeth in a box!" This was just one of the odd things that his mother had saved for him.

THE SOLUTION

The way to keep your child's memorabilia under control is to save a reasonable amount, keep it all in one place, and then look at it every year to decide again what is really worth saving.

Decisions, Decisions

You have to be reasonable about what you keep. It's often said that the key to organizing is making decisions. I completely agree with this statement and have seen it demonstrated with many of my clients. The people with the most clutter and the most "old stuff" can't seem to make a decision and let go of the past. When it comes to savoring your children's lives with little pictures and tokens of their stages of growth, it's best to do it on a year-by-year basis. Think of it as finding the "best of" that year. Chose the best, toss the rest, and move on! There's so much more ahead.

Another key point to consider is to only save what gives you happy memories. Believe it or not, there are people who save mementos of unhappy occasions. I have seen people save bloody blankets from when their dog was hit by a car, newspaper clippings of national tragedies and obituaries, teeth that they lost as children, and pieces of casts from broken arms. And I have to think, *Why?* Why would you want to be reminded of something sad, tragic, or unpleasant? I guess it's a matter of opinion and preference, but I would like to think that if you are saving things for your child to have when he gets older, you would want only the happy memories to be preserved. So when considering what to keep for your child, ask yourself and your child, "Does this bring a smile to your face?"

Categorize, Purge, and Rearrange

If you've already accumulated lots of memorabilia for your child, you'll have to gather it all into one room first to get it under control and organized. If you have more than one child, work on one child's memorabilia at a time. It's a great excuse to have some one-on-one time together.

Allot a few hours for this process because you may get lost in reminiscing, and that's OK! If you don't think you'll get through it all, make sure you have an area set aside where you can leave the stuff until you do finish your project.

I suggest using my tried-and-true process of CPR (Categorize, Purge, and Rearrange. See pages 190 and 246 for a full explanation). Your categories might be: photos, artwork, baby blankets and clothes, baby photo albums or scrapbooks, trophies and awards, religious articles, schoolwork, and stuffed animals, just to name a few. Of course your personal categories will depend on the age of your child and how much you have saved thus far. As you categorize, ask your child, "Do you want to save this?" If the child says no, you've got to honor that. You can also decide if something is necessary to save just by your child's reaction. If there are lots of "oohs" and "aahs," and "I remember this," you probably want to keep it. If you get a "What is that?" it's probably a toss.

As parents who are trying to hand off some responsibility to your children, you can't force your child to save everything, but you can make suggestions. You also have to let him make some decisions, too. So if your ten-year-old had a lousy experience on a soccer team, there's no reason why you have to save the team picture. Now there are going to be items that you find adorable and your child will find meaningless, I guarantee it. For those items, make a separate pile for yourself. Those items are now yours to store and not your child's.

Toys and clothes are two categories where I see many parents saving way too much. Let's face it, if your child is a teenager and you still have his stuffed animals, every toddler toy, and every piece of clothing he wore in his first year, you've got some paring down to do. Save the special clothes like a christening outfit or the outfit he wore home from the hospital. Save a special stuffed animal, toy, or book that he loved. The rest could be given to charity.

Create a Memory Box

Once you have made all your decisions about what to keep, toss, and donate, take a look at your piles. Papers, artwork, and awards can be kept in a folder, portfolio, or accordion file, and loose photos can be put in an album (see Chapter 32 on photos). If you are someone who likes to do scrapbooks, then small and flat items may be used for that. Look at the size of your collection as it is spread out on the floor in piles, and think about a nice container in which your child could keep his memories. Some options are: plastic containers with locking lids, steamer trunks, or wooden hope chests. Remember, too, that this will be a collection you will add to every year, so get a container with extra space. When choosing where to store your memory box, consider how many years it took to fill one box and plan for up to eighteen years. For instance, if you fit three years' of memories in one box, then you will need six boxes by the time your child is an adult. Of course, at some point you will not be the keeper of items, it will be your child's decision, so he may decide to keep more or less than you did.

Hand Over the Responsibility

Once you have rearranged your child's memories into a nice container, you will need to establish a process to keep up with all the new stuff that is going to come into your home from this point forward. I suggest finding a box, a drawer, or an accordion file in which you can store these items for one year. One of my children uses a drawer in his desk to store memorabilia; my other son has a drawer in his dresser; and my daughter has an accordion file on her bookshelf. Throughout the year we toss extra pictures, award certificates, playbills, buttons, and special greeting cards in the memory drawer or file. In the summer, we go through that drawer to categorize and purge and find a home for everything. Most flat items end up in their scrapbooks. We cut pictures from the greeting cards to decorate the pages and toss any cards we don't use. The bigger items get put in the memory boxes, which are stored in the bottom of their bedroom closets. At the beginning of the school year, they each have an empty drawer or file to fill up again. At the end of the school year, it's time to go through and weed out.

Accordion File. *An accordion file is a great place to store memorabilia accumulated during the school year.*

Review, Reminisce, and Refresh

Establish a routine of going through your child's memory box with him every year. This routine is a great way to keep down the clutter and to limit the decisions you'll need to make in the future. Throughout the year you only have to decide what to put in the memory collection spot. It's not a final commitment. Once a year you decide what goes into a scrapbook, photo album, or memory box. As you are putting in the new stuff, it's a great time to look at the old. You may find some cute things that make you laugh, cry, or smile along with your child. Sometimes you will find old things that have lost their significance so you can let those go. It's amazing what a few years will do. The child's memory box will then be refreshed.

THREE STEPS TO SAVORING CHILDHOOD MEMORIES

1. Gather up what you have saved. Decide, with your child, what to keep and what to toss.
2. Find an appropriate container for keeping your child's memorabilia and a place to collect new memories for the year.
3. Go through the new memory items each year and add the "keepers" to the memory box. Then go through the memory box and toss old things that no longer have meaning.

32. File Those Photos

THE PROBLEM

Photos, like other memorabilia, seem to multiply once you have children. Parents take pictures, grandparents send you doubles, and when children get older, they start taking their own pictures of friends, school trips, and special events. You have digital photos on the computer, framed photos on your walls and shelves, and perhaps boxes of loose photos that are bursting at the seams. If you are someone who has not gotten control of your photos, then your child may be following in your footsteps and creating her own backlog. Together you can conquer this problem and create a system.

THE STORY

A friend of mine came from a large family with eight children. Her mother was an excellent organizer, especially when it came to photos. On her twenty-first birthday her mother presented her with a photo album that captured all the special moments in her life. I found out that she had done this for all her children. I thought, "What a wonderful present!" not only because it was thoughtful and special, but because it also represented a rite of passage. My friend's mother had preserved her child's memories in a photo album, and now she was letting go of the past and acknowledging that her child was an adult. It was now her child's responsibility to create and preserve her own memories.

THE SOLUTION

As with mail, we are constantly obtaining more and more photos, so a backlog grows pretty rapidly. I am often asked, "What should I do with photographs?" There are many answers to this question, and the solution lies with you and your child. You have to decide how you like to look at your photos, not just how you want to *store* them. Once you organize your backlog, you have to develop a plan for going forward.

Take Care of the Backlog

If you would like to one day hand your adult child a special gift like a chronological photo album, first you have to clear out your own backlog of photos. Start by gathering your loose photos in one location. Separate them into piles or boxes based on who you are saving the photos for: yourself, your child, your friends, or other family members. As you sort, purge any pictures that are dark, out of focus, or just plain bad.

> *Purge any pictures that are dark, out of focus, or just plain bad. Mail any doubles you've been saving for other people.*

Many people hang on to photos with the intention of giving them away to friends or family. If you have any photos in this category, now is the time to take care of them. As you come across these photos, grab some envelopes and your address book and get them in the mail with a short note. Even if you are going to see that person soon, it's better to get them out the door than to hold on to them until the next time you see that person. Plus, who wouldn't enjoy receiving a friendly note and some old pictures in the mail?

Separate the pictures that you are saving for your children by placing them in boxes for each individual child. From there you can make a photo album, a scrapbook, or at least pass on the box for your child to decide what to do with the photos.

Help Your Children Decide Where to Keep Their Photos

Set aside some time to work on your child's photos with her. Bring in your photos for her and help her gather up all of her own photos. Then ask your child, "How do you best enjoy looking at your photos?" There are so many options: in frames, in albums, in collages, on bulletin boards, or on the computer. Next you can gather up any photo accessories that you may have around the house. These would include empty photo albums, picture frames, and bulletin boards. If you don't have any of these tools, wait until you know the size of the photo pile before you buy anything new. For instance, if your child wants a bulletin board for photos, you have to know whether it should hold fifteen photos or one hundred. You can choose one or more of these options when creating your own unique system. Let's review each of these options and how to use them:

Wait until you know the size of your child's photo collection before you buy any photo accessories such as frames, albums, or bulletin boards.

Frames. Put your favorite pictures that you love to look at every day in frames. If you don't have the frames right now, take the pictures with you when you go to purchase the frames. You'll want to consider the size, color, and style of frame that will make your photo really pop. You'll also need to consider whether the frames will be stand-up (for shelves or desktops) or hanging on your wall.

Collages. Picture collages are a great way to get a lot of pictures in a small space. Whether it's on a page of a "paste in" photo album or in a picture frame, a collage is fun to make and fun to look at. You can take pictures from a single event or from a specific time and crop them to fit on one sheet. Examples would be: a collage from your child's field hockey season, summer camp, graduation, or a play that she was in. Collages also make great gifts for friends!

Bulletin boards. Like the collage, a bulletin board allows you to see a bunch of pictures at once. This is even easier to create than the collage because you don't have to crop or paste the pictures. Simply stick a pin in it and you're finished!

Computers. If your child is taking her own photos now, chances are the photos are digital. So if the child has her own computer, she can create slide shows that run while the computer is not in use, or she can put them on a digital photo frame.

Digital photos give you many options for preserving your family's memories. However, the common problem I hear is that the digital photos go into the computer and never come out! In an effort to go paperless, some families are missing out on the pleasure of flipping through photo albums with their kids. So think about whether you want hard copies of some or all of your photos.

Albums. If you take a lot of photos and you like to have hard copies of them, the album is your best bet. I like the ones with slip-in sleeves for easy filing. If

Slip-in Album. Try a slip-in photo album as a quick, easy way to organize and store your photos.

Digital Scrapbooks

I FIND DIGITAL SCRAPBOOKS to be an excellent and efficient way to capture your photos from special events or trips. They come in various sizes and you can even choose page layouts that give you room to write little stories about what happened. The book itself is saved as a project file on a Web site so you can also go back and order multiple copies of the same book if necessary. To find out more about these digital scrapbooks, check out these Web sites: www.shutterfly.com and www.snapfish.com.

you put photos in each time you get some printed, you will automatically have a chronological album of events. Many slip-in albums also have room for you to write captions. Write a quick note about who's in the photo, where and when the photo was taken, and what event was happening to enhance your memory when you look at your photos in the future.

Ongoing Maintenance

Each of the options discussed is a great starting point. However, there is only so much space in your child's bedroom or your home to display all of these photos. So you've got to develop a system for ongoing maintenance of your photos. Here are some suggestions for routines you and your child can follow to organize your photos from this point on:

Once a month. Have your pictures developed once a month. If you have a digital camera, this entails uploading the pictures from your camera to your computer or taking your camera to a photo center where they can take the memory card from your camera and print the photos for you. When uploading to your computer, it's a good idea to save all the photos in one folder on your computer marked "Photos," and then subfolders can be named with the month and the year (e.g., September 2013). This makes it easy to go back and find photos from a special occasion (as long as you can remember the month and the year of that occasion). Once the photos have been uploaded, order prints of the ones you want from an online service and delete the images from your camera. Keeping up with this routine helps you know which pictures have already been developed. Anything that is left on your camera should be from the current month. Once you have your prints, put them in an album, in frames, or on a bulletin board.

Send a digital photo album instead of prints to family and friends.

After a big event. Some months you may have more photos than usual because of big events. In our family, May is always a busy time because we have birthdays, graduations, sacraments, and Mother's Day. For these special occasions, you may want to make a photo folder that is named by the event: "John's Grad 2013," for example. Again, upload the photos from that event and delete them from your camera. Then order the prints that you want and put them in frames, photo albums, or a scrapbook for that event. If you don't have the time to make an album right away, at least you will have all the photos in one digital file so you can refer back to it when you are ready to get creative!

Once a year. Pick a point in the year when you like to refresh your photos. It may be over Christmas break or at the start or the end of summer. At this time, gather up all your framed pictures and decide on which ones to keep and which ones to change. You can always just put a new picture on top of an old one in a frame. Each time you change the picture, you get to enjoy the memory of what is underneath, like a hidden treasure. Also look at your digital photo frame and your bulletin board and take off the old to make room for new. If you like the digital photo albums, you can go back to each file named for a month of the year and choose your favorites to put into one album, like a year in review. I love to do this at Christmastime and send copies to my children's grandparents. This replaces the process of sending them doubles of all the kids' cute photos taken throughout the year.

THREE STEPS TO FILING YOUR PHOTOS

1. Gather all your photos in one place. Categorize and purge the bad ones.
2. Decide how you want to display and/or file your photos.
3. Create a routine: monthly—upload your digital pictures, order prints, and put them in albums; yearly—refresh your display photos.

33. Shelve the Books and Magazines

THE PROBLEM

Books are good things. We want our kids to read, right? In some cases they have to read certain books for school, so we are surrounded by children's and young adult literature. When children are young, their parents often read parenting magazines for advice on everything from fun activities to discipline. When children get older, they start to acquire their own choices of books and magazines. So the piles start. We keep adding to our collections of books, but many of us are reluctant to subtract. That's where the problem begins. Reading materials from different sources start to commingle and we lose track of what goes where. And if you're a regular at your local library, you might suddenly find that you are a persona non grata until you return those books you checked out last month.

THE STORY

I recently attended a high school reunion where we had a great time reminiscing and looking at old photographs. When we pulled out the ones from our graduation ceremony, we couldn't help but notice that in one photo our friend Chris had a puzzled look on her face as she shook hands with the principal of our school

> *Treat library books like bills. Keep them separate and visible so you can return them before their due dates.*

and glanced at her diploma. She told us that when she opened the folder that we all assumed would have our diplomas in it, she found a notice that said, "Overdue library books. Please report to the librarian."

We all had heard the announcement, "You can't graduate until all library books are returned and all school bills are settled." But none of us took it seriously or thought that this announcement was meant for us. Chris had received a few notices in the mail, but had not really addressed them during her busy senior year. There were so many more exciting things to think about! Who would've thought that an overdue library book could cost you a diploma?

THE SOLUTION

OK, so keeping order and organizing your reading materials is not exciting. My solution is to make a simple system that works. Keep up with it on a regular basis and you'll never have to worry about losing library books again, and you won't be walking between stacks of books in your home.

Keep Library Books Separate

I consider library books like bills because they have a due date and they may cost you money. You don't want to lose your bills in a stack of papers, so you keep them separate and visible. Library books should be treated the same way.

If your children are very young and you are the person checking out the library books, the first thing to do is to write *library* on the day of your calendar that your current books are due. That becomes one of your tasks, and it's a visual reminder. Secondly, find a basket or shelf where you can keep the library books separate from other books you own. This should be near the place you usually read books to your children. If your children are inclined to mess up the books or misplace them, make sure your spot for library books is out of their reach.

As your children get older and are in elementary school, there is usually one day a week when their classes go to the library. Make sure this day is marked on your weekly chart (see Chapter 23), and then help your child choose a place in his bedroom where his library books will always be kept. By the time your children are in high school, they should have made this a habit.

Make Preschool Books Accessible

Books play an important role in the development process of young children. Most families that I work with have lots of picture books and simple word books for their preschoolers. These books may be in the playroom, the living room, and the bedroom, which is fine if that's where they are being used. Think about whether your child looks at his books as much as you would like him to. If not, the books may be in the wrong place or they might not be accessible to your child. If you have books scattered everywhere and you'd like to get them consolidated into one room or on one shelf, I recommend you consider where you use the books and then place the books in that area, containing them on a low shelf or in a basket that the children can reach.

If you have an enormous amount of books that is hard to contain on one shelf, you may also want to go through the books once a year to weed out any that your child has outgrown. If there are younger siblings who will have the books next, pass them down. If there are no other younger children in your house, consider donating the books to a library, school, or children's hospital in your area.

If your children don't look at their books as much as you'd like, make sure the books are easily accessible to the children and in a location where the children will use the books most often.

Give Every Child a Bookshelf

Your preschoolers will grow up and have their own tastes in books. Hopefully they

The Great Book Clean Out

IF BOOKS HAVE TAKEN OVER YOUR HOME, if you have boxes of books stashed away, if your children don't even know what books they have, or they look at their shelves and say, "I've read all of these, I want something new to read," it's time for a Great Book Clean Out. This organizing project involves the whole family and all your books, so get ready.

1. Gather all the books into the room where they are kept. Personal books could go in the child's bedroom, and the family books could be in a common room such as the living room, family room, or den.

2. Start with the oldest child first. Have him go through every book he has and ask, "Have you read this?" and "Will you read this?" Essentially you're making two piles: Books to Read and Books to Pass On. In some cases he might read a book again, or he might want to hang on to a book to share with a friend; keep those with the Books to Read pile.

will be purchasing books through the school book fair and receiving books as gifts. So their collections will grow as they do. It's a great idea to have a bookshelf in each of your children's bedrooms so they can keep their books separate from the rest of the family's books. Bookshelves are essential, but often overlooked. You'd be amazed at how many homes I help organize that have books everywhere, but very few bookshelves. Shelving doesn't have to be big or expensive, a simple two-shelf bookcase might work for your child's room. These can be

3. Pass any books that your child will not read again on to a younger sibling, even if he is not at that reading level yet. These will go on the next child's "Books to Read" shelf. If there are no other siblings, consider donating these books.

4. Go through each child's books (in order of age), doing the same process. Then go through the family books. Again, the practical solution to book clutter is to only keep books that someone in your home will read or reread someday. I'm all for saving the classics, but if you are trying to save every book your child has ever read, you're fighting a losing battle.

5. Once all of your books have a home (a room, a bookshelf, or a basket), keep up with your system by going through them at least once a year.

6. Find a worthy charity or used bookstore where you can take the books your family is finished reading.

purchased at a yard sale, a consignment shop, or a home store. Put the shelf where your child usually reads—in most homes that's the bedroom, but it doesn't have to be.

Contain and Keep Up with Magazines

As your children start to develop their own interests, they may like to subscribe to magazines that cater to their hobbies and activities. These are fun because not only do they have something of their very own to read, but they also get mail on a regular basis. My daughter is always excited when her new copy of *American Girl* magazine arrives, and my son has been reading *Sports Illustrated Kids* for a few years now. As adults, we know that magazines can clutter up our living spaces and pile up if we don't recycle old issues regularly. Start this habit early. Ask your child how long he would like to keep his magazines. Some children might read an issue cover to cover and put it in the recycle bin as soon as they finish. Others might want to keep certain

Book Storage. *Let your bookshelves double as a nightstand in your child's bedroom to save space while keeping books in a convenient location.*

pages in their magazines. And others might never want to part with any of their magazines because they "just might need it someday."

Find out what your child prefers. If he wants to save magazines for a long time, decide on a container that will keep them together. I love floor baskets because they go well in all types of rooms. Another option is a cardboard magazine holder, which can be found at stationery and office supply stores. In either case, let your child know that you can't keep buying more baskets and magazine holders when one gets full. Instead, when the container is full, it's time to pare down and recycle some issues. Set a limit ahead of time—maybe six months of magazines or two containers worth, whatever your storage space will allow. Or you could use the one in, one out method. In other words, when the new edition arrives, recycle the oldest edition of that magazine. If your child likes to pick and choose to save some pages of the magazine, then there should be a purpose for each page. If the magazine contains pictures your child likes, post them

If space is really an issue in your home, consider a tall bookcase that uses vertical space. Or use end tables that have shelves underneath them.

on a bulletin board. If your child wants to save craft or recipe ideas, beauty tips, or summer activity ideas, have her start a binder with tabs that indicate what is in it. She can call it her "Ideas Binder" and keep it on her bookshelf.

If you don't have room for a large bookshelf, a nightstand with two small shelves works well.

Display Family Books in a Common Room

Some books may not belong to anyone in particular in your family, so these we will consider family books. Some examples of family books might be: classics that you have saved and want to pass down to your children, coffee table books, travel books, family histories, Bibles, dictionaries, thesauri, or collections of poems.

Because you want the whole family to have access to them at any given time, it makes sense to store them in a family room. Some families even consider books to be part of their décor.

If you feel like you have more books than space to keep them, here's a trick you can do to know exactly how much space you need. Line up your books on the floor with the binding up (as if they were on a shelf), then measure across to see how much shelf space you need.

You can spend anywhere from two thousand dollars for custom-made built-in bookshelves to ten dollars buying a used bookshelf at a garage sale. Or you could do it yourself and make a bookshelf from wood you can buy at a home store. If space is really an issue in your home, consider a tall bookcase that uses vertical space. Get one as close to your ceiling height as possible or use end tables that have shelves underneath. There are many options out there. You might have to use a little creativity to find one that works for your family.

THREE STEPS FOR KEEPING READING MATERIALS ORGANIZED

1. Keep borrowed books in a separate location from books you own and write their due dates on your family calendar.
2. Give everyone in your family an appropriate bookshelf or container to hold their books and magazines.
3. Go through your books annually and donate the unwanted ones to a charity. For magazines, decide on the amount of time that you will keep them. Maintain your system by using the one in, one out method.

Get Your Categories In Order

You now have a plan to help organize your child's belongings.

REMEMBER

1. Set realistic expectations about where things like toys, sports equipment, memorabilia, and personal electronics can be kept. Decide on the room first, then the container.

2. Clean out toys, clothes, and sports equipment with your child a few times a year to move out the old stuff and rearrange items.

3. Work with your child to develop a daily or weekly routine for getting things back where they belong.

4. Display collections, photos, and art to appreciate them.

5. Retire collections once your child has lost interest in them.

6. When going through a category of belongings, keep decision making simple. Hold up the item and let your child decide yes (to keep) or no (to purge).

7. Consider your child's opinion when deciding where to put his things so everything is easy to access.

8. Go through your child's memorabilia, books, and artwork once a year. Toss old things that no longer have meaning to make room for new items.

9. Upload digital photos on a monthly basis and order prints that you want. Refresh photos on display once a year.

Once you have your children's belongings organized, you can help organize their spaces. In Part VI we will address your child's backpack, desk, locker, and bedroom.

Part VI: Conquer the Space Invaders

WHEN CHILDREN PLAY HOUSE they are making little spaces that mimic grown-up ones: little offices, little kitchens, little tool benches. As your children start to need their own space, you can help them create functional areas at school and home: space to create, space to learn and study, and space to relax. Creating a functional space for your child helps to set her up for success and make it easier for her to focus on tasks at hand.

A certain amount of chaos and clutter is inevitable when you have school-aged children. But once you have what you need in the right place, and you have a system for keeping schoolwork flowing from home to school and back again, you will be able to conquer those space invaders.

> "The greatest gifts you can give your children are the roots of responsibility and the wings of independence."
>
> —DENIS WAITLEY, PRODUCTIVITY CONSULTANT

34. Schoolbags & Paperwork: Pack 'em Up & Move 'em Out!

THE PROBLEM

Your child's schoolbag is really her vehicle for transporting items to and from school. The problems occur when your child begins to use this vehicle as a permanent home for everything from papers to cosmetics. Everything seems to go in, but nothing comes out! The bag gets messy and heavy. When the backpack becomes overloaded, physical problems can occur for your child. I thought the great solution for heavy backpacks was the rolling backpack, but my children thought differently. "They're not cool, Mom," I was told. Even though you will find rolling suitcases a big hit in the corporate and travel industries, the majority of students I see are sticking with the backpack.

THE STORY

Last spring, my son's school held its annual Field Day. I signed up about a month before to help out. As the date got closer, I asked my son if he had received any papers for me that would give me my assignment. He told me no. When the date got even closer, the Field Day was actually postponed from a Friday to a Monday because of rain. Still no note from school, so I assumed they had enough volunteers and didn't need me. A few days later I was putting something in my son's backpack and I noticed some papers crumpled at the bottom. One was an envelope with a permission slip and a check and the other was my Field Day assignment sheet! Now, my son usually does his homework on his own and we had no reason to micromanage his backpack with regard to schoolwork. However, he obviously needed some supervision when it came to parent–teacher communications.

THE SOLUTION

The solution to an unorganized or dysfunctional backpack depends on the root cause of the problem. So ask your child these questions:

1. Is your schoolbag too heavy?
2. Is it difficult for you to remember to bring home your homework?
3. Are you forgetting to turn in your homework?
4. Can you find what you need in your schoolbag?

All of these are common problems for school-aged children. If you believe your child's backpack is unorganized, then identify the problem before you take a look at the following solutions. It may just be that the bag is messy, but if your child does her homework, turns it in on time, and always has the books and papers she needs at home and at school, there may be no problem at all.

Absolute of Organizing Your Family: If it isn't broken, don't fix it. In other words, focus on what's not working.

Too Heavy

If you are concerned about your child's backpack being too heavy, then weigh it. Show her exactly how much she is lugging around. Then ask your child, "What do you need to bring back and forth every day?" There are different types of things such as: schoolwork, lunch, personal items, and after-school paraphernalia. Start by taking everything out of the backpack and sorting it into those categories. You can use my CPR organizing process (see pages 190 and 246) to begin organizing a full backpack. First, categorize the contents. Then purge, which means throw out the trash and remove any items that don't belong in the backpack. Finally, rearrange or get things back to where they belong. Put schoolwork in the largest compartment of the backpack. Important items like money, keys, and ID cards should go in a smaller zippered compartment inside the backpack. If your child likes to carry a water bottle in school, use the outside mesh pockets on the side of the backpack.

Important items like money, keys, and ID cards should go in a smaller zippered compartment inside the backpack.

Even after cleaning out and rearranging the contents of your child's backpack, it might still be overloaded. Try to identify the heaviest or bulkiest item. If it is a large binder or accordion folder that is meant to

Backpack

Small Compartment
Keys, money, ID card

Big Compartment
Books, folders, binders, lunch, assignment pad

Water bottle

Outside Pocket
Extra pens, pencils, cell phone

Make sure you are not enabling your child's forgetfulness by constantly going back to school or borrowing a book from a neighbor.

hold everything so the child doesn't forget, ask the teacher if you can keep some papers at school or at home. In general, a good system to have is to keep school papers in the designated binder or folder until it is test time. After the test, you should be able to clean out the papers and put them in a file at home (see Chapter 36 for ideas on how to file the papers). That way the only papers that are traveling back and forth are for the current topic in each of your child's classes.

If textbooks are the problem, find out if the books can be supplied on a disk or if pages can be copied and sent home. Some schools may be able to give you an extra textbook to keep at home as well as the one your child uses in school. There are many options out there for teachers, sometimes they may just need to hear the suggestion from a concerned parent.

Not Remembering to Bring Work Home

If your child often forgets a crucial piece of homework, ask her about her end-of-the-day routine at school. Get a sense of what is happening. How much time does she have to pack up? What does the assignment book look like? When and how does she write down assignments? Are there too many folders and notebooks to sort through? If necessary, talk to your child's teacher about adapting the end-of-the-day routine to benefit your child. Or ask if you can just use one folder to be the "take home" folder with one side marked "take home" and the other side marked "back to school." This is the typical system used for younger children. In my first grader's class, they give every child a red folder. Red stands for "hot" or "action" so they know they have to do something with that folder every day. As your child gets older, their middle school may use an accordion filing system for all subjects, or ask you to have multiple folders with one for each subject. If that is not working for your child, let the teachers know. Every child thinks and remembers differently, so find out what is best for your child. Sometimes all you have to do is ask, "What would make it easier for you to remember your homework?" Also, make sure you are not enabling her by constantly going back to school or borrowing a book from a neighbor. This is fine once in a while, but if you make it a habit, your child has no incentive to remember.

> Absolute of Organizing Your Family: Don't be afraid to talk to
> your child's teacher or principal about organizational help.

Not Remembering to Take Work Back to School

If your child has no problem bringing the work home, and does her homework but just doesn't turn it in on time, then you have to look at the routine or process for doing homework and packing up the schoolbag each night. Typically parents are involved with younger children who are doing homework, but as the children get older, we may assume they are finishing their work and putting it back in folders in their schoolbags on their own. At the first indication that homework is incomplete or not turned in on time, you may want to oversee the homework process even for your middle school and high school students.

It all starts with the assignment book. Take a look and make sure everything is written down. If it helps your child, suggest that she check off items as she completes each homework assignment. She may even want to take the books out of her school-bag all at once, and then return them to the bag after the work is complete. That way, when the desk or table is clear, you know she's finished. Have your child put all papers in a folder or binder; this will prevent the assignments from getting crumpled at the bottom of her schoolbag.

To help your child remember long-term assignments, plan interim dates in their month-at-a-glance calendar and write them in their weekly assignment book.

Long-term assignments are a bit of a different story. Sometimes it's actually easier for kids to remember the daily assignments and to miss the big ones that they have had a month or more to complete. As described in Chapter 23, you can help your child plan out their big projects using a month-at-a-glance calendar. The trick is to put the interim dates in the daily planner or assignment book, as well. If the child's assignment book has dates this is easy to do ahead of time. But if she simply writes in a blank notebook, she will need to consult her monthly calendar each night before she starts her homework. For example, in addition to her Tuesday night homework, she may need to type up her outline for a research project that's due in a couple weeks. It's important to help children set these deadlines for themselves so you are not cramming it all in the night before a project is due.

Can't Find What You Need

If the problem your child has with her schoolbag is finding what she needs in it, then you need to dig a little deeper and fine tune the organizing process within the schoolbag. I find that different teachers require different organizing systems. A few of the methods I have seen are:

1. *One homework folder.* Often used for elementary school children, this is the simplest way to get papers from point A to point B. One side says "take home" and one says "back to school." All homework papers and tests go in this folder.

2. *Color-coded folders and notebooks for each class.* These are sometimes used in elementary school, and children may choose to do this for themselves in the older grades. Color coding is an easy visual way for students to keep notebooks and folders together for each subject: for example, a blue copybook and blue folder for math. This system works well if your child is changing classes often (as in middle and high school). When going to her locker she can see quickly which folders and notebooks she needs to grab. It's also a good idea to keep the notebook and folder with the textbook for that class.

Communication Envelopes

We all know that in addition to all your child's homework and class papers there is a large amount of communication that comes home from school on paper. This includes fliers about upcoming events, permission slips for field trips, fundraiser information, and lunch schedules. To lessen the student's paper overload, many schools have adopted a communication envelope system. If your school has not done this yet, you might want to suggest it at your next parent–teacher meeting. Here's how it works:

- The school designates one day a week (or every other week) when the envelopes will come home.
- One envelope is assigned per family and all the fliers and forms that need to go home get stuffed into that envelope by parent volunteers.
- The envelope used is the "interoffice" style, which has a place for signatures and dates. When the parents receive the envelope, they empty it, sign and date it, and return any necessary forms in that envelope, which goes back to school.

To save even more paper, some schools do this via e-mail. That way each family can determine whether they need to print out a form or flier on their own.

As a parent, I treat the communications envelope just like I would mail coming in each day. It all gets sorted into piles: To Do, To Read, To File, and Recycle.

3. *Accordion file for all subjects.* I've seen teachers ask students to use this method in the older grades, like seventh and eighth. It works well if they have a large amount of handouts, and if students are expected to take this back and forth each day, they are less likely to forget a paper. However, the danger here is that the folder will get too heavy, and it's hard to find a particular paper for a subject by the end the year. These need to be cleaned out on a regular basis. The teacher can help you determine if it is best to clean after each test, or after each grading period. The older papers can be kept at home in a file if there will be a need to reference them for end-of-the-year exams.

4. *One binder for all subjects.* Like the accordion file, this is a catchall way to keep all papers together. However, unless students have a three-hole punch ready at home or school, there is even more of a chance that they will forget to file the papers. Binders also increase the chance that papers will get torn out and lost. This is not my favorite option for students, but some children and schools do like it. The good point about large binders is that notebooks can also be kept in them and many binders now have zippered closures, handles, and side pockets like a folder has.

5. *A binder for each subject.* This method is more common in the older grades. You can categorize the papers within the binder as such: homework, notes, tests and related articles. Keep the most recent in the front of each tabbed section. When the binder gets too full or heavy, ask your child or her teacher if some older papers (from the last test period or grading period) can be purged, and keep those at home in a file.

Decide with your child which system works best for her. If it is not the system the teacher has decided on, talk with the teacher about adapting it in an effort to help your child spend more time completing homework and less time looking for it.

If you are trying to get organized along with your child, this may be a good time to examine your own pocketbook or work briefcase. Identify if you have a problem, try a new system, and then maintain that system on a daily or weekly basis.

ORGANIZING THE PAPERWORK ON YOUR END

Whether or not your children's school uses communications envelopes, you'll still have to organize the papers you need to see and sign. As I said in the sidebar on page 331, I treat school information just like I would mail coming in each day. I sort it into four piles:

- *To Do*: This would include forms that need to be filled out, fundraiser material, money that needs to be sent in, calls that need to be made for volunteers, and dates that need to be written on the family calendar. If I cannot do these action items right away, this pile will go on my desk.
- *To Read*: This would include newsletters, policy updates, and community or school event fliers. Once I read them, they will move to another pile. If I can't read these right away, they get moved to my reading chair.
- *To File:* This would include lunch calendars, phone lists, class lists, handbooks, yearly calendars, Web site instructions, and any information you might have to reference throughout the year. I file these immediately in a file marked "school information," and I have one for each school.
- *Recycle:* This includes any fliers for events or programs that I am not interested in, and anything that I already have marked on my calendar.

Set aside a place in your home for your To Do, To Read, and To File piles. Mark the To Do items in your calendar immediately so you don't forget, or if you have time, complete the task right away. Likewise, do your filing and reading immediately, or set these piles in a spot for later. A good time to go through these things is during homework time.

THREE STEPS TO AN ORGANIZED SCHOOLBAG

1. Keep it light with only essential items needed at both home and school.
2. Help your child develop a routine for loading up the schoolbag each afternoon using her assignment pad. Create another routine at home for putting all her homework and necessary forms back in the bag.
3. Decide which filing system works best for your child: one homework folder, a binder or an accordion file, or separate folders for each subject.

35. No More Chutes & Ladders. Now It's Desks & Lockers

THE PROBLEM

The harsh reality is our school-aged children are away from us most of the day. When they were at home, their time was spent playing games, taking naps, reading for fun, and watching TV. But now that they are students, they've got responsibilities. They also have their own spaces outside the home that need to be at least somewhat organized and functional. And they've got to do it on their own! One of the problems I see is that desks in elementary schools are flat and small. In the older grades, lockers are tall and skinny, and students only have a few minutes between classes to grab what they need. So if your child has to tear his locker apart each time he changes classes, he's going to be late. As parents, we have to let go, but we can start our children off with some pointers on how to keep their desks and lockers organized enough to be functional.

THE STORY

Girls and boys certainly view their lockers differently. In my children's school district, the students' first experiences with having lockers occur in middle school. I asked a few students how their lockers were working out for them during that first semester of sixth grade. As expected, the tricky part seemed to be getting the lock open and figuring out when they could stop at their lockers to switch books. I also noticed that the girls took great pride in their lockers. "I put in a mirror, some pictures of Justin Bieber, a whiteboard, and an extra hook for my lunch bag," one girl described. "It's hard to fit everything in," a boy responded. That same boy actually had to ask a teacher for help in extracting some bags from his locker after it had become so packed with books, gym bags, and sweatshirts that he couldn't pull anything out!

The best time to get a desk or locker organized is right at the beginning of the school year.

THE SOLUTION

The best time to get a desk or locker organized is right at the beginning of the school year. Here are a few questions and suggestions you can discuss with your child about how to maintain an organized desk and/or locker.

Questions to Ask Your Child During the First Week of School

- How big is your desk?
- What does your teacher expect you to keep in the desk?
- How big is your locker?
- How many sections does your locker have?
- What does your teacher expect you to keep in there?
- When can you go to your locker?
- How much time do you have to switch books between classes?
- When do you pass by your locker?

Answers to these questions will give you an idea of how your child has to organize his things while in school. If you have never been inside your child's school, you may want him to draw you a picture of the desk or locker so you really

Have a Plan for Locker Organizers

WHEN SETTING UP A LOCKER for the first time, let your child use the locker for a week in order to find out what he really needs to help him stay organized there. As with any organizing project, you don't want to make the mistake of buying the containers or accessories first and then trying to make them work in your space. Decide what you need first, then go shopping. Most home stores will have locker accessories on sale in August and September for back-to-school shopping. Here are a few Web sites that carry excellent locker accessories:

- www.organizeit.com has adjustable double shelves that you can place on the bottom of lockers to add extra shelves.
- www.stacksandstacks.com has hanging pockets made of fabric if your kids prefer that type of organizer.
- www.containerstore.com has magnetic mesh bins for small items if your child has a metal locker.

understand how much space he has to work with. Or find a day when you can go into school and actually see the locker or desk with your child.

Suggestions to Give Your Child During the First Week of School

- Take your daily schedule of classes and arrange your books in that order.
- In your desk or locker, make sure the binding of your textbook is showing so you can easily read the subject.

School Locker

Lunch box

Hooks for backpack, jacket, and gym bag

Mirror

Class schedule

Dry erase board (for quick reminders to yourself)

Books lined up in order of your classes

- Keep folders, notebooks, and textbooks for each subject together.
- Clean out your desk and/or locker every Friday.

Troubleshooting When Your Child Can't Find or Remember Items at School

Once you give your child suggestions on how to set up his locker and desk, you have to let it go. See how things are working for a while. If your student is keeping up with assignments and remembering what to bring to class and what to bring home, then you have no problem. However, if your child or your child's teacher gives you an indication that there is a problem with organization, you can offer some suggestions. Benjamin Franklin's adage "a place for everything and everything in its place" is a good rule of thumb. Help your child find a place for everything in his locker or desk.

Benjamin Franklin's adage "a place for everything and everything in its place" is a good rule of thumb. Help your child find a place for everything in his locker or desk.

Lockers. Here are some tweaks you can do to a standard locker to make it more accommodating:

- Put after-school gear in a drawstring bag to hang from a hook.
- For additional hooks, try strong magnetic hooks made for metal lockers.
- If books are falling from a high shelf, consider using the bottom of the locker. Use a store-bought "add-a-shelf" wire rack to add a level if necessary.
- Post the class schedule on the door to the locker.
- Hang a small whiteboard on the door for quick reminder notes.
- Lots of loose items causing clutter? Consolidate pens, pencils, and crayons in a box or pencil case. For girls, personal items can be placed in a cosmetic bag.
- Lunch getting squished? Put it on the highest shelf or hang it from a hook if the lunch bag has a handle.

Organizing a Desk

I KNOW A TEACHER who works with kindergarten-age children who have special learning needs. She has her students use a color-coded system to organize their desks. At the beginning of the year she tells her students what items will be kept in their desks. Each item is assigned a color, and the teacher gives each student colored stickers to put on their items. They place corresponding stickers inside the desk so the children can match up the colors to know what goes where. Desk styles vary by school, and this school uses desks that flip open from the top so the dots are easily seen. If some students are still confused, the teacher has each student place a stop sign that reads, "Stop! Where does this belong?" in the middle of the desk. This is a visual reminder for the children to keep up with the system. This is a very structured method and most children won't need this much direction, but it is a great solution for children who need structure and systems to follow.

Once your child's locker has all the necessities in place, you can allow him to put up any personal decorations that make the locker more "homey."

Desks. Desks are usually the main storage spaces for elementary school children, so they can become overloaded or cluttered pretty easily. Here are some tips to share with your younger children on how to keep a neat and organized desk:

- Keep one pencil and eraser on top of the desk. All others belong in a pencil case or box inside the desk.

- Pile your books, folders, and notebooks in order of your classes inside the desk.
- If you cannot see all the way inside your desk, put accessories in the same spot every time so you can easily find them. For example, ruler on the left, crayons on the right.
- Never put loose papers in the desk. Always put them in a folder.

Ways Parents Can Check Up

If you have helped your child set up his locker and desk and you still believe there might be a problem, there are creative ways to sneak a peek at what's happening. If you are volunteering at school during the day, you can pop in your child's classroom when the kids are at lunch and the teacher is in the room. You can also do this during a parent–teacher meeting if the classrooms are open. If you do not often get to your child's school (which is typically when your kids are in middle or high school), offer to pick him up and meet at his locker. If he needs to bring in a

School Desk

Notebook, text book, folder for one or two subjects

Pencil case or box

Eraser

Homework assignment pad and pencil or pen

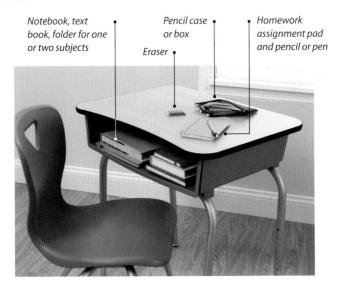

huge project for school you can offer to take him in the morning. No need to be completely sneaky about the reason. In fact, you might offer before the holiday break to help your student clean out his locker or desk. Use these methods only if you have evidence that there is a problem—such as a note from a teacher or continually missing assignments. Don't check in just to be nosy or to make sure the children follow your level of organization. Remember, even if it looks messy to you, there is no problem if your child is able to find what he needs and bring the appropriate items to class.

Absolute of Organizing Your Family: If it isn't broken, don't fix it. In other words, focus on what's not working.

Routines

Remember that routines not only bring comfort, they also lessen the chances that things will be forgotten. In elementary school the teachers are usually good at teaching the children routines for the school day. Ask your child about the routines he goes through when he first arrives at school and when he's getting ready to leave at the end of the school day. Because you know your child better than the teacher, you should know whether these classroom routines will work for him or not. If not, you can always make suggestions to improve the routine and make it custom fit for your child so he can succeed at school.

In addition to the classroom routines, you might also suggest to your child that he clean out his desk and locker every Friday while packing up to come home. By cleaning out any trash, tucking any loose papers in binders or folders, and bringing home any lunch items, extra coats, hats, and umbrellas on the weekend, your child can have

Only check up on your child's locker if you have evidence that there is a problem—such as a note from a teacher or continually missing assignments.

a fresh start every Monday and have the clothing items and accessories he needs for the weekend. Remind your older children to mark this clean-out time in their schedules so they remember to do it.

If you, as a parent, have spaces that are overcrowded or cluttered at home (such as your desktop or kitchen counter), Friday is a good time for you to clean up those surfaces as well. Use my CPR method (see pages 190 and 246) to show your child a good example.

THREE STEPS TO ORGANIZED DESKS AND LOCKERS

1. Set up your school books in the order of your class schedule.
2. Decide on a place for everything and then stick to the system.
3. Clean out desks and lockers every Friday, so that parents will only have to step in if there is a problem with lost items or forgotten assignments.

36. Set Up a Home Office for Your Student

THE PROBLEM

Children need different kinds of environments to help them focus on homework. Some need quiet and solitude; others need parental supervision. Some children like to spread books and papers out, others do fine with just a small area in which to work. Often the ideal homework conditions seem impossible to attain in a small home or a busy household. And even if you have a pretty good system going now, things may change as your children progress from grade school to middle school to high school. So if your child has a hard time focusing on homework, or is reluctant to get started on it, what can you do to help her?

THE STORY

Growing up in a small house with six kids and two parents, I found it almost impossible to find a quiet area to do my homework during grade school and high school. I remember doing a lot of projects lying on my bed in the room I shared with three sisters. This literally was the only space I had to myself. Other times I would wait in line for the family typewriter and type up my reports at the kitchen table late at night. Conditions were less than optimal, let's say, but all in all I was able to

Set your children up for success in their schoolwork by setting up a homework area that meets their needs as best as you can.

maintain a good grade point average and I always handed assignments and homework in on time. It was at that time of my life when I had to develop my own organizational style to keep up with my school work.

When I went away to college I thought I had achieved homework nirvana. I only had to share the room with one other person and we each had our own built-in desk and shelf at the entrance to our dorm room. For graduation I had received a typewriter, so no more waiting in line for me! I was living large. I quickly turned my study cubby into a functioning office. I had my textbooks on a shelf and my school supplies either on my desk or in a milk crate below it. There was plenty of tabletop space to spread out and I used the "left-to-right" system. Homework to be done was placed on my left, and as I completed it, I stacked it to my right.

THE SOLUTION

In the story above, it was only after I had the space to set up an office in my dorm room that I felt I had a functional homework area. In fact, one of the motivations for me to move away to college was the homework factor. I couldn't imagine how I could focus on college-level work in a crowded, busy, and noisy household. I was a student who needed quiet and my own space to do my best. As parents, you can help your children now by understanding their needs and setting up a homework area that meets those needs as best you can. By doing so, you will be setting them up for success in their schoolwork.

Define the Needs

To begin setting up the optimal homework environment for your children, first you have to define their needs. This can be done by asking questions and observing what they are doing now. For example, with regard to the area in your home where they like to do homework, is it a quiet, solitary space? Or do they like to be in the main living area of the house with parental supervision and interaction? If you're not sure, have your child try a week in each type of location and see what goes better. How about noise level? Do they need absolute quiet or can they easily tune out other people talking or the television? Again, if you and your child are not sure, try a week doing homework in quiet and another week with moderate background noise. See in which environment your child is better able to focus.

Once you know a little about the environment your child prefers for homework, how about the physical items she needs? Here are a few suggested items that students may need, depending on their grade level, and their school:

- Computer, printer
- Calculator
- Dictionary
- Thesaurus
- Loose-leaf paper
- Markers
- Crayons
- Old magazines
- Large calendar
- Scissors
- Tape, glue stick
- Stapler
- Three-hole punch
- Pens, pencils, and erasers
- Pencil sharpener
- Assignment book

Find out what your child or children need and then accumulate all those items in one place. This will give you an idea about what type of storage you need in the designated homework area.

Define the Space

Now that you have a good idea about what your student needs, you, the parent, can decide what room in your house works best to fit those needs. Is it the kitchen, the dining room, the child's bedroom, a spare room, or a portion of the family room? These are all possible areas that can be set up for homework. All you need is a table or desk and an area to store the other materials that your child needs to do her homework. If you are using a common area of the house, it doesn't always have to look like a school desk. You can be creative about where you store your

Kitchen Desk

Dictionary,
thesaurus

Arts and craft
supplies

Calendar

Wall organizer
for project in-
structions. One
pocket per child

Old magazines

Pens, pencils,
scissors, stapler

Tape, glue,
ruler, paper

supplies. It's a good idea to ask your child to clean up the homework area when she is finished with the work for that night. Here are some specific ideas about ways to set up a home office for your student:

Kitchen or Dining Room. Most families have a table for eating in either the kitchen or dining room, so this may be the simplest place for children to do their homework, especially when they are younger. If they do their homework after school, this area is ideal because a parent can make dinner and supervise at the same time. If you are lucky, you might have an extra cabinet or drawer for storing homework supplies right in the kitchen. If not, you can either put up a shelf on the wall, or have a basket or bin on the counter for these items. Another option is a cupboard in the dining room or a small bookshelf in an adjacent room for storing all the homework supplies. The key is to have the supplies all together, accessible to the children, and in a place where they can be put away once the homework is finished so they don't clutter up your eating space.

Family or Living Room. You may choose to stay away from the eating areas in your home if you have the space for a desk or table in your family room. This would keep the children in the main living area of the home but give them their own desk to keep set up for homework. The desk doesn't have to be anything fancy. Actually, a small desk or table with a few drawers is perfect. You can put supplies and extra paper in the drawers and a small bookshelf on the wall to hold any reference books. If your desk does not have drawers, you can purchase a set of plastic drawers at any home store and slide it under the table and out of sight. Just make sure all your supplies will fit before you buy the drawers.

The kitchen is ideal for younger children because the parent can supervise the homework while making dinner.

If your child needs a calendar, place one on the desktop or hang one above the desk. If you have a computer on this desk, make sure there is still room to write and have a separate table or shelf to hold the printer.

Living Room and Bedroom Desk

Dictionary, thesaurus

Tape, glue stick, stapler, three-hole punch

Pens, pencils, highlighters

Bulletin board for calendar and other reminders

Notepads, sticky notes, software discs

Current files of tests, reports, projects, extra school supplies

Photo courtesy of The Container Store

Your Child's Bedroom. The same setup that was used in the family room can be used in your child's bedroom. If your child needs a desk, I recommend getting an older desk from a secondhand shop. These usually have a narrow drawer for pencils and pens, at least one small drawer for papers or books, and one file drawer that you can use for hanging files or for holding school work and artwork that comes home throughout the year. If you use it as holding place, at the end of the school year, clean it out and only keep the memorable pieces. Some pros to having the homework done in the bedroom are that your child could be more comfortable with a bed or chair for studying and reading, and it is a quiet area. Also with this setup, your child takes on the responsibility of keeping this area clear and functional.

Spare Room. If you have a spare room in your house, it can be a great place for the student who needs quiet and fewer distractions in order to concentrate. It is also ideal if your older student needs a computer for her homework because you can set it all up in one room: the desktop space to write, the shelves or drawers for storing supplies, and the computer and printer tables for doing research and typing up reports. You can probably get all this in a small area of the room and still have space for a single bed, a lamp and a chair to make this a guest room as well. It's also ideal if your child needs to leave some papers hanging around for long-term projects or weekly assignments. These can be placed in a wall bin or in a two-pocket folder that is kept on the desk. You may also have the wall space in this room for a bulletin board or calendar to be used for visual reminders about schoolwork.

If your child does her homework in her bedroom, make her responsible for keeping the area clear and functional.

No matter what room you decide is best, make sure there are limited distractions for your child and optimal lighting.

DEFINE THE SYSTEM

Now that you have defined what your child needs and set up a little area for homework in some room in your home, you'll want to discuss the homework-area system with your child.

The system is basically how your child or children are to use the homework area and how they are to maintain it. If you have multiple children using the same area, each child needs to be respectful of the other children. In some cases, you may have to make a time schedule for when each child gets to use the computer or writing area. This shouldn't be too rigid, but it may just be that one child uses the computer after school, and the other uses it after dinner. Or if you have younger children who play while the older ones do homework, you may have to direct them to another room. Another part of maintaining the homework area is keeping up with all those papers that fly back and forth between school and home.

> *If you have multiple children using the same area, you may need to make a time schedule for the area.*

Paper Filing System

Teachers in elementary school are usually very clear about which papers can go home and which need to come back to school. Students themselves should know by the time they reach middle school and high school what can stay home and what needs to stay in their schoolbags. As a parent, it's a good idea for you to help your child develop a system at home for papers she wants to keep. In order to do this, you'll need to consider the Who? What? Where? When? Why? and How? of filing school papers.

Who (as in who files the papers): Parents can direct and let the child do the actual filing. This teaches your child good organizational skills and helps her remember where things are.

What (as in what papers to keep): I recommend keeping all graded papers that the teacher sends home. That would include quizzes, tests, and projects. If you are seeing a trend with your child getting things marked wrong on classwork or homework, you should also save those papers. These can be used as study guides for future tests, to mark a trend, or to seek help from the teacher. If everything is fine with ungraded classwork and homework, look at it, then recycle it. In the younger grades, children may be bringing home a few pages

Assign your children the responsibility of filing their graded tests, reports, and projects.

of classwork each day. It's unrealistic and usually unnecessary to save every one.

Where (as in where to keep the papers): If your child has her own desk with a filing drawer, create hanging folders for each subject she has this year. If you do not have a file drawer, use a milk crate (preferably with wheels) that can be kept in the homework area. If you have an especially interesting classwork page, or a great test grade your child is proud of, you can treat it like artwork and post it on the refrigerator for a while, then file it.

When: Filing of school papers can be done on a daily basis. If you have already spoken with the teacher about when your student can clear out her binder or accordion folder—after a unit test or after a grading period, for example—that is another time to file. This will help lighten the load in your child's backpack.

Why: Saving graded papers is especially helpful if your child takes a final exam at the end of the year because the tests from each chapter or unit can serve as a study guide. If you have a question about your child's grade on a report card, these paper files can also be used to support the grade she deserves.

How: To set up the filing drawer or box in the beginning of the school year, keep it simple: one folder for each subject. Only subdivide into "Classwork" and "Tests" if the file gets too full. Have your child clearly label each hanging file. If she likes to color code, use a different color for each subject. Let your child arrange the files however she wants. Alphabetical may seem logical to you, but she may want to organize in the order of her class schedule. As your child is doing homework you can quickly flip through the papers that have come home that night.

Sign any tests that need to go back to school, and sort papers that are coming home based on the criteria on pages 352–353 (what to file). Make two piles: Recycle and File. Let your child take care of the piles after she finishes her homework for the day. At the end of the school year, go through all the papers with your child and only keep a few memorable projects for the memory box (see Chapter 31).

If your child's needs change or there is a change in your household, go back to step one and reconsider your homework setup.

Computer Filing System

Although I didn't use a typewriter until high school, today most children will be using a computer as early as elementary school. You'll want to help them save some of their projects on the computer (at least temporarily), so let's talk about an electronic method of filing. First of all, each child in your household should have his or her own folder on the computer system. Within that folder, you can set up subfolders named by the subject and year, and then leave each individual report or paper as a document.

For example:

Mary (folder)

Science 2013-2014 (subfolder)

Recycling (document)

Maintenance

Like the files in your file drawer, computer files can be deleted at the end of the school year, unless you have a reason to save a report for a younger sibling. Make sure each child knows where her files are, both on the computer and in the homework area. Show them where they can find materials such as the dictionary, paper, and art supplies. And make it a rule that all these materials go back to the correct container, drawer, or bin each night. By keeping up with organization on a daily basis, the children can prevent clutter from accumulating and items from getting lost. Use this system until it stops working. If your child's needs change, or there is a change in your household, go back to step one and reconsider your homework setup.

THREE STEPS TO SETTING UP A HOME OFFICE FOR YOUR STUDENT
1. Define your child's needs.
2. Designate the room and set it up.
3. Discuss a system for doing homework, filing papers, and keeping the area organized.

37. A Room of Their Own—Simple and Cozy

THE PROBLEM

Many parents I speak to complain about their children's bedrooms as the worst rooms in the house. When I ask why, I get a multitude of reasons: The room is too small; everything is shoved in the closet; he never picks up his clothes; he keeps stepping over stacks of things on the floor. Ultimately, the parent is not in control of the child's bedroom, especially once the child becomes a preteen or teenager. After all, we have to give them some privacy and some responsibility. To deal with the messy bedroom, some parents choose avoidance. They simply close the door and don't look in. Well, that's one approach. Another is to help your child identify problem areas in his bedroom, design a room that is set up for his comfort and efficiency, insist that he straighten his room on a regular basis, and then let him be. Now which approach sounds like that of an organized parent?

THE STORY

If you think that it's easier to be organized when you have one child with his own bedroom and bathroom, think again. Sometimes too much space is a problem. One of my fellow professional organizers in NAPO, Diane Albright of All Bright

Ideas, relayed a story to me about one of her young clients. Diane had been called in to organize a girl whose mother had just ordered new furniture to accommodate her daughter's growing wardrobe. Not surprising, because we all know how teenage girls love clothing. But as Diane started to pull out the clothes and sort them, she and the client were in for a big shock. Hiding in the recesses of this girl's current dressers were forty-five tank tops, 150 T-shirts, plus numerous pairs of jeans and sweaters. When they entered the bathroom to do the same sorting technique, they found thirty bottles of shampoo! The only reason this mother-daughter duo had reached this point was that when the daughter needed something, they simply purchased it instead of searching through what she already had to find what she needed. Obviously new furniture was not the answer. Instead they needed to purge the excess and arrange it so this over-buying wouldn't happen again.

Organizing your child's room is a great Saturday morning project that can take anywhere from two to six hours.

Another organizer, Sanka Coyle of reSolutions Organizing & Design, relayed to me a story about one wealthy family who had so many extra rooms in the house that they allowed their child to move into a guest room if her bedroom got too crowded and cluttered! The organizer was called in when the family finally ran out of open bedrooms.

THE SOLUTION

If your child's bedroom has reached a stage of critical mass, meaning it's just so cluttered that neither one of you knows where to start, take some time to overhaul this room using my CPR process (see pages 190 and 246). This is a great Saturday morning project that can take anywhere from two to six hours depending on the size of the room and the amount of stuff in it. Plan for this project by choosing the day and time with your child. Have your spouse or someone else occupy the other children if you have them. Look at this project as an opportunity for some one-on-

one time with your son or daughter. On the day you choose to organize, make sure you have trash bags or boxes handy. Put on some music that your child likes, have snacks and drinks at the ready, and then get down to business.

Set Your Goals

Make sure the goals for this project are clear to your child. You are not just cleaning his room. At the end of your Saturday organizing session you should have:

1. Purged old things he really doesn't want or use.
2. Moved other people's items out of the room.
3. Identified the functions of the child's bedroom.
4. Rearranged the room to maximize comfort and to support its functions.
5. Identified some new things that he may need to add to the room to make it easier to stay organized.

Categorize

To get started, you are going to need some room to work. So if floor space is limited, look for any large items that you would like out of the room and move them first. Then you can begin to categorize. Pick a corner of the room. (It's best to pick the worst corner.) Start taking everything off shelves, dressers, and walls. Keep like things together as you make piles on the floor or bed. Think in big categories first and don't get caught up spending a lot of time on little items found in a junk drawer or in desk drawers.

Purge

As you categorize, you may want to purge simultaneously. Purged items can fall into several categories themselves, for instance:

- Trash: anything broken and unusable
- Recycle: papers, plastics, glass
- Donate: anything you don't use or want anymore
- Move out: items that belong in another room of the house or items that need to be returned to someone else

Make sure each of these categories is clearly labeled so you don't have to guess which pile is which. Once all the items in the room have been categorized, have your child take a look at the piles and ask himself, "Do I have too much of one thing?" and "How much do I really need?" Then purge some more from those categories. If he is having trouble deciding what to keep and what to purge, use the "fire" rule.

Absolute of Organizing Your Family: To prioritize, use the "fire" rule. Ask your child, "If there were a fire, what five things would you want to save?"

Another way to get past a sticking point in the purging stage is to ask your child what he would like to keep. In my example story, the organizer asked her client to choose her favorite fifty of the 150 T-shirts instead of asking her to part with 100. If you find that clothes are the biggest problem, you may want to save that project for another day. Get them into the closet or dresser, and if there is overflow, put those clothes in a box. After dealing with all the other items in the room, you can tackle the clothing. Refer to Chapter 28 for this project.

If your child is having trouble purging items, ask him what he would like to keep as opposed to what he wants to get rid of.

Rearrange

The final step of my CPR process is rearrange. This is the step where you can plan out your bedroom just like an interior designer. Think about the function of your child's bedroom, how he really uses it now, and how he might like to use it in the future. If you want to get creative, you can make a paper model of the room. I use a simple method of measuring the room and converting feet to inches. So I draw a room that is 10' × 15' on a piece of paper that is 10" × 15". On that sheet of paper, mark where the doors and windows are. Now, measure all the big furniture and use the same scale to cut out shapes of colored paper to represent the furniture. Next you can plan out the arrangement of your room.

To make a plan, use my Space Planning Worksheet on page 371.

Decide on the function. The first thing you and your child need to decide on is the function of the room. Obviously, the bedroom is used for sleeping. However your child might have additional functions in mind. Some of these might be: reading, doing homework, practicing hobbies (like music, art, building models), playing with toys, watching TV, or using video games. When you are discussing this with your child, make sure you limit the functions to three, or else the room may become too cluttered. Then you need to make sure all the items in the room support those functions, nothing more, nothing less.

Absolute of Organizing Your Family: Give your children a few options that you can live with, and let them choose.

Define what's working and what's not. Following the Space Planning Worksheet, write down what you like about the room. In your rearranging step, make sure you don't change the good things.

What don't you like? That's where you focus. Can your problems with the room be fixed by moving some things out of the room or into the room? I recommend moving things out first.

Arranging a Young Child's Room

When arranging a bedroom for your preschooler or elementary schooler, think simplicity. The more you have going on in there, the more likely it is to get disorganized. Have one container for toys if you want your child to play in his room. Likewise, have one bookshelf for storing books. With a tall bookshelf, you can use the top for display items and the bottom for items that your child wants access to. A beanbag chair is nice if he wants to sit on the floor to read or play. A desk is a good idea if you want your child to be able to write or draw in his room. The drawers in the desk are also a good place to keep supplies and completed

Example Bedroom Layout for Elementary School Children

Shelves

Display

Toys

Framed art

Window

Tall book-shelf for books and favorite toys

Bulletin board

Dresser

Desk

Beanbag chair

Trash can

Closet

Door

Mirror

Nightstand with book shelf

Bed

drawings. Don't forget wall space, too. You can hang up artwork in clear plastic frames, which make it easy to update and change pictures. You could also hang a bulletin board above the desk so your child can post pictures or a calendar. If you have a lot of knickknacks that your child wants to display, small display shelves work well. You can always change what is displayed from time to time to give the room a little face-lift.

Arranging a Preteen or Teenager's Room

When your children get older, their bedrooms become more of a retreat for them. Therefore, the room may have to serve different functions and may require more stuff. Start with the basics: a bed, a dresser, a desk, and a bookshelf, and then see how much space you have for additional items. If you like, you can set up a little entertainment center with a TV, stereo, video game console, and bean-bag chair. If you have the space for a second dresser or armoire, the second one can be used for out-of-season clothing or clothing to grow into. Putting the dressers and a mirror near the closet creates a little dressing zone. At this age, your child also may have more items they consider memorabilia. I think steamer trunks are ideal for storing these items. When the trunk is out in the room, it's easy to place items in it, and it can serve as an extra table or bench. If you don't have the room to leave it out, you can tuck it under a bed or in a closet. The desk,

In his room, your teenager may need a drop zone where he can put his jacket, hat, and sports bags when he gets home from school.

bookshelf, and bulletin board go together to create the homework zone. Finally, you may need a "drop zone." The older they get, the more stuff they need to drop when they come home from school. I like the idea of a coat tree or hooks on a wall to make it easy to put away their everyday items such as jackets, purses, ball caps, and sports or activity bags. For any bedroom, make sure that you have good lighting for reading and doing homework, and don't forget open space. No one

Example Bedroom Layout for Middle School/High School Teenagers

TV

Window

Stereo, video games

Night-stand

Bed

Tall book-shelf

Beanbag chair

Trunk for memorabilia

Desk

Dresser

Closet

Door

Coat rack or hooks for caps, purses, jackets, etc.

Mirror

Dresser for out-of-season clothes

Bulletin board

can relax in a room that is jammed from floor to ceiling. You have to work with the space you have and set realistic expectations. Use the scaled-down drawing to play around a little bit with the arrangement. Then make sure you have some strong helpers when you are ready to move furniture.

Containers

Once the big stuff has been arranged, you can focus on the little stuff. First consider the containers you have on hand. Shelves, baskets, bins, and plastic containers can all be used for storing items in the room. If you find that you need more containers, decide

You can purchase containers for small items as a reward for a job well done on organizing the room.

what size and what kind you want and write those down on a shopping list. Here are some suggestions on where to keep the little stuff that can sometimes take over a child's bedroom:

- A basket on top of the dresser to hold odds and ends
- A clear plastic shoe organizer inside the closet door to hold his favorite small toys
- One small drawer in the desk or dresser designated as the junk drawer
- Display shelf on the wall for trophies, sculptures, and plaques
- Bulletin board for pictures, postcards, or small cutouts

By allowing your child one little container to hold all his small stuff, you are essentially containing the clutter. These organizers will need to be cleared out once they get too full or when your child can no longer find what he needs.

Maintain the System

Make sure that your new containers make it easy to clean up. Simple instructions work well with all children. Be specific. Telling your child to put books on the bookshelf, toys in the toy box, dirty clothes in the hamper, and clean clothes in the drawers or closet is preferable to just saying, "Clean that room!" If there are certain things that your child likes to leave out because the items are used every day, set aside space on a rack or shelf for them. When you make it easy for your child to keep these items picked up and off the floor, you are working with him to create a functional organizing system. Let him know when you expect him to get things back to normal in his room. This might be a daily straightening up in the morning or evening, or a weekly task to keep things under control.

THREE STEPS TO ORGANIZING YOUR CHILD'S BEDROOM

1. Decide on the functions of the room first.
2. Plan the time to go through everything in the bedroom using my CPR process (pages 190 and 246).
3. Help your child establish a routine of straightening up (either daily or weekly) using simple containers that work for him.

Make a Space For Everything

After setting up your child's spaces, such as his desk and locker, his homework area, and his bedroom, you can sit back and watch him work. Only step in when he asks for help or you see that things are getting out of hand.

REMEMBER

1. Keep in the backpack only essential items that need to be taken to and from school.
2. If remembering homework is a problem for your child, help him develop a routine for packing his schoolbag both at home and at school.
3. To keep track of individual papers, decide which system works best for your child: a folder for every subject, one binder, or one accordion file.
4. Have your child decide on a place for everything in his desk or locker, and then stick to that system.
5. Help your child get in the habit of clearing out schoolbags, desks, and lockers every Friday.
6. Set up books in the locker and/or school desk in the order of the child's class schedule.
7. Help define your child's needs when it comes to creating a homework area.
8. Set up a simple homework desk in an appropriate room in your house for your child.
9. Set up your child's bedroom with zones for each function.

Appendices

ABSOLUTES OF ORGANIZING

1. C.P.R. is the method: Categorize, Purge and Rearrange.
2. Keep purging simple with "Yes" and "No" piles.
3. Keep only what you use.
4. If you don't plan it, it won't happen.
5. Keep like things together.
6. Start with a good list.
7. Subtract before you add.
8. Finish one thing before you start another.
9. Organize from large to small.
10. Daily routines are a must.

ABSOLUTES OF ORGANIZING YOUR FAMILY

1. If you lead, they will follow.
2. Keep it simple.
3. If you push too hard, they'll fight back.
4. Give your children a few options that you can live with, and let them choose.
5. You can't overload your children's schedules and complain that you're too busy or they're too cranky.
6. Kids need downtime. Factor that in.
7. There is comfort in routine.
8. To prioritize, use the "fire" rule. Ask your child "If there were a fire, what five things would you want to save?"
9. Don't be afraid to talk to your child's teacher or principal about organizational help.
10. If it isn't broken, don't fix it. In other words, focus on what's not working.

DEBBIE LILLARD'S ROOM ORGANIZING WORKSHEET

Room: _____

Function of room
1. _____
2. _____
3. _____

What do you like about the room currently? _____
_____

What don't you like about the room currently? _____
_____

What is in the room now? (List categories of items)

_____   _____
_____   _____

What do you want to keep in this room?

_____   _____
_____   _____

What if anything needs to be added to the room? _____
_____

What contractors do you need to hire? _____
_____

If needed, get three labor/materials estimates:
1. _____
2. _____
3. _____

DEBBIE LILLARD'S SPACE PLANNING WORKSHEET

Space: _____

Function of space

1. _____
2. _____
3. _____

What do you like about the space currently? _____

_____

_____

What don't you like about the space currently? _____

_____

_____

What is in the space now? (List categories of items)

_____

_____

_____

What do you want to keep in the space?

_____

_____

_____

What, if anything, needs to be added to the space?_____

_____

_____

_____

WHAT EVERY MOM NEEDS

There are certain organizational items that I believe no mom or family should be without. You may have some of these already, but you really need all of them to run your family efficiently.

1. Daily planner
2. Family calendar
3. Stair basket
4. House Projects Plan book
5. Home office
6. Notebook—kept where you do your best thinking
7. Coupon caddy
8. Perpetual food list
9. Folder for children's activities and school information
10. A memory box for each family member

RESOURCES AND TOOLS THAT EVERY PARENT NEEDS
AND WHERE TO FIND THEM

PRODUCT	WHERE TO FIND IT
Blotter-style calendar for students	Office supply store
Wall calendar for all the family's activities	Stationery store, bookstore, office supply stores, or kiosks set up in malls around the end of the year
Portfolio for oversized artwork	"My Art Place Portfolio" at www.hearthsong.com
Daily planner for your child	Office supply stores or FranklinCovey.com
Display shelves for trophies, medals, artwork, memorabilia	Any arts-and-crafts store. My favorite is an unfinished plate rack with pegs.
Charging station for small electronics	www.ballarddesigns.com or www.potterybarn.com
Sports racks for the garage or mudroom	www.thecontainerstore.com or www.rubbermaid.com
Bins for memories, toys, or out-of-season clothes	Rubbermaid plastic bins with lids or steamer trunks found most often in August at home stores.
A mail table for incoming papers	Discount home good stores or second-hand shops. Ideally get one that is narrow and has drawers or cabinets.
Desks and bookshelves	Second-hand stores, office supply stores

TIME PLANNING WORKSHEET

	MORNING	MIDDAY	AFTER SCHOOL	EVENING
Monday				
Tuesday				
Wednesday				
Thursday				
Friday				
Saturday				
Sunday				

Index

NOTES

Chapter 24

1. Raising Children Network, "Family Routines," Raising Children Network, http://raisingchildren.net.au/articles/family_routines:_how_and_why_they_work.html (accessed April 10, 2009).

2. American Academy of Pediatrics, "Caring for Your School-Age Child: Ages 5 to 12," American Academy of Pediatrics, http://www.aap.org/publiced/BK5_Family_Routines.htm (accessed March 19, 2009).

ABOUT THE AUTHOR

Debbie Lillard is the owner and operator of Space to Spare Professional Organizing Service, which has been in operation since 2003. She has a BA in Communications and Business from Marymount University. In high school and college she was the consummate "student leader" on the newspaper staff, student council, cheerleading squad, campus ministry, and Residence Hall Council. Debbie is also one of six children and the mother of three. It's easy to see that her organizing expertise stems from her real-life experience of handling the responsibilities of first being a busy student, then parenting, volunteering, and running her own business. Many of her clients are in the same situation.

Debbie has appeared on HGTV's *Mission: Organization*, *The 10! Show* in Philadelphia, and on numerous talk radio shows nationally. Her organizing tips and articles have appeared in such magazines as *Woman's Day*, *Better Homes & Gardens*, and *Disney FamilyFun*.

Debbie is a member of the National Association of Professional Organizers, Philadelphia Chapter (NAPO-GPC) and is a Certified Provider of NAPO in the Schools, a community outreach program. This program sends professional organizers into elementary classrooms with a totally interactive presentation that teaches students basic organizing principles and the benefits of being organized. For more information about her services or to sign up for her online newsletter, go to www.spacetospare.com.

Erinn Aloi, a fresh focus photography

The material in this compilation appeared in the following previously published North Light Books and Betterway Home Books, and appears here by permission of the author.

Lillard, Debbie	Absolutely Organized c. 2008
Lillard, Debbie	Absolutely Organize Your Family c. 2010

Other fine Betterway Home Books are available from your local bookstore, or direct from the publisher. Visit our Web site at www.betterwaybooks.com.

ISBN: 978-1-4403-2488-8

16 15 14 13 12 5 4 3 2 1

Distributed in Canada by Fraser Direct
100 Armstrong Avenue, Georgetown, ON, Canada L7G 5S4, Tel: (905) 877-4411

Distributed in the U.K. and Europe by F&W Media International, LTD
Brunel House, Forde Close, Newton Abbot, Devon, TQ12 4PU, Tel: (+44) 1626 323200,
Fax: (+44) 1626 323319, E-mail: enquiries@fwmedia.com

Distributed in Australia by Capricorn Link
P.O. Box 704, S. Windsor NSW, 2756, Australia, Tel: (+61) 4 577-1400

Designer: Clare Finney
Production Editor: Jacqueline Musser
Production coordinator: Debbie Thomas

Photo on page 176 by Tim Grondin; photos on pages 235, 254, 262, 266, 267, 280, 292, 298, 303, 304, 308, 318, 327, 338, 341, 348 by Ric Deliantoni; Illustrations on pages 16, 20, 39, 60, 67, 74, 75, 83, 88, 94, 95, 106, 107, 111, 142, 159, 173 by Christine Erikson; illustrations on page 362 and 364 by Len Churchill. Items on pages 267, 282 and 318 from The Container Store.

![B] **BETTERWAY HOME BOOKS**

Find More Helpful Organizing Books

*Organize For a
Fresh Start
by Susan Fay West*

*Organized Simplicity
by Tsh Oxenreider*

*The Easy Organizer
by Marilyn Bohn*

Available online and in bookstores everywhere!

Online Organizing Videos

Looking for more help getting organized? Find inspiration and great step-by-step advice from Professional Organizers Jennifer Ford Berry, Susan Fay West and other Betterway Home authors.

Sign up for our free newsletter at **betterwaybooks.com** to receive a link to these free presentations.

To get started join our mailing list at **betterwaybooks.com**.

FOLLOW US ON:

*Become a fan of our Facebook page:
facebook.com/BetterwayHomeBooks*

*Find more great advice on
Twitter: @Betterway_Home*